"These nineteenth- and early-twentieth-century biographies, now republished by Chelsea House, reveal an unsuspected significance. Not only are a good many of them substantively valuable (and by no means entirely superseded), but they also evoke a sense of the period, an intimacy with the attitudes and assumptions of their times."

—Professor Daniel Aaron

Cottonus Matherus
S. Theologiæ Doctor Regiæ Societatis Londinensis Socius.
et Ecclesiæ apud Bostonum Nov-Anglorum nuper Propositus.
Ætatis Suæ LXV. MDCCXXVII.

COTTON MATHER
BARRETT WENDELL

INTRODUCTION BY
DAVID LEVIN

American Men and Women of Letters Series

GENERAL EDITOR
PROFESSOR DANIEL AARON
HARVARD UNIVERSITY

CHELSEA HOUSE
NEW YORK, LONDON
1980

Cover design by Abner Graboff

Copyright © 1980 by Chelsea House Publishers, a division of
Chelsea House Educational Communications, Inc.
Printed and bound in the United States of America

Library of Congress Cataloging in Publication Data

Wendell, Barrett, 1855-1921.
    Cotton Mather.

    (American men and women of letters)
    Reprint of the ed. published by Dodd, Mead, New
York, in series: Makers of America.
    Includes index.
    1. Mather, Cotton, 1663-1728.   2. Puritans--
Massachusetts--Biography.   I. Series.   II. Series:
Makers of America.
[F67.M43W46 1980]   285.8'32'0924 [B]   80-23335
ISBN 0-87754-166-3

Chelsea House Publishers
Harold Steinberg, Chairman & Publisher
Andrew E. Norman, President
Susan Lusk, Vice President
A Division of Chelsea House Educational Communications, Inc.
133 Christopher Street, New York 10014

CONTENTS

THE VISITABLE PAST
Daniel Aaron

THE TWENTY-FIVE BIOGRAPHIES of American worthies reissued in this Chelsea House series restore an all but forgotten chapter in the annals of American literary culture. Some of the authors of these volumes—journalists, scholars, writers, professional men—would be considered amateurs by today's standards, but they enjoyed certain advantages not open to their modern counterparts. In some cases they were blood relations or old friends of the men and women they wrote about, or at least near enough to them in time to catch the contemporary essence often missing in the more carefully researched and authoritative later studies of the same figures. Their leisurely, impressionistic accounts—sometimes as interesting for what is omitted as for what is emphasized—reveal a good deal about late Victorian assumptions, cultural and social, and about the vicissitudes of literary reputation.

Each volume in the series is introduced by a recognized scholar who was encouraged to write an idiosyncratic appraisal of the biographer and his work. The introductions vary in emphasis and point of view, for the biographies are not of equal quality, nor are the writers memorialized equally appealing. Yet a kind of consensus is discernible in these random assessments: surprise at the insights still to be found in ostensibly unscientific and old-fashioned works; in some instances admiration for the solidity and liveliness of the biographer's prose and quality of mind; respect for the pioneer historians among them who made excellent use of the limited material at their disposal.

The volumes in this American Men and Women of Letters series contain none of the startling "private" and "personal" episodes modern readers have come to expect in biography, but they illuminate what Henry James called the "visitable past." As such, they are of particular value to all students of American cultural and intellectual history.

Cambridge, Massachusetts
Spring, 1980

INTRODUCTION
TO THE
CHELSEA HOUSE EDITION

David Levin

Just in time for the two hundredth anniversary of the witchcraft trials that had made Cotton Mather's unique name a byword of fanatical superstition, Barrett Wendell published in 1891 this remarkably sympathetic, compact biography. Ninety years later Wendell's portrait remains one of the most wisely balanced characterizations of that legendary figure.

Wendell wrote before Mather's diaries had been published; they had only recently become available in manuscript. He therefore had some scholarly justification for his decision to work from a simple premise: that the only fair way to judge Mather was to "strive to see him as he saw himself." The point was not for the biographer to substitute Mather's standards of judgment for his own. Wendell insisted that the best way to express his modern biographical judgment was to narrate much of the life in Mather's own words. "By no other means," he said, "could I show so simply what seems to me the truth: that with a depth of human nature which makes him above most men who have lived a brother to all of us, he never ceased striving, amid endless stumblings and errors, to do his duty."

Why so much emphasis on *judging* a historical figure? Only a handful of names in American history provokes us so immediately as Cotton Mather's moves us to an affirmative or negative judgment. He was a prodigious child, a pious child, and a loyal son and grandson, determined to honor the names and carry on the work of his eminent progenitors. He was also an irrepressibly energetic writer, constantly devising new schemes for doing what he considered good in the political, religious, and scientific affairs of seventeenth-century Massachusetts. Throughout his 450 books, even in the considerable number that he published anonymously, one can recognize a strong, often vain personality, an insistent will. Whether punning to entertain us or displaying his learning to instruct us, he makes it difficult for any reader to ignore his personal presence.

As an indefatigable writer, moreover, he undertook not only the history of New England's saints but also the defense of belief in angels and devils. He was convinced that the Millennium was about to begin, foreshadowed by great revolutions in England and France, and he interpreted both New England's version of the Glorious Revolution (1689) and the subsequent outbreak of witchcraft in Boston and Salem as signs pointing to the imminent culmination. His narrative of the Salem trials, *The Wonders of the Invisible World* (1693), defended the judges even while admitting that their procedures had already been discredited and that the Devil had probably gained as much by provoking Christians to "maul one another" with hysterical accusations as he had gained by the actual assault of his witches and demons.

Mather's belated, shrill defense of the special court would have discredited him even if there had been no sequel. What sealed his reputation as a credulous bigot was his angry controversy with a merchant named Robert Calef, who in 1700 published a devastating book called *More Wonders of the Invisible World*. There Calef ridiculed Mather's demonology, challenged Mather's account of the Salem trials, and published a manuscript Mather had sent him during a private debate about the diabolical possession of a young woman in Boston.

Because Mather wrote so much and so personally, he thus became for his detractors and in American literature what he had devoutly hoped to become: the representative of the Old

New England Way that he had tried to preserve in a time of declining piety. Washington Irving's "Legend of Sleepy Hollow" (1820), James Fenimore Cooper's *Wept of Wish-ton-Wish* (1829), and Nathaniel Hawthorne's "Main Street" (1849) treat Mather's generation as a narrow imitator of the founders. In Hawthorne and Cooper, as in the histories written by George Bancroft and Richard Hildreth, the founders, too, had been rigid, but their piety had been genuinely ardent and not, in Hawthorne's word, the *counterfeit* fabricated by their grandsons. In 1867, moreover, Charles W. Upham triumphantly completed the most thorough of all studies of Salem witchcraft, and his verdict against Cotton Mather endorsed the received judgment.

Even today the impulse to judge Mather is stimulated by our literary and historical tradition. Mather's name is known to millions who know very little about him. For Katherine Anne Porter and Robert Lowell he represented, in Lowell's words, "the professional man of letters employed to moralize and subdue." An editorial in the *New York Times* called Richard Nixon's secretary of the treasury "the Cotton Mather of twentieth-century finance." A reporter for the *Washington Post* concluded an article on the vindictiveness of Boston baseball fans by remarking that "Cotton Mathers do not forgive a sinner. They only give him a free road map to the eternal fire."

If Barrett Wendell's method relies too much on Mather's own words, and sometimes too uncritically on Mather's interpretations, we can still see why it made good sense for Wendell to confront modern readers with Mather's language. Quotations might bring them closer than any conventional portrait could bring them to the historical actuality of this man of words. If readers could repeatedly see Mather's own version of his thoughts through decades of striving, the human reality might rival the legendary figure.

Wendell, of course, had other reasons besides the bicentennial of the witchcraft trials for believing that his readers ought to make a special effort to understand a pious man. Wendell, like Mather, wrote at the end of a century in which material progress and secular knowledge had undermined human faith in spiritual or intuitive ways of knowing. Wendell hoped, as Mather had hoped, to reconcile scientific knowledge with modern versions of age-old intuition. His hypothesis about the witchcraft in Salem (near the beginning of Chapter VI) is only the most striking example of that aspiration. By concentrating on the genuineness of Mather's piety, the passionate dedication to a merging of devotion and strenuous duty, Wendell rejected the traditional distinction between the first New England Puritan generation and the third. For him Cotton Mather was "the Puritan priest," not a monster degenerated from authentic ancestors but an imperfect "brother to us all." Wendell, moreover, was a scholar working to preserve traditions of humane learning throughout his forty years on the Harvard faculty, and (as Alan Heimert has shown) he felt that he himself lived in a time marked by the decline of a great New England tradition.

Critical though he was of Puritanism, Wendell thus did as much as anyone before the 1920s to prepare the way for the recent flourishing of New England studies. He argued in *Cotton Mather* that "this great tradition of Puritanism" consisted of much more than the "grim, untruthful formalism" toward which Calvinist doctrines tended. Long before Perry Miller wrote eloquently of "the Augustinian strain" of piety in New England, Wendell appealed to the reader's historical imagination:

... whoever cannot feel beneath the austere pettiness of Puritanism the passionate enthusiasm that made things unseen—Hell and Heaven, the Devil, and the Angels, and God—greater realities than anything this side of eternity, can never even guess what Puritanism meant.

In his quiet way Wendell also pointed out a connection between the piety of Puritans and the energy of Yankees. Even as he praised Mather for endlessly striving to do his duty, he perceived both the almost inevitable self-deception in a priest's "histrionic" function and the blurring of distinctions between the acquisitive man and the elected saint. He was probably the first historian to call Sir William Phips, the poor New Englander who found a fortune and a knighthood by salvaging a sunken Spanish treasure ship, "this archetype of self-made Yankees."

With similar acuteness, Wendell penetrated beyond Mather's articulated thoughts in the weeks after Mather's first vision of an angel, at age twenty-three. Wendell quotes and translates the extraordinary paragraph of Latin in which Mather described the vision—the angel's brilliant appearance and his frightening yet exhilarating predictions of personal glory in the young man's service of the Lord. Wendell reminds us of Mather's concluding prayer for protection "from the wiles of the Devil" and then points quietly to another influence on the young diarist's consciousness that year: "He was very anxious to be married, too; a fact which probably had more than he knew to do with his state of mind."

The clarity, the brevity, and the insight of this book deserve as much praise as its fidelity to Cotton Mather's self-portrait. Yet those

benefits do have a price. Wendell reports that
Increase Mather "broke down" for months
when Cotton was only six years old, but the
biography makes no effort to consider that
episode in relation to the child's development,
and Wendell is similarly uninquisitive about the
origins, the effect, and the cure of Cotton
Mather's boyhood stammer. Theological con-
troversies receive very little serious attention in
the book, even when the Mathers are deeply
engaged in a conflict over the founding of a
new church that threatens to overturn a central
doctrine of Congregational government. Wendell also neglects the importance of Mather's
chiliasm. And except for a few admirably perceptive comments on Mather's great church-
history of New England, *Magnalia Christi
Americana,* Wendell's biography says very little
about some of this voluminous writer's most
important works: *Bonifacius, The Christian
Philosopher, The Angel of Bethesda,* and others.
Wendell's research relies mostly on the diaries
of Mather and Samuel Sewall, and on Mather's
printed works about the chief figures in his life,
including his biographies of his famous grandfathers, Richard Mather and John Cotton, and
his biography of Increase Mather, written only
three years before Cotton himself died.

One good consequence of Wendell's reliance
on Mather's historical and biographical works

for much of his factual information is the reminder of their high quality. In Cotton Mather's *Parentator,* we see, Increase Mather does live as a unique character, and so does John Cotton in some of the incidents Wendell cites from the grandson's biography of him. Barrett Wendell performed the same service, somewhat less obtrusively, for Cotton Mather. This biography deserves a sympathetic reading, not only because it reports Mather's scientific curiosity and his brave defense of smallpox inoculation, but also because it treats his religious devotion with equal seriousness.

Charlottesville, Virginia
May, 1980

AUTHOR'S NOTE
TO THE
1891 EDITION

WHOEVER finds anything in this little book must share my gratitude to the possessors of Cotton Mather's manuscripts, who have so generously put them at my disposal. To the Massachusetts Historical Society, the American Antiquarian Society, the Congregational Library, and Mrs. Skinner of Chicago, our most earnest thanks are due.

I heartily regret that I have not been permitted to examine the exhaustive life of Cotton Mather left in manuscript by the late Rev. Mr. Marvin, of Lancaster, Massachusetts.

COTTON MATHER

COTTON MATHER

I

INTRODUCTION

Two hundred years ago there was living in Boston a man whose name is still remembered. Few nowadays know why we have heard of Cotton Mather; but even in this last decade of the nineteenth century few Yankees do not know his name. My object is to tell what manner of man he was, what manner of world he lived in, why — with all the oddities and failings that are to us so grotesque — he seems well worth remembering. For this Cotton Mather was of those who take life in earnest; and the life he took in earnest was, throughout the sixty-five years he passed on earth, the life of that New England which we who come of it like to believe the source of what is best in our own America. If, for a while, we can make ourselves see life as he saw it, we shall have done what I have in view.

Cotton Mather's diaries, together with his published works, express his views of life with rare completeness. So far as may be, then, I shall tell his story in his own words. In so doing, I shall doubtless expose myself to little less than the contempt of many serious students of Colonial history. The man's veracity has been seriously

questioned; and one can see why. In the first place,
he was the champion of a cause that, even in his own
time, was hopelessly lost, — the cause of the old hierarchy of New England, that once hoped to govern the
Western world in accordance with no laws but those of
God and Calvin; and not the least tragic fate of men
whose cause is hopelessly lost is that victorious posterity
rarely appreciates how they can have been honest.
Again, Cotton Mather was a priest, and in this world
priests are generally accepted in one of two ways:
whoever will not bow to their authority is lost in horror
of their priestcraft.   Finally, Cotton Mather was a man
of such passion as rarely worries a human being from
the cradle to the grave: throughout his life his emotions swept him into ecstasies which he found sometimes
divine, sometimes diabolical; and, having a ready
tongue and pen, he gave utterance to many hasty things
not always consistent with fact or with each other.
Wherefore such of posterity as have not loved his
memory have inclined now and again to call him by
a name he would probably have been the first to use in
their place, — a very great liar.

To me he seems otherwise. The better I know him,
the more firmly I believe that from beginning to end
he meant to be honest. Beyond doubt, like emotional
people about us, — abolitionists, nationalists, what not,
— he often saw things not as they were but as he would
have had them. What counted for him was God's
own work, what counted against him the Devil's; and
God's work, of course, was all good, and the Devil's
refreshingly free from any redeeming trait. But I do
not believe that he often wrote or spoke a word that he

disbelieved when it was written or spoken. He writes as follows in the Magnalia : —

"I have not commended any person, but when I have really judged, not only that he *deserved* it, but also that it would be a benefit unto posterity to know wherein he deserved it ; . . . yett I have left unmentioned some censurable occurrences in the story of our Colonies, as things no less unuseful than improper to be raised out of the grave, wherein Oblivion hath now buried them."

If we cannot accept him, then, as a veracious historian of all that went on before him, it is rather that his eyes were blinded than that his pen put down what he knew was error. And we may accept him, I believe more and more, as a singularly veracious historian of himself, who shows us year after year not exactly what things were, but exactly what he felt God bade him believe them.

In the chapters that follow, I shall try first to give some account of the race he sprang from, and of the place and the period in which he found himself. Then I shall try to tell, from his own point of view, the story of his own career. And I shall be sorry if I do not make it seem that there is still good ground for believing that it was a good man they buried on Copp's Hill one February day in the year 1728.

THE PURITAN FATHERS: COTTON AND MATHER

1585–1662

To understand the founders of New England we must recall more than tradition has preserved. All the world knows that to a rare degree the settlers of Plymouth and of Massachusetts alike were men of character. Cromwell himself is no bad type of them. Among the descendants of one of the emigrant ministers, indeed, a tradition is preserved that Cromwell, at the height of his power, once said that he had been more afraid of their ancestor at football than of "armies in the field." One may almost say that all the notables during the first generation of New England were men who might have played at football with Cromwell, and who, if they had, would probably have kept his hands full. All the world knows, too, that these men came hither to found a state where for once the laws of God and of man should coincide. But in the course of two centuries the world has forgotten that their conception of the laws of God was very different from what prevails nowadays. Yet to understand the Puritans at all we must in a general way understand their creed.

To the time of the Reformation, England, with the rest of Europe, had virtually accepted the doctrines of

Christianity as expounded by the Catholic Church. The Reformation and the Renaissance, affecting England together, produced there a new state of religious thought, which was greatly fostered by the political accidents of the time. Under Queen Elizabeth the first duty of Englishmen was to fight Spain; and Spain was the head and front of the powers that professed allegiance to the Church of Rome. Protestantism, in that sense of the word which means repudiation of Rome, was the spirit that must be nurtured. Bibles in the English language were chained to public reading-desks in the churches; so were great folios of Foxe's Book of Martyrs: whoever could read might go and read the truth. The truth they read was not favorable to ecclesiastical authority. When the danger of Spanish aggression was passed, the Church of England found that in fostering patriotic Protestantism it had permanently strengthened a class of people not free-thinking enough to discard religious authority, but firmly resolved to accept no other authority than Scripture. The Scriptural creed thus developed in England, but formulated most definitely at Geneva, was the creed of the founders of New England.

Stripped of subtlety and technicality, it may perhaps be stated as follows:[1] In the beginning God created man, responsible to Him, with perfect freedom of will. Adam, in the fall, exerted his will in opposition to the will of God: thereby Adam and all his posterity merited eternal punishment. As a mark of that punishment they lost the power of exerting the will in harmony with the will of God, without losing their

[1] Magnalia, V. I.

hereditary responsibility to Him. But God, in His infinite mercy, was pleased to mitigate His justice. Through the mediation of Christ, certain human beings, chosen at God's pleasure, might be relieved of the just penalty of sin, and received into everlasting salvation. These were the elect: none others could be saved, nor could any acts of the elect impair their salvation. Now there were no outward and visible marks by which the elect might be known: there was a fair chance, then, that any human being to whom the Gospel was brought might be of the number. The thing that most vitally concerned every man, then, was to discover whether he were elect, and so free from the just penalty of sin, ancestral and personal. The test of election was ability to exert the will in true harmony with the will of God, — a proof of emancipation from the hereditary curse of the children of Adam: whoever could ever do right, and want to, had a fair ground for hope that he should be saved. But even the elect were infected with the hereditary sin of humanity; and, besides, no wile of the Devil was more frequent than that which deceived men into believing themselves regenerate when in truth they were not. The task of assuring one's self of election, then, could end only with life, — a life of passionate aspirations, ecstatic enthusiasms, profound discouragements. Above all, men must never forget that the true will of God was revealed, directly or by implication, only and wholly in Scripture: incessant study of Scripture, then, was the sole means by which any man could assure himself that his will was really exerting itself, through the mediatory power of Christ, in true harmony with the will of God.

Such, if I read the "Magnalia" aright, was the creed of the fathers of New England, at least as Cotton Mather understood it. To live in accordance with this, they crossed the Atlantic. To lead unmolested their lives in accordance with this, they confined the franchise to actual communicants, and dealt so summarily with whoever proclaimed other opinions, — Mrs. Hutchinson, Roger Williams, and the crazy fanatics whom they called Quakers. To preserve this unaltered, they founded Harvard College. In obedience to the implications of this, they rated far above other men the official ministers of the Gospel.

Cotton Mather sprang from a race of these ministers. His very name combined two of those most distinguished among the emigrant clergy of Massachusetts. In his chief book, the "Magnalia," he has written the lives of his grandparents. And these lives, combining the historical and the domestic traditions amid which he grew to manhood, deserve our attention, if we would understand the life he strove to live throughout in accordance with these traditions.

Among the ministers who came from England in the full flush of their powers, none was more eminent than John Cotton.[1] Born at the town of Derby in 1585, the son of a pious and industrious lawyer, he was sent at the age of thirteen to Trinity College, Cambridge. Early chosen a fellow of Emanuel, he distinguished himself by

"an University sermon, wherein, aiming more to preach *self* than *Christ*, he used such florid strains, as extremely recommended him unto *the most*, who relished the *wisdom of words* above the *words of wisdom :* though the pompous

[1] Magnalia, III. I. 1.

eloquence of that sermon afterwards gave such a distaste
unto his own *renewed soul*, that with a sacred indignation
he threw his notes into the fire." For at this time, "such
was the secret enmity & prejudice of an *unregenerate soul*
against *real holiness*, & such the *torment* which our Lord's
witnesses give to the consciences of the *earthly-minded*,
that when he heard the bell toll for the funeral of Mr. Per-
kins, his mind secretly rejoiced in his deliverance from that
powerful ministry, by which his conscience had been so oft
beleagured : the remembrance of which thing afterwards
did break his heart exceedingly." Converted by the preaching of a certain Dr. Sibs, he signalized his regeneration by
preaching at St. Maries a sermon so plain in substance and
diction that "the vain wits of the University . . . discovered their vexation .   . by their not *humming*,[1] as according to their sinful & absurd custom they had formerly
done. . . . Nevertheless, the satisfaction which he enjoyed
in his own faithful soul, abundantly compensated unto him
the loss of any favour or honour."

Shortly after this he was invited to become the minister of Boston, in Lincolnshire, where, in spite of the
Bishop's opposition, he was settled at the celebrated
church of St. Botolph for twenty years. Throughout
this period his non-conformity steadily increased : his
conscience bade him discard every rite and vestment
for which he could not find authority in Scripture. At
length, neither his learning, nor his character, nor the
moral excellence of his work, nor the friends he had
made among those in power, could save him from the
consequences of a charge, brought by "a debauched
fellow in the town," that the magistrates under his cure
did not kneel at the sacrament. The debauched fellow, in fulfilment of a prediction of "the renowned
Mr. John Rogers of Dedham,"

[1] Cf. page 19.

"quickly after this, died of the *plague*, under an *hedge*, in Yorkshire ; and it was a long time ere any one could be found that would bury him. *This 't is to turn persecutor.*"

But Cotton was driven into hiding.

Doubtful whether to remain in Boston, preaching in private, he consulted an elderly divine, who gave the opinion

"'That the removing of a minister was like the draining of a fish-pond : the good fish will follow the water, but eels, & other baggage fish, will stick in the mud.' Which things, when Mr. Cotton heard, he was not a little confirmed in his inclination to leave the land."

So he ultimately came to New England in a ship which brought two other notable ministers, — Hooker and Stone. It was pleasantly said at the time that this ship brought New England "three great necessities : *Cotton* for their *clothing, Hooker* for their *fishing,* and *Stone* for their *building.*" Among them the three managed to solace the voyage by a daily sermon ; and in favorable weather by three sermons a day. Hooker and Stone became the ministers of Hartford : Cotton remained in

" New-Boston, which in a few years, by the smile of God, . . . came to exceed Old Boston in everything that renders a town considerable." On his arrival "he found the whole country in a perplexed & a divided state, as to their *civil constitution*" ; and being requested to suggest convenient laws "from the laws wherewith God governed his ancient people," he recommended among other things "that none should be *electors,* nor *elected,* . . . except such as were *visible subjects* of our Lord Jesus Christ, personally *confederated* in our churches. In these & many other ways, he propounded unto them an endeavour after a *theocracy,* as near as might be, to that which was the glory of Israel."

This theocracy came near getting him into trouble. In spite of the passionate defence of Cotton Mather, there is little room for doubt that he was almost perverted by the heresies of Mrs. Hutchinson; but he retraced his steps in time, learning for once in his life to conform.

"Nineteen years & odd months he spent in this place, doing of *good* publickly & privately, unto all sorts of men, as it became 'a good man full of faith, & of the Holy Ghost.' Here in an expository way, he went over the Old Testament once, & a second time as far as the thirtieth chapter of Isaiah; & the whole New Testament once, & a second time as far as the eleventh chapter to the Hebrews. Upon the Lords-days & lecture-days, he preached thorow the Acts of the Apostles; the prophesies of Haggai & Zechariah, the books of Ezra, the Revelation, Ecclesiastes, Canticles, second & third Epistles of John, the Epistle to Titus, both Epistles to Timothy, the Epistle to the Romans, with innumerable other scriptures on incidental occasions."

At last, in 1652, going to preach at Cambridge, he caught cold; his voice failed in the midst of his sermon. It had been

"his declared wish 'That he might not outlive his work!' . . . he had rather *be dead* than *live dead*. . . . On the eighteenth of November he took in course, for his text, the four last verses of the second Epistle of Timothy,[1] giving this reason for his insisting on so many verses at once, 'Because else (he said) I shall not live to make an end of this Epistle';

---

[1] "Salute Prisca and Aquila, and the household of Onesiphorus. Erastus abode at Corinth: but Trophimus have I left at Miletum sick. Do thy diligence to come before winter. Eubulus greeteth thee, and Pudens, and Linus, and Claudia, and all the brethren. The Lord Jesus Christ be with thy spirit. Grace be with you. Amen."

but he chiefly insisted on those words, ' Grace be with you all.' Upon the Lord's day following he preached his last sermon on Joh. i. 14,[1] about that 'glory of the Lord Jesus Christ,' from the *faith* to the *sight* whereof he was now hastening."

In a day of secret humiliation and prayer, he took solemn leave of " that *study* which had been *perfumed* with many such days before." As he lay sick, friends came to take leave of him.

" When his colleague, Mr. Wilson, took his leave . . . with a wish that God would lift up the 'light of his countenance' upon him, he instantly replied, ' God hath done it already, brother ! ' He then called for his children, with whom he left the gracious *covenant* of God, as their never-failing portion : & now desired that he might be left *private* the rest of his minutes, for the more freedom of his applications unto the Lord. So lying *speechless* a few hours, he breathed his blessed soul into the hands of his heavenly Lord, on the twenty-third of December, 1652, entring on the sixty-eighth year of his own age : & on the day — yea, at the *hour* — of his constant weekly labours in the lecture, wherein he had been so long serviceable, even to all the churches of New-England."

Cotton was

" an indefatigable student," who " judged ordinarily that more benefit was obtained . . . by conversing with the *dead* [in *books*] than with the *living* [in *talks*]. . . . He was an early riser, taking the morning for the Muses; &·in his latter days forbearing a supper, he turned his former supping time into a reading, a thinking, a praying-time. Twelve hours a day he commonly studied, & would call that *a*

---

[1] " And the Word was made flesh, and dwelt among us, (and we beheld his glory, the glory as of the only begotten of the Father,) full of grace and truth."

scholar's day." He read, wrote, and spoke Hebrew, Greek, and Latin. "For his *logic* he was completely furnished therewith to encounter the subtilest adversary of the truth." As for theology, even his "incomparable modesty" could not prevent his telling a private friend, "That he knew not of any difficult place in all the whole Bible, which he had not weighed, some what unto satisfaction. . . . And being asked, why in his latter days he indulged *nocturnal studies* more than formerly, he pleasantly replied, 'Because I love to sweeten my mouth with a piece of Calvin before I go to sleep.'"

Two or three anecdotes, preserved by Cotton Mather, show that he had a vein of humour. On one occasion,

"an humourous & imperious brother" complained to him "that his ministry was become generally either dark or flat: whereto this meek man, very mildly & gravely, made only this answer: 'Both, brother, it may be, both: let me have your prayers that it may be otherwise.'" Again, "a company of vain, wicked men, having inflamed their blood in a tavern at Boston, & seeing that reverend, meek, & holy minister of Christ . . . coming along the street, one of them tells his companion, 'I'll go,' saith he, '& put a trick on old Cotton.' Down he goes, & crossing his way, whispers these words into his ear: 'Cotton,' said he, 'thou art an old fool.' Mr. Cotton replied, 'I confess I am so: the Lord make both me & thee wiser than we are, even wise unto salvation.'" One can see why "the keeper of the inn where he did use to lodge, when he came to Derby, would profanely say to his companions, that he wished Mr. Cotton were gone out of his house; for 'he was not able to swear while that man was under his roof.'"

In family devotions he was very short, accounting "that it was a thing inconvenient many ways to be tedious in family duties." But his Sabbath-keeping was something marvellous.

"The Sabbath he began the evening before; & I suppose," adds Cotton Mather, "'twas from his reason and practice that the Christians of New England have generally done so too.[1] When that evening arrived, he was usually larger in his exposition in his family than at other times: he then catechised his children & servants, & prayed with them, & sang a psalm; from thence he retired unto study & secret prayer, till the time of his going unto his repose. The next morning, after his usual family worship, he betook himself to the devotion of his retirements, & so unto the publick. From thence towards noon, he repaired again to the like devotions, not permitting the interruption of any other dinner, than that of a small repast carried up unto him. Then to the publick once more; from whence returning, his first work was closet-prayer, then prayer with repetitions of the sermons in the family. After supper, he still sang a psalm; which he would conclude with uplifted eyes & hands, uttering this doxology — 'Blessed be God in Christ our Saviour!' Last of all, just before his going to sleep, he would once again go into his prayerful study, & there briefly recommend all to that God, whom he served with a pure conscience."

Such was John Cotton, at least as Cotton Mather believed him. He left a widow. The mothers of New England were not fond of widowhood. Before long, she became the second wife of the Reverend Richard Mather, minister of Dorchester.

This Richard Mather[2] was born in Lancashire, in 1596. His parents, though in reduced circumstances, gave him a liberal education. At fifteen he went as

---

[1] Cf. page 43.   [2] Magnalia, III. II. xx.

schoolmaster to Toxteth Park, near Liverpool, where
the

"difference between his own walk & the most exact, watchful, fruitful, & prayerful conversation of some in the family
. . . where he sojourned, . . . caused many sad fears to
arise in his own soul that he was himself *out of the way.*
. . . But . . . about the eighteenth year of his age, the
good Spirit of God healed his broken heart, by pouring
thereinto the evangelical consolations of 'His great &
precious promises.'"

A little later he went to Oxford ; and in 1618 he returned to Toxteth as minister. When the Bishop of
Chester ordained him, the prelate startled him by requesting a private interview.

"Mr. Mather was now jealous that some informations
might have been exhibited against him for his Puritanism;
instead of which, when the Bishop had him alone, what he
said unto him was, 'I have an earnest request unto you, sir,
& you must not deny me : 't is that you would pray for me ;
for I know (said he) the prayers of men that fear God
will avail much & you I believe are such a one.'"

At Toxteth Richard Mather preached fifteen years.
In his private manuscripts he wrote thus of the trial by
which he was finally suspended for non-conformity : —

"In the passages of that day I have this to bless the
name of God for, that the terrour of their threatening words,
of their pursevants, & of the rest of their pomp, did not
terrifie my mind, but that I could stand before them without being daunted in the least manner, but answered for my
self such words of truth & soberness as the Lord put into
my mouth, not being afraid of their faces at all: which
supporting & comforting presence of the Lord, I count not
much less mercy, than if I had been altogether preserved
out of their hands."—"But all means," adds Cotton

Mather, "used afterwards to get off this unhappy *suspension* were ineffectual; for when the visitors had been informed that he had been a minister *fifteen* years, and, all that while never wore a *surpliss*, one of them swore, 'It had been better for him that he had gotten seven bastards!'"

Once suspended, his thoughts turned to New England.

"He drew up some arguments for his removal thither, which arguments were, indeed, the very reasons that moved the first fathers of New-England unto that unparellelled undertaking of transporting their families with themselves, over the Atlantic ocean:

I.   A removal from a *corrupt* church to a *purer*.

II.   A removal from a place where the truth & professors of it are *persecuted*, unto a place of more *quiet* & *safety*.

III.   A removal from a place where all the *ordinances* of God cannot be enjoyed, unto a place where they *may*.

IV.   A removal from a church where the *discipline* of the Lord Jesus Christ is wanting, unto a church where it may be practised.

V.   A removal from a place, where the ministers of God are unjustly inhibited from the execution of their functions, to a place where they may more freely execute the same.

VI.   A removal from a place, where there are fearful signs of *desolation*, to a place where one may have well grounded hope of God's protection."

So in 1635, after a stormy voyage, he came to Boston. The first church founded in Dorchester had followed its minister to Connecticut. Within a year, Richard Mather had gathered there a new church, where

"he continued, a blessing unto all the churches in this wilderness until his dying day, even for near upon four and thirty years together. . . He never changed his habitation after this till he went unto the 'house eternal in the heavens'; albeit his old people of Toxteth vehemently solicited his return unto them when the troublesome Hierarchy in England was deposed."

In 1669 he died of the stone, "wherein, according to Solomon's expression of it, 'the wheel was broken at the cistern.'"

"As he judged that a preacher of the gospel *should* be, he *was* a very hard *student:* yea, so intent was he upon his beloved studies, that the morning before he died, he importuned the friends that watched with him to help him into the room, where he thought his usual *works & books* expected him; to satisfie his importunity they began to lead him thither; but finding himself unable to get out of his lodging-room, he said, 'I see I am not able; I have not been in my study several days; & is it not a lamentable thing, that I should lose so much time?'"

His temperament was sombre, self-conscious.

"He was for some years exercised with . . . uncertainties about his everlasting happiness. . . . In those *dark hours* . . . a *glorious light* rose unto him . . . which I find in his private papers thus expressed: 'My heart relented with tears at this prayer, that God would not deny me an heart to bless him, & not blaspheme him, that is so holy, just, and good; though I should be excluded from his presence, & go down into everlasting darkness & discomfort.'" On his death-bed, "though he lay in a mortal extremity of pain, he never shrieked, he rarely groaned, with it; & when he was able, he took delight in reading Dr. Goodwin's discourse about patience, in which book he read until the very day of his death. When they asked 'how he did?' his usual answer was, 'Far from well, yet far better than mine iniquities deserve.'"

His last recorded words were a solemn charge to his son as to who might properly be admitted to baptism, — a question then seriously disturbing the churches of New England. The only bright touch in Cotton Mather's picture of him is that which tells how, one Saturday evening in 1661, two of his sons, both ministers, arrived at about the same time, — one from England, one from

"a Remote place where he was now Stationed in the Country ; And the Comforted Old Patriarch, sat shining like the Sun in *Gemini*, & hearing his two Sons, in his own Pulpit entertain the People of GOD, with Performances, that made all People Proclaim him, An Happy Father."[1]

Richard Mather's first wife[2] was

"Mrs. *Katharine Holt;* a Gentlewoman Honourable for her *Descent;* but much more so, for her *Vertue.* . . . She sometimes told her Son, while he was yet scarce more than an *Infant*, but very much her *Darling*, That she desired of the Glorious GOD only two things on his behalf; the one was, The *Grace* to Fear & Love GOD; the other was, the *Learning* that might Accomplish him to do Service for GOD. . . . Among her Instructions, it is to be *Remembred* that she mightily inculcated the Lesson of *Diligence* upon him, & often put him in Mind of that Word, *Seest thou a Man Diligent in his Business: He shall* STAND BEFORE KINGS. . . . When he was about Fifteen Years Old, she Died Marvellously Triumphing over the *Fear of Death*, which thro' *all her Life* she had been Afraid of.

"If a pretty late Abortion might have Passed for a *Birth*, it might have been said of this Gentlewoman, she was a Mother of *Seven Sons*. . . . *Four* proved Useful, & Faithful, & Famous Ministers of the Gospel. INCREASE

[1] Parentator, p. 23.   [2] Ibid, pp. 3-5.

was the *Youngest* of them; Whom his Father called so
. . . because of the never-to-be-forgotten *Increase*, of every
sort, wherewith GOD favoured the country, about the time
of his Nativity. . . . Had he been Indisputably a *seventh
son*, yet he would not have Countenanced the Foolish,
Profane, Magical Whimsey of the silly People which fur-
nishes the *seventh Son*, with I know not what *uncommon
Powers;* 'T was among the *Vulgar Errors* always derided
with him.   However, we shall hear of *Strange Things*
done by him, & for him."

Born at Dorchester in June, 1639, Increase Mather,[1]
to use his own words,

" Swam quietly in a Stream of Impiety & Carnal Security
for many Years together, till it pleased the Lord in the year
1654, in Mercy to Visit me with a sore Disease, which was
Apprehended to be the Stone."

The serious frame of mind thus induced resulted in
his conversion.   In 1656 he took his first degree at
Harvard College,

" At which time the Præsident,[2] who was deep in the Dark
Principles with which the *Stagyrite* has for so many Ages
Tyrannized over Human Understanding, upon a Dislike of
the *Ramæan* Strains in which our Young Disputant was
carrying on his Thesis, would have cut him Short; but Mr.
Mitchel Publickly Interposed, *Pergat, Quæso, nam doctis-
sime disputat.*"[3]

In 1657,

"on his *Birth-Day*, he Preached his *First Sermon*, at a
Village belonging to Dorchester.   And on the next Lord's-

---

[1] Throughout my account of Increase Mather, I follow Cotton Mather's " Parentator."

[2] Charles Chauncy, who was inclined to Baptist heresies.

[3] " Let him go on, I beg, for he is arguing like a great
scholar."

Day he Preached in his Fathers Pulpit, . . . When the whole Auditory were greatly Affected with the *Light* & *Flame*, in which the Rare Youth Appear'd unto them: Especially was his Father so, who could scarce Pronounce the *Blessing*, for the Tears which from the *Blessing* he had himself now so Sensibly Received, he was thrown into."

A month later, young Increase Mather sailed for England, whence he presently went to Dublin, where his brother Samuel was settled as a minister. The next year he proceeded Master of Arts at Trinity College, where

"the Scholars were so Pleased with the Wit & Sense & Polite Learning brilliant in his Exercises, that they Publickly *Hummed*[1] him; which being a Complement that he had never heard Paid unto any one before, at first had like to have given too much Surprise unto him."

Declining a fellowship, he preached for one winter in Devonshire; and in 1659 became chaplain to the garrison of Guernsey. But the Restoration was upon him. In 1660, finding that he must "either conform to the Revived Superstitions in the Church of England, or leave the Island," he gave up his charge. Refusing a living in the Established Church, disappointed in a chance to travel on the Continent, his thoughts turned homeward. "In fine, all things Conspired for the moving of the *Star*, to illuminate the *Western* Hæmisphere."

In June, 1661, he sailed from Weymouth; in August he came to his "comforted old patriarch" of a father

---

[1] Cf. page 8. A capital example this of Cotton Mather's "Inconsistency."

at Dorchester, who had now for six years been the husband of John Cotton's widow. The following winter Increase Mather passed in preaching alternately for his father and "to the New Church in the North-part of Boston." In the course of the year, Mrs. Mather's daughter, Maria Cotton, conquered his affections.

"On March 6, 1662, he Came into the Married State; Espousing the only Daughter, of the celebrated Mr. *John Cotton;* in Honour to whom he did . . . call his First-born son by the Name of COTTON."

Of such parentage, whose story I have told chiefly in his own words, Cotton Mather was born, in Boston, on the 12th of February, 1662–63.

III

THE YOUTH OF COTTON MATHER

1662–1678

At this time the Plymouth Colony was about forty years old, the Charter of Massachusetts about thirty. Their story has been told again and again. Founded shortly before Laud became Archbishop of Canterbury, the Colonies were first strengthened by such emigration as was stimulated by the persecutions in England, and then confirmed in their strength by the independent responsibility thrust upon them by the civil wars, which kept the attention of England centred on herself. During the Commonwealth, home matters were too important to permit much attention in England to subjects beyond the Atlantic; for the rest, these professed a faith and a policy not very different from those which for twelve years prevailed in the mother country.

What that faith was, we have seen; and in some degree what that policy was, too. It was based on a hope that the government of the visible world might, by the grace of God, be brought into harmony with the system by which God governed the invisible. At the outset the Puritans were met by a difficulty they never quite realized. The government of God, as they understood it, was the reverse of democratic. But the very

fact that drove them to a wilderness for the founding of their system was the assumption at home of
divinely autocratic power by kings and bishops for
whose claims they could find no authority in Scripture.
On Scripture only they were determined to rest; but
who should interpret Scripture? "All things in Scripture," they themselves professed, "are not alike plain
in themselves, nor alike clear unto all."[1] Clearly no
bishops, no ecclesiastical tradition, could do their business; they must fall back on active ministers of the
Gospel. But whence came the authority of these ministers, which might be held final? Again, only from
Scripture, or from such occasional presences of God as
we shall see revealing themselves in the ministrations
of the Mathers. And who should designate the Scrip-
turally authorized interpreters of the Scripture on which
all authority must ultimately rest? Scripture, unhap-
pily, contained no prophetic catalogue of its proper
exponents. They fell back on the visible members of
churches, on those of themselves whose public profession of religious experience had proved, as far as
earthly processes could prove, their regeneration. The
elect of God became the electors of God's chosen. In
other words, their system at once claimed autocratic
power, temporal and spiritual, and yet rested its claim
on something remarkably like the consent of the governed. They strove to establish a thing that can never
exist, — a Protestant priesthood.

The democratic spirit implied in all Protestantism, in
all revolution, was greatly strengthened by the political
circumstances in which they found themselves. Under

[1] Magnalia, V. I. i. vii.

the first Charter of Massachusetts, virtually that of a trading corporation, the freemen elected the magistrates. And though for more than a generation the theocratic principles of John Cotton prevailed, and none were freemen but the members of churches, there was neither among the churches nor among their members that heavenly unanimity which alone could prevent voters from now and then — and more and more — voting as they pleased. "The will of man," their creed admitted, "is made perfectly and immutably free to good alone in the state of glory only."[1]   In the first thirty years of their life in America, the theocratic spirit was strong enough to establish the terms of the franchise, to banish Roger Williams and Mrs. Hutchinson, to hang the Quakers; the democratic meanwhile had established and maintained civil order, and had been forced by the presence of Indians and other harassing neighbours into strengthening demonstrations of military power, as well as into that Confederacy of New England whose memory is dear to lovers of Union. The democratic spirit, I take it, made Sir Henry Vane Governor in 1637; a year or two later, the theocratic drove him in disgust from the Colony. It was the growth of the democratic that stopped the hanging of Quakers before Cotton Mather was born.

In 1660, Charles II came to the throne of his father. Massachusetts had grown unaccustomed to paying much attention to what went on in England. She sent him a complimentary address; but it was more than a year before she was brought to the point of officially proclaiming him sovereign.   Theocracy and

[1] Magnalia, V. I. i. ix.

democracy, priesthood and protestantism, agreed in profound disinclination to be meddled with. Together they met in peaceable but dogged resistance to the effort of royal commissioners to assert in New England a power superior to that of the Charter. In their common cause their mutual antagonism was forgotten. What is more, the two spirits were not sharply distinguished : both were inherent in the original constitution of the Colonies. Theoretically, pretty much everybody believed at once in the divine authority of the clergy, and in the right of godly men to say who should preach to them and who govern them.

It was at this time that Cotton Mather came into the world. Little record is preserved of his childhood; but he was of a temperament at once so sensitive and so precocious that we must consider the aspects of life that first presented themselves to him.

For above a year, Increase Mather hesitated to accept the charge of the Second Church in Boston, having

"some Views . . . of greater service elsewhere. At last, the Brethren of the Church kept a *Day of Supplications* unto Him who has all Hearts in His Hands, to pray that GOD would Incline him and Perswade him, to Accept the Invitation which they had given him. From *This Day*, he felt another *Biass* on his mind, and soon Complied with their Desires; and on *May* 27, 1664, he did with a great Solemnity, wherein his Father publickly gave him his *Charge*, Accept the *Pastoral Care* of the Flock ; with which, (Them and Their Children,) he *Continued Serving the Lord, with many Tears and Temptations, and keeping back nothing that was Profitable for them,* for more than Threescore Years together."

Early in his work he was assailed by Satanic temptations to doubt the existence of God : these he overcame, not by reasoning, — " it puts too much Respect upon a *Devil,* to Argue and Parley with him, on a Point which the *Devil* himself *Believes and Trembles at,*" — but by " flat contradiction," fortified by the reflection that, since some of his prayers had been answered, there must evidently be a God to answer them. Failing in this direct attack, the Devil betook himself to the hearts of the parish, which he so hardened as to keep Increase Mather's salary for some years decidedly below his expenses. Amid the heavy debts that naturally followed, the good man had recourse to prayer, sometimes tempered with thanksgivings for such blessings as he was graciously permitted to enjoy. After a while, the church paid him well, to the very end of his life, — a consummation which Cotton Mather attributes chiefly to these prayers. In fact, the form which the answer to these prayers probably took was a growing and well-grounded conviction on the part of the members of the Second Church that unawares, in calling to their ministry a promising young man, they had secured to themselves the ablest and most eminent minister in America.

An indefatigable worker he seems to have been. His diary records devices for saving and employing every moment, and for maintaining incessant seriousness of heart. And in 1669, when his father died, and his brother Eleazar, of whose death he had supernatural warning, he broke down. The mood in which, some months later, he recovered, is best phrased in his own diary, for the 11th of June, 1670 : —

"The Threefold Wish of the Chief of Sinners. I *Wish!*
I *Wish!* I *Wish!* 1. That I may do some *Special Ser-
vices* for my dear GOD in JESUS CHRIST before I leave this
World. 2. I would fain *Leave Something* behind me, that
may be doing of Good upon *Earth*, after I shall be in
Heaven. 3. After I have finished my *Doing Work*, I
would fain *Suffer* for the Sake of my dear GOD, and for
JESUS CHRIST." [1]

In 1674, " observing the *Sins of the Times,* & therewith Discerning the *Signs of the Times,*" he preached
a prophetic sermon on the text, " The Day of Trouble
is near." The next two years were the most dreadful in the history of New England. The Colonies,
which since the discomfiture of the royal commissioners had been disturbed by no more insidious tests of
their civil strength than discussions about baptism,
and the intrigues concerning the presidency of Harvard
College that broke the heart of Leonard Hoar, were
plunged into the horrors of King Philip's war. Palfrey
tells in detail the story of that helpless struggle of the
native savages, and of the organized military power
which at last exterminated them with no foreign aid.
Sewall's Diary gives glimpses of the ghastly news of
massacre that now and again found its way to Boston.
But neither Palfrey nor Sewall emphasizes the sentiments concerning the Indians that pervade the long
accounts of the struggle which form an interesting part
of Cotton Mather's " Magnalia." In the view of the
Puritans, the Indians were the wretched remnant of a
race seduced to the Western Hemisphere by the Devil
himself, that he might rule them undisturbed by the

[1] Cf. page 47.

rising light of the Gospel. The landing of the Pilgrims
was an invasion of the Devil's own territory; the mis-
sionary work of Eliot and the Mayhews was a direct
storming of his strongholds, almost unprecedented in
his experience. The outbreak of the Indians was his
natural retort; every arrow, every bullet, every war-
song and magic chant, of the expiring natives of New
England was a missile aimed by Satan himself against
the power of Christ. The laity met the attack with
gunpowder; the clergy were no less active with
prayer. To which should be attributed the final victory, — a victory not so much over Philip and his
followers as over Philip's Satanic master, — opinions
may differ. But Increase Mather was not disposed
to undervalue his petitions to the Lord: his estimate
of them was confirmed by a singular experience in
August, 1676.

" He had for diverse *Lords-Days*," writes Cotton Mather,
" made the Death of that Miserable King, a Petition which
in his *Public Prayers* he somewhat Enlarged upon. But
on one Lords-Day he quite forgot it; for which *Forgetful-
ness* I well *Remember*, that I heard him wondring at, and
Blaming of, himself in the Evening. However, he was
more Satisfied, when a few Hours after, there came to
Town the Tidings, That before *That* Lords-Day, the
Thing was Accomplished." — " I will not *Theologize*,"
writes Cotton Mather a little later, "much less will I
Philosophize, upon the Original and Operation of those
Præsagious Impressions about *Future Events*, which are
often Produced in Minds, which by *Piety* and *Purity*
and *Contemplation*, and a Prayerful and Careful walk
with GOD, are made more susceptible of them. I am
only to Observe that this *Holy Man of God* was no
stranger to them."

He was no stranger, either, to ecstasies of an even more mysterious kind.

"As I was Praying," he wrote in 1672, "my Heart was exceedingly Melted, and methoughts, saw GOD before my Eyes in an Inexpressible Manner, so that I was Afraid I should have fallen into a Trance in my Study." — "In his latter years," writes Cotton Mather, "he did not Record so many of these *Heavenly Afflations*, because they grew so frequent with him. And he also found . . . that the Flights of a Soul rapt up into a more Intimate Conversation with Heaven, are such as *cannot be exactly Remembred* with the Happy Partakers of them."

Such was the career of Cotton Mather's father during the first sixteen years of the boy's life. During these years must have been founded and confirmed the passionate personal affection that marked their relations throughout life. Increase Mather, I take it, was of a temper whose affections were most conciliated by enthusiastic acquiescence. Cotton Mather never observed any other law of God quite so faithfully as the Fifth Commandment. And the father he delighted to honour, the father who handed down traditions of ancestors equally honourable, was at the same time clothed with the divine authority of the ministry, to all appearances specially favoured by God, and revered by the public both personally and in his official capacity as minister of the Second Church and Fellow of Harvard College. Under these circumstances, nothing could have made a stronger or more lasting impression on the boy's mind than the example and the teachings of his father. How that example impressed him, his accounts of his father and his grandparents show. Exactly what those teach-

ings were is not recorded. Two or three records of
domestic life at this time, however, may help us guess
what Increase Mather's teachings must have been.

To understand these records nowadays, we must
recall afresh the creed that at almost every moment
made the concerns of another world than this the chief
reality in the minds of the Puritans. It was our duty,
they held, to live for the glory of God; only by so
living, with all our hearts, could we assure ourselves of
the election which alone could save us from the eternal
penalty of Adam's sin and our own. The first thing for
us to learn was acquiescence in the will of God, — in
His eternal justice, His unmerited and for all we could
see capricious grace; without such acquiescence our
wills must inevitably exert themselves in unregenerate
baseness. At worst we could be no worse off than our
damnable deserts; and if at any time we had the in-
effable joy to find ourselves elect, nothing could more
exquisitely torture us than the memory of early godless-
ness. As soon as children could talk, then, they were
set to a process of deliberate introspection, whose mark
is left in the constitutional melancholy and the frequent
insanity of their descendants.

In the light of these facts, two entries in Sewall's
Diary are even more significant than grotesque.

"Nov. 6," 1692, runs the first, "Joseph [1] threw a knop
of Brass and hit his Sister Betty on the forhead so as to
make it bleed and swell; upon which, and for his playing
at Prayer-time, and eating when Return Thanks, I whipd
him pretty smartly. When I first went in (call'd by his
Grandmother) he sought to shadow and hide himself from

[1] Born 15 August, 1688.

me behind the head of the Cradle: which gave me the
sorrowfull remembrance of Adam's carriage."

The second is for January 13, 1695–96 : —

"When I came in, past 7 at night, my wife met me in the
Entry and told me Betty[1] had surprised them. . . . It
seems Betty Sewall had given some signs of dejection and
sorrow ; but a little after diñer she burst out into an
amazing cry, which caus'd all the family to cry too ; Her
Mother ask'd the reason ; she gave none ; at last said she
was afraid she should goe to Hell, her sins were not pardon'd.   She was first wounded by my reading a Sermon of
Mr. Norton's, about the 5th of Jan.   Text Jno. 7. 34, Ye
shall seek me and shall not find me.   And those words in
the Sermon, Jno. 8. 21, Ye shall seek me and shall die in your
sins, ran in her mind, and terrified her greatly.   And staying at home Jan. 12, she read out of Mr. Cotton Mather —
Why hath Satan filled thy heart, which increas'd her Fear.
Her Mother ask'd her whether she pray'd.   She answer'd,
Yes; but feared her prayers were not heard because her
Sins not pardon'd.   Mr. Willard,[2] though sent for timelyer,
. . . came not till after I came home.   He discoursed with
Betty who could not give a distinct account, but was con-
fused as his phrase was, and as had experienced in himself.
Mr. Willard pray'd excellently.   The Lord bring Light and
Comfort out of this dark and dreadful Cloud, and Grant that
Christ's being formed in my dear child, may be the issue
of these painfull pangs."

A familiar example of infant piety, from the "Magnalia,"[3] shows what elect children are expected to be.

"Anne Greenough . . . left the world when she was but
about five years old, and yet gave astonishing discoveries

---

[1] Born 29 December, 1681.
[2] Minister of the Old South Church.
[3] Appendix, VI, VII.

of a regard unto God, and Christ, and her own soul, before she went away. When she heard any thing about the Lord Jesus Christ, she would be strangely transported, and ravished in her spirit at it; and had an unspeakable delight in catechizing. She would put strange questions about eternal things, and make answers her self that were extreamly pertinent. Once particularly she asked, 'Are we not dead in sin?' and presently added, ' But I will take this way: the Lord Jesus Christ shall make me alive.' She was very frequent and constant in secret prayer, and could not with any patience be interrupted in it. She told her gracious mother, 'that she there prayed for her!' and was covetous of being with her mother, when she imagin'd such duties to be going forward. When she fell sick at last of a consumption, she would not by sports be diverted from the thoughts of death, wherein she took such pleasure that she did not care to hear any thing else. And if she were asked 'whether she were ready to die?' she would still cheerfully reply, ' Ay, by all means, that I may go to the Lord Jesus Christ.' "

Such domestic influences as these surrounded Cotton Mather's childhood. The Boston in which they flourished was between thirty and forty years old. From a bare peninsula of such gravelly hills as one may still see about the harbour, it had become a flourishing seaport, in aspect not unlike the older parts of Newburyport or Portsmouth to-day. The population of Massachusetts in 1665 was, according to Palfrey, about twenty-five thousand, of whom a large minority resided in the capital. New England, in short, was becoming too important to be much longer abandoned to its own devices. By far the most vivid pictures of the social life of the time are in Sewall's Diary. People were forced by public opinion to the willing

performance of their several duties : they attended to
their business, they took conscientious interest and
part in politics, they went to church as often as possible, — which was at least three times a week, — and
their most edifying festivals were the frequent funerals
incident to the physical hardship of the period.   Perhaps the most suggestive fact concerning their extreme
simplicity of manners is, that young people of the
better sort habitually went into domestic service.   The
Sewalls were people of consideration ; but in 1676
Sewall's sister Jane came from Newbury to live with
Mrs. Usher ; and, finding that this lady had supplied
herself with help, went. to live at Sewall's " Father
Hull's," who wanted a maid, and discovered that it
was hard to find a good one.[1]   At this time Seth
Shove, a minister's son, and later a minister himself,
was also living at Mr. Hull's, where on the day of his
arrival a neighbour, mistaking him in the dark for a
stray dog, had knocked him over the head, — a circumstance which led Sewall to fear that "the Devil
seemed to be angry at the child's coming to dwell
here." [2]   And a little earlier Sewall gives a very curious
account of the spiritual experience of one Tim Dwight,
son of a gentleman in Dedham, and likewise appren-
ticed to Father Hull.[3]   Just after prayers one day, Tim
fell in a swoon, and, recovering, in a most incoherent
condition lamented that his day of grace was out.
Sewall reproached him, saying that " 't was sin for any
one to conclude themselves Reprobate."   But Tim was
not to be comforted.

[1] Sewall's Diary, I. 34, 35.
[2] Ibid., 30.   [3] Ibid., 15, 16.

" Notwithstanding all this semblance of compunction," adds Sewall, " 't is to be feared that his trouble arose from a maid whom he passionately loved : for that when Mr. Dwight and his master had agreed to let him goe to her, he eftsoons grew well." A fortnight later, Sewall "spake to Tim of this, asked him whether his convictions were off. He answered, no. I told him how dangerous it was to make the convictions wrought by God's spirit a stalking horse to any other thing. Broke off, he being called away."

In such a society, and among such domestic influences as we have seen, Cotton Mather grew up. Late in life, he wrote for his son Samuel some account of his early years.[1]

" I desire to bewayl unto the very *end* of my Life, the early Ebullitions of *Original Sin*, which appeared at the very Beginning of it. Indeed your Grandfather, tho' he were a wise and strict parent, would from the observation of some Dispositions in me, comfort himself with an Opinion of my being *Sanctified by the Holy Spirit of God in my very infancy.* But he knew not how vile I was, he saw not the instances of my *going astray*, even while I was yet an infant. However, there were *some good things* in my childhood, in which I wish *my child* may *do better* than I. I began to *pray*, even when I began to speak. I learned myself to *write* before my going to school for it. I used *secret prayer*, not confining myself to *Forms* in it: and yett I composed *Forms* of *prayer* for my school-mates (I suppose when I was about seven or eight years old), and obliged them to *pray*. Before I could *write Sermons* in the public Assemblies I commonly *wrote* what I remembered when I came home. I rebuked my play mates for their wicked *words* and *ways;* and sometimes I suffered from them, the persecution of not only *Scoffs* but *Blows* also, for my

[1] Paterna. MS. in the library of the late Judge Skinner, of Chicago.

Rebukes, which when somebody told your Grandfather, I
remember he seemed very *glad*, yea, almost *proud* of my
Affronts, and I then wondered at it, tho' afterwards I better
understood his Heavenly principles."

The principal schoolmaster of this godly youth was
the celebrated Ezekiel Cheever, to whose memory Cotton Mather paid a heartfelt tribute :

"'T is Corlett's praise and Cheever's, we must own,
    That thou, New England, art not Scythia grown." [1]

Sewall gives a graphic account of the last days of
this famous pedagogue,[2] ending with this sketch of
his life : —

" He was born January 25, 1614. Came over to N. E.
1637, to Boston : To New-Haven 1638. Married in the Fall
and began to teach School; which Work he was constant in
till now. First, at New-Haven, then at Ipswich ; then at
Charlestown ; then at Boston, whither he came 1670. So
that he has Laboured in that Calling Skillfully, diligently,
constantly, Religiously, Seventy years. A rare Instance of
Piety, Health, Strength, Serviceableness. The Wellfare of
the Province was much upon his Spirit. He abominated
Perriwigs." [3]

What Cotton Mather studied, and how he comported
himself under this master, appears from the manuscript
he left his son.[4]

---

[1] Corderius Americanus (1708).

[2] Diary, II. 230, 231 (August, 1708).

[3] This was always a serious matter with Sewall : " Friday,
Nov. 6 [1685]. Having occasion . . . to go to Mr. Hayward,
the Publick Notary's House, I speak to him about his cutting
off his Hair, and wearing a Perriwig of contrary Colour : mention the words of our Saviour, Can ye not make an Hair white
or black. . . . He alledges, the Doctor advised him to it."
Diary, I. 102. And cf. II. 36, 37.

[4] Paterna.

"One special Fault of my childhood (against which I would have you *my son* be cautioned) was idleness. And one thing that occasioned me very much *idle time*, was the Distance of my Father's Habitation from the *School;* which caused him out of compassion for my Tender and Weakly constitution to keep me at home in the *Winter.* However I then much employed myself in *Church History;* and when *Summer* arrived I so plied my Business, that thro' the Blessing of God upon my endeavours, at the Age of little more than *eleven years* I had composed many *Latin* exercises, both in prose and verse, and could speak *Latin* so readily, that I could write notes of sermons of the English preacher, in it. I had conversed with *Cato, Corderius, Terence, Tully, Ovid,* and *Virgil.* I had made *Epistles* and *Themes;* presenting my first Theme to my Master, without his requiring or expecting as yett any such thing of me; whereupon he complimented me: *Laudabilis Diligentia tua.*[1] I had gone through a great part of the New Testament in *Greek,* I had read considerably in *Socrates* and *Homer,* and I had made some entrance in my *Hebrew* grammar. And I think before I came to Fourteen, I composed Hebrew exercises and *Ran* thro' the other Sciences, that *Academical Students* ordinarily fall upon."

At twelve he had been admitted to Harvard College. What the College was then like may be guessed from the "Laws, Liberties, and Orders," printed in the Appendix to Quincy's "History of Harvard University,"[2] In brief, the students had to observe rules of pious decorum inconceivable in the nineteenth century, and ultimately to prove their fitness for the bachelor's degree by showing that they could "read the original of the Old and New Testament into the Latin tongue, and resolve them logically." To be sure, human depravity

---

[1] "Your diligence is praiseworthy." [2] I. 515.

had so manifested itself among undergraduates as early as 1659 that the authorities of the College thought proper to authorize the town watch to keep order in the college yard. But in general whoever looks through the pages of Sibley's " Harvard Graduates " must feel sure that during the first half-century of its existence Harvard College to a rare degree fulfilled the purpose for which it was founded, and gave the Colonies a notably vigourous, learned, devoted ministry. In the " Magnalia " [1] Cotton Mather gives a catalogue of the Congregational ministers officiating in New England in 1696; he names one hundred and twenty-one; of these only eleven were not graduates of Harvard.

Of his academic studies, Cotton Mather writes thus :

" I composed *Systems* both of *Logick* and Physick, in *Catachisms* of my own, which have since been used by many others. I went over the use of the *Globes*, and proceeded in *Arithmetic* as far as was ordinary. I made *Theses*, and Antitheses upon the main *Questions* that lay before me. For my *Declamations* I ordinarily took some Article of *Natural Philosophy* for my subject, by which contrivances I did Kill two birds with one Stone. Hundreds of books I read over, and I kept a Diary of my studies. *My son* I would not have mentioned these things, but that I may provoke *your* emulation." [2]

Meanwhile his spiritual life had been growing.

" I can't certainly remember," he writes,[2] " (having by an unhappy casualty [3] lost some of my records) when it was that I began to keep *Days of Prayer with Fasting* alone by myself. But I think it was when I was about *fourteen* years old. And I remember well That I made *Mr. Scudder's Christian's Walk* my Directory in those Duties."

[1] I. VII.   [2] Paterna.   [3] See page 271.

He notes that he was melancholy, and thought he had every distemper he read of. His self-consciousness was enhanced by what often afflicts people of active mind, — an impediment of speech.[1] He "had great benefit from a Society of Young Men, who met every *Evening* after the Lord's Day for the Services of Religion." Two other small facts about his undergraduate career are recorded in the Mather Papers: he sent to his uncle abroad a carefully drawn map of the region, wherein his uncle was surprised to find that the Blue Hills were not, as he remembered them, north of Boston; and during some vacations he was invited to act as tutor to some kinsmen older than he. At sixteen, he became a member of the Second Church.

Slight enough these facts; but they should help us to imagine what manner of boy it was who in 1678 presented himself for the bachelor's degree. At that time he was the youngest who had ever applied for it at Harvard; to this day but two have applied younger.[2] And this is what President Urian Oakes said to him in his Commencement oration: —

"Alter vero Cottonus Matherus nuncupatur. Quantum Nomen! Erravi, fateor, Auditores; dicissem etenim, quanta Nomina! Nihil ego de Reverendo PATRE, Academiæ Curatore vigilantissimo, municipii Academici socio primario, dicam; quoniam coram et in os laudare nolim; sed si Pietatem, Eruditionem, Ingenium elegans, Judicium Solidum, Prudentiam et Gravitatem AVORUM Reverendissimorum JOANNIS COTTONI et RICHARDI MATHERI, referat

[1] S. Mather, Life of Cotton Mather.
[2] Paul Dudley, 1690, and Andrew Preston Peabody, 1826. Sibley III. 6.

et representet, omne tulisse Punctum dici poterit; nec despero futurum, ut in hoc juvene Cottonus atq: Matherus tam re quam Nomine coalescant et reviviscant." [1]

[1] Sibley, III. 6, 7.—"The next is named Cotton Mather. How notable a name! I am wrong, my friends; I should rather have said what notable names! I will say nothing of his reverend father, the most watchful of guardians, the most distinguished Fellow of the College: I dare not praise him here, to his very face. But if this youth bring back into being the piety, the learning, the elegant accomplishment, the sound sense, the prudence, and the gravity of his very reverend grandfathers, John Cotton and Richard Mather, he may be said to have done his highest duty. Nor is my hope small that in this youth Cotton and Mather shall, in fact as well as in name, join together and once more appear in life."

IV

THE FALL OF THE CHARTER — THE BEGINNING
OF COTTON MATHER'S MINISTRY

1678–1686

THE next eight years were among the most critical
in the history of Massachusetts. From the settlement
the Colony had been governed under a royal charter,
granted to the Governor and Company of Massachusetts Bay in 1629. Under this, as we have seen, none
but church-members had been freemen. Church-members had elected all political officers; they had established their own system of law; on their actions, and
on their actions alone, rested everything in the rapidly
strengthening community; not so much as the title to
an acre of land came from any other source. The relation of the Colony to the Crown, in short, was comprised in the fact that the Crown had originally granted
the Charter. As we have seen, the disturbed condition of England during the Civil Wars and the Commonwealth conspired with the original insignificance of
the Colony to allow it virtual independence; and its
political history is that of a conflict between the theocratic and the democratic spirits inherent in its original
constitution.

A new factor had now appeared, however. Theoretically, New England, in virtue of its discovery by the
Cabots, was the private property of the sovereign. Only

the voluntary act of the sovereign, in the Charter, gave
the colonists any rights at all; their position resembled
that of tenants on a private estate. And from the
beginning the Charter had been contested by some
gentlemen, who maintained that it was in violation of
previous royal grants to them. Under Charles II this
attack was renewed, partly perhaps because New England was growing too prosperous to be let alone. During King Philip's War there came to Boston for the
first time Edward Randolph, agent of the Lords of
Trade, with a royal letter requiring the Governor and
Assistants of Massachusetts at once to send representatives to England, there to answer the claims of those who
contested the Charter. The contest thus begun lasted
till 1684. Massachusetts fought to the death, but no
diplomacy could save her. What is more, a party appeared in the Colony itself which favoured submission
to royal authority. This party seems to have been built
up chiefly by the exertions of Randolph, who constantly
went back and forth from England, and achieved a popular detestation not yet quite forgotten. At the head of
the Royalists was Joseph Dudley, son of Thomas Dudley,
second Governor of the Colony. In 1684 came the end:
the Court of Chancery vacated the Charter of Massachusetts. Without a government, without a single legal
right, the Colony lay at the mercy of the Crown. It
was the intention of Charles II to send over as governor, vested with absolute authority, that Colonel Percy
Kirke whose "Lambs" a few months later did such
notable work in suppressing the traces of Monmouth's
rebellion.[1] But before anything definite was done,

[1] See Macaulay's History of England, Chapter V.

Charles was dead, James on the throne, Monmouth in arms, and Kirke busy cutting undefended throats. Meanwhile, in Massachusetts, one more election was held under the forms of the vacated charter: the last Governor elected by the people was Simon Bradstreet, who was likewise the last survivor of the magistrates who nearly sixty years before had founded the government now at an end.

With these facts in view, certain dry notes in Sewall's Diary[1] grow dramatic. He tells how, on the 14th of May, 1686, the Rose frigate arrived at Nantasket; how Randolph came to town by eight in the morning, and took coach for Roxbury, where Dudley lived; and how, with other magistrates, he himself was summoned to see the judgment against the Charter with the Broad Seal of England affixed. He tells how, on the following Sunday, Randolph came to the Old South Church, where Mr. Willard in his prayer made no mention of Governor or government, but spoke as if all were changed or changing. He tells how next day the General Court assembled, and how Joseph Dudley, temporarily made President of New England, exhibited the condemnation of the Charter and his own commission under the Broad Seal of England; how the old magistrates began to make some formal answer, and how Dudley said he could not acknowledge them as a court nor in any way capitulate with them; and how, when Dudley was gone, a sorrowful group of the old magistrates decided that there was no room for a protest: "The foundations being gone what can the Righteous do?" He tells how Increase Mather with

[1] I, 137-140.

other ministers vainly strove to persuade Dudley not to accept the presidency. And finally comes this note : —

"Friday, May 21, 1686. The Magistrates and Deputies goe to the Governour's. . . . Mr. Nowell prayed that God would pardon each Magistrate and Deputies Sin. Thanked God for our hithertos of Mercy 56 years, in which time sad Calamities elsewhere, as Massacre Piedmont; thanked God for what we might expect from sundry of those now set over us. I moved to sing, so sang the 17. and 18. verses of Habbakkuk.[1] The Adjournment . . . was declared by the weeping Marshall-General. Many Tears Shed in Prayer and at Parting."

This dry note marks the end of the pristine government of Massachusetts. From that day to this church and state have been finally separate there. Until the American Revolution, the people never had a word in the choice of another Governor. The dream of the Puritans — the dream of a state governed only by the dictates of Scripture — had passed, with other dreams of men, into the region of things that may not be.

For seven months Joseph Dudley was President of the provincial government of New England. On Sunday, May 30, Sewall notes that he sang

"the 141 Psalm . . . exceedingly suited to the day. Wherein there is to be worship according to the Church of England, as 't is called, in the Town House, by countenance of Authority."

In August, he had grave doubts as to whether he

[1] Hab. iii. 17, 18. "Although the fig tree shall not blossom, neither shall fruit be in the vines; the labour of the olive shall fail, and the fields shall yield no meat; the flock shall be cut off from the fold, and there shall be no herd in the stalls: yet I will rejoice in the Lord, I will joy in the God of my salvation."

could conscientiously serve in the militia under a flag
in which the cross was replaced; in November, he
finally resigned his commission as Captain of the South
Company. On Saturday, September 25, the Queen's
birthday had been celebrated with drums, bonfires,
and huzzas. Next day, " Mr. Willard expresses great
grief in 's Prayer for the Profanation of the Sabbath
last night."

On Sunday, December 19, while Sewall was reading
to his family an exposition of Habakkuk, he heard a
great gun or two which made him think Sir Edmund [1]
might be come. Sure enough he was, " in a Scarlet
Coat laced." That day the President went to hear
Mr. Willard, who " said he was fully persuaded and
confident God would not forget the Faith of those who
came first to New England, but would remember their
Posterity with kindness." Between sermons the President went down the harbour to welcome Sir Edmund.
The next afternoon Andros landed in state, and was
escorted by the eight companies to the Town-House.
Here his commission was read, declaring his power to
suspend councillors and to appoint others, and vesting
the legislative power in him and his Council. Then he
took the oath of allegiance, and stood by with his hat
on while eight councillors were sworn. The same day
he demanded accommodation in one of the meeting-houses for the services of the Church of England.
This was too much for the Puritans. At a meeting of
the ministers and four of each congregation, it was
agreed that they could not with a good conscience
consent that their meeting-houses be made use of for

[1] Andros, the Governor appointed by James II.

the Common Prayer worship; and "Mr. Mather[1] and
Willard thorowly discoursed his Excellency about the
Meeting-Houses in great plaiñess." So for a while
Sir Edmund was content to worship at the Town-
House. But Sewall notes, on January 25, that "this
day is kept for St. Paul, and the bell was rung in the
Morning, to call persons to Service. The Governour
(I am told) was there"; and on January 31 there was
a similar service "respecting the beheading Charles
the First."

Meanwhile there had been minor symptoms of the
change that was coming to New England. As early as
November, 1685,

"the Ministers Come to the Court and complain against a
Dancing Master who seeks to set up here and hath mixt
Dances, and his time of Meeting is Lecture-Day; and 't is
reported he should say that by one Play he could teach
more Divinity than Mr. Willard or the Old Testament.
. . . Mr. Mather[1] struck at the Root, speaking against
mixt Dances." Early in September, 1686, "Mr Shrimp-
ton . . . and others come in a Coach from Roxbury about
9 aclock or past, singing as they come, being inflamed with
Drink: At Justice Morgan's they stop and drink Healths,
curse, swear, talk profanely and baudily to the great disturbance of the Town and grief of good people. Such
high-handed wickedness has hardly been heard of before in
Boston." And though on Christmas day shops were "open
generally and persons about their occasions," there was a
sad affair on Shrove Tuesday: "Joseph Maylem carries a
Cock at his back, with a Bell in 's hand, in the Main
Street; several follow him blindfold, and under pretence of
striking him or 's Cock, with great cart-whips strike passen-
gers, and make great disturbance."

[1] Increase.

During these eight years the career of Increase Mather was steadily advancing. No figure was more conspicuous among those who resisted the change. We have seen how he vainly tried to dissuade Joseph Dudley from accepting the presidency of New England, and how he told Sir Edmund " in great plainness " that the meeting-houses of Boston should not be used for the rites of the Established Church. But we must turn to Cotton Mather for a full account of his life, public and private.[1] In 1679 Increase Mather was among the leaders of that Synod which assembled to consider " What are the Evils that have Provoked the Lord to bring his judgments on New England? and what is to be done that so these Evils may be Reformed? " A general revival followed, in which the earnest work of the preachers resulted in many renewed covenants with the Lord. A year later, on the verge of a severe illness, he was called to preside at a second meeting of the Synod, which formulated the elaborate Confession of Faith printed in the " Magnalia." [2] He " kept them so close to their *Business* that in *Two Days* they dis- patch'd it : and he also Composed the *Præface* to the *Confession*. On this he immediately took to his Bed under a dangerous fever." But, in accordance with many prayers of many good people, he recovered ; and preached his first sermon on the text, " To me to Live is CHRIST." At the death of Urian Oakes, in 1681, he acted for a while as President of Harvard College. Four years later, after the death of John Rogers, he finally accepted the presidency.

[1] Parentator, Arts. XVIII.–XXII.
[2] V. L.

It was in 1683 that the demand came from Charles II that Massachusetts should " make a *full Submission and entire Resignation* of their Charter to his pleasure." At a meeting of the freemen of Boston, Increase Mather was invited to give them his thoughts on the *Case of Conscience* before them.

" I verily Believe," he said, " We shall Sin against the GOD of Heaven if we vote an Affirmative. . . . Nor would it be *Wisdom* for us to Comply. We know, *David* made a Wise Choice, when he chose to fall into the *Hands of GOD* rather than into the *Hands of Men*. If we make a *full Submission and entire Resignation* to Pleasure, we shall fall into the *Hands of Men* Immediately. But if we do it not, we still keep ourselves in the *Hands of GOD ;* we trust ourselves with His Providence : and who knows, what GOD may do for us ? " — " Upon this pungent Speech," writes Cotton Mather, " many of the Freemen fell into Tears ; and there was a General Acclamation, *We thank you, Syr ! We thank you, Syr !* The Question was upon the Vote carried in the Negative, *Nemine Contradicente*. And this Act of Boston had a great influence upon all the Country."

The next year came one of the most critical incidents of Increase Mather's life. A letter signed with his initials and addressed to a friend in Holland was intercepted and brought to the notice of the authorities in England. It contained sentiments which, if not treasonable, were in the highest degree offensive to the King. Nothing could more seriously affect his public influence abroad. The Mathers always declared this letter a forgery, which they attributed to Edward Randolph ; their enemies, then and now, have pronounced the letter genuine and the defence a lie. The question of veracity can never, perhaps, be satisfactorily settled.

But a note on the subject from Increase Mather's diary seems to me honest : —

" The Lord has had respect unto all the WISHES Written down before Him; on Jun. 11, 1670[1]— Yea he had so far Gratified my Desire of *Suffering for Him*, that my Name hath been cast forth as Vile, and Wicked Men in *England, Scotland, Ireland, Barbadoes,* and the Leeward Islands, and elsewhere, have been *Speaking all manner of Evil of me falsely.* And the Ground of these my *Sufferings* has been, because I have desired to Approve myself faithful unto the Lord JESUS, and unto His Kingdom and Interest."

A less depressing experience came on the 6th of February, 1685 ; at this time Kirke was expected as governor.

"THIS DAY," wrote Increase Mather, " as I was Praying to GOD for the Deliverance of *New-England,* I was very much Moved and Melted before the Lord, so that for some time I was not able to speak a word. But then, I could not but say, *GOD will deliver* New-England ! *GOD will deliver* New-England ! *God will deliver* New-England ! So I rose from my knees, with much Comfort and Assurance, that GOD had heard me. These things, I hope, were from the Spirit of GOD. Before I Prayed, I was very sad, and much dejected in my Spirit; but after I had Prayed, I was very Cheerful and joyful; I will then *Wait* for the *Salvation of GOD !* "

Sure enough, Kirke never came to Massachusetts.

It is during these eight years that we begin to have definite accounts of Cotton Mather's private life. Twenty-four of his diaries are preserved ; and of these, four fall within this period.[2] The diaries always

[1] Cf. page 26.

[2] Those for 1681, 1683, 1685, and 1686; all in the possession of the Massachusetts Historical Society.

begin on his birthday; and as he begins the year, after the old fashion, on the 1st of March, the first three weeks of each volume bear date of the year before the rest of it. By far the greater part of the entries concern his spiritual experiences; yet among them are notes of other matters sufficient to give us a pretty vivid notion of what manner of life he led. It is characteristic of Cotton Mather that, until 1711, none of the diaries are original copies. For some years he took the trouble to copy from his records such as he deemed worth preserving, and then to destroy the notes. But the presumption of error which this process raises is greatly weakened in my mind by the fact that his diaries, after he gave up the practice of revision, show no change in the general character of the entries; and this is particularly true of one volume, which his third wife, who was occasionally insane, stole, and hid before it was finished, and which, apparently, he never saw again.

Until 1681 I find nothing concerning him beyond what his son tells.[1] Suffering from an impediment of speech, he at first believed himself unfitted for the ministry, and studied medicine; but, following the advice of a friend to " oblige himself to a *dilated Deliberation* in speaking," he " procured with Divine Help an happy delivery." On August 22, 1680, he preached in his grandfather's church, at Dorchester, his first sermon, in which, " because of the Calling he had relinquished, he did . . . consider our blessed Saviour as the glorious *Physician of Souls;* chusing those words for his first Text in Luke iv. 18. *He hath sent me to heal the broken-*

[1] S. Mather, Life of Cotton Mather, 26, 27.

hearted." Just six months later he was unanimously invited to assist his father at the Second Church.

This was his occupation during 1681, the year covered by his first extant diary. The notes in this concern little but spiritual experiences. The first is a long devotional passage, full of good resolutions, "penned by *Cotton Mather,* a Feeble and worthless, yett [Lord by THY GRACE] desirous to approve himself a Sincere & Faithful Servant of Jesus Christ." On the following Sabbath,

"The Singular Assistencies which the God of Heaven gave unto mee, in my public ministrations . . . were such as caused me to draw up this conclusion: *I believe I shall have a Glorious Presence of God with me through my whole Ministry.*" And about this time he was gratified by a subscription of seventy pounds, "for my Encouragement in my public service the ensuing year."

On the 13th of March, "in the Assurances, the glorious and Ravishing Assurances of the Divine Love, my joyes were almost insupportable." On the 19th, he was depressed; on the 3d of April, he was again ecstatic; on the 8th, he suffered from a "silence of God" in prayer-time — a punishment for "an Idle Fraud of Soul"; on the 10th, he recovered his poise of temper: "If it be thy Will," he wrote, "I would *live,* to do some Special Service for thee, before I shall go hence and bee no more seen." I cite this experience in some detail, because its course and period of emotional action and reaction is typical of what followed him throughout life. In March he was

"taken with a violent *pain,* . . . which looked like a messenger of Death. Here I am," he wrote; "Afflict mee;

4

Do what thou wilt with mee; Kill mee ; for thy Grace
hath made mee willing to Dy : *Only, Only, Only,* Help mee
to Delight in thee, and to glorify thy dearest Name."

Two months later, he had a toothache, which induced two reflections : —

"I. Have I not sinned with my *Teeth?* . . . By sinful, Graceless, excessive Eating. And by Evil *Speeches,*
for there are *Liberal Dentals* used in them. II. This is
an Old Malady, from which I have yett been free, for a
considerable while. Lett me ask then : Have not I of late
given way to some old Iniquity?"

The iniquity which troubled him most seems to have
been the one he mentions most definitely in October.

"I desire to walk Humbly before the Lord, all my Dayes,
in the Remembrance of the Lothsome Corruptions, which
my Soul has been from my Youth polluted withal. *Lord,
Wherewithal shall a young man cleanse his way?* Altho'
I have been kept from such Out-breakings of Sin, in Actions towards others, as have undone many in the world,
yett I have certainly been one of the Filthiest Creatures
upon Earth."

Another besetting sin was revealed to him in June.
A good woman told him how one of his sermons had
convinced her that she had fallen into the sin of pride.
Reflecting that pride is "the sin of young ministers,"
he straightway discovered it in himself. A day of passionate prayer followed, which the Lord was pleased to
reward with " glorious Assurances that Hee would never
Leave the Work which Hee had begun in my soul."
A week later came a day of secret Thanksgiving.
" *Oh Lord,*" he wrote, "*Not unto mee, Not unto mee, but
unto thy Name is All, All, All the Glory due;* and thou

shalt have it. There shall *Hallelujahs* be sung to thee forever and ever "— for the "great works" which Cotton Mather, thus freed from the sin of pride, shall accomplish. But before he closes this grotesque day, he earnestly thanks God, too, for " the Life and Health of my dear Father, whom I may reckon among the Richest of my Enjoyments."

Meanwhile, several of his experiences had been comforting. In May, a man whom he had warned of Divine displeasure for not joining a church, fell off a roof,

"and received a Blow, whereof he Lay, for some while, as Dead. But coming to himself one of the first things he thought on, was what I had said unto him ; under the sense whereof, hee quickly went and joined himself unto the *South* church."

In October, he preached in the pulpit of his Grandfather Cotton,

" with a very singular Assistance of the Lord. Yea, such was his powerful presence with mee, that some afterwards declared their melted and Broken Hearts could hardly forbear crying out in the Assembly."

About the same time, he fixed on certain habits of devotion which he found permanently edifying: one was

"to start the day with a Scripture . . . which might be of some special consequence to my everlasting Interests "; and his first meditation was on Zech. 13, 1,[1] "cast into Three Observations. The *Blood* of the Lord Jesus Christ is fitly compared unto a *Fountain*. This is an *Open Fountain*. And, the End of it is, for the *Washing away* of Sin, which is Uncleanness."

[1] "In that day there shall be a fountain opened to the house of David and to the inhabitants of Jerusalem for sin and for uncleanness."

A little earlier he had had a still more comforting experience : —

"As I was in Meditation . . . *How I might glorify God?* I happened to Look thro' the window upon the Heavens; and this Thought was after a most powerful and Refreshing manner cast into my mind, Surely, If the Lord intended not forever to glorify mee in Heaven, Hee would never have put it into my Heart, that I should seek to Glorify Him on Earth."

But perhaps his most characteristic experience in 1681 was this : —

"I bought a Spanish Indian; and bestowed him for a Servant on my Father. This Thing I would not Remember . . . but only because I would observe whether I do not hereafter see some Special and Signal Return of this Action. . . . I am secretly persuaded, *That I shall do so!*"

In the course of his life he had a great many secret persuasions and particular faiths : this is the first he records. In the " Magnalia " he defines them : —

" Good men, that labour & abound in prayer to the great God, sometimes arrive to the assurance of a *particular faith* for the good success of their prayer. . . . Many a real Christian . . . is a stranger to . . . this thing; . . . it is here & there a Christian, whom the sovereign grace of Heaven does favour with the consolations of a particular faith. . . . The *wondrous meltings*, the *mighty wrestlings*, the *quiet waitings*, & the *holy resolves*, that are characters of a particular faith, which is no delusion, are the works of the Holy Spirit, wherein his holy angels may be instruments." [1]

A particular faith which proved no delusion, then, was above most things else an assurance of election: it was, as it were, a momentary sharing of the foresight of

[1] IV. II. I. § 6.

God. To justify his faith about the Spanish Indian, Cotton Mather had to wait sixteen years : then a knight whom he had laid under many obligations bestowed a Spanish Indian on him.[1]

The actual facts he noted this year are few. On August 9th,

" I took my Second Degree, proceeding Master of Arts. My Father was *president*, so that from his Hand I Received my Degree. Tis when I am gott almost Half a year beyond *Eighteen* in my age. And all the circumstances of my Commencement were ordered by a very sensibly kind providence of God. My *Thesis* was, *Puncta Hebraica sunt Originis Divinæ.*" [2]

In October he was active in forwarding a plan, objected to by some as superstitious, that devout people should devote a given hour every Monday to prayer for persecuted churches abroad. In November he declined a call to New Haven. Towards the end of December, he was elected pastor of the Second Church, with a salary of seventy pounds. In February, 1682, he again refused a call to New Haven.

" My Reason was, because the Church of *North Boston* would have entertained uncomfortable Dissatisfactions at my Father, if after so many Important *Votes* of Theirs for my Settlement here, he had anyway permitted my Removal from them."

He remained minister of the North Church all his life.

" Horae plusquam amoenae, nunquam rediturae," [8]

is the motto of his diary for 1683. From now on, each

---

[1] S. Mather, Life, etc., p. 12.
[2] Hebrew vowel points are of divine origin.
[8] " More than delightful hours, never to return."

of his diaries bears some motto on the outer leaf; and begins with a devout and generally searching birthday meditation. Towards the middle of the year he copied one of his original notes which shows the course of his daily life : —

"28 d. 6 m. Legi Exod. 34, 35, 36 | Oravi | Examinavi adolescentes | Legi Cartesium | Legi Commentatores in Joh. 6. 37 | Jentacul | Paravi concionem | Orationi interfui Domestica | Audivi pupillos Recitantes | Legi Salmon pharmacop: | pransus sum | Visitavi plures Amicos | Legi Varia | Paravi concionem | Audivi pupillos Recitantes | Meditat: On, *the exceeding Willingness of the Lord Jesus Christ to Do good unto them that come unto Him.* And, I Resolve As to be Encouraged in my Addresses unto the Lord Jesus for His Mercy from the Thoughts of his mercifulness, then also the Endeavor that I may be Like unto Him in Humble and Ready *Helpfulness* to others | Oravi | Coenavi | paravi Concionem | Orationi interfui Domestica."[1]

He made, and often put in practice, any number of good resolutions : some concerning other people, as to encourage rich gentlemen to support a country minister, and to pay an old hawker to distribute good books ; some more personal, as to govern his speech carefully, to close visits with some suitable text of Scripture, and to contrive "what Noble Attainments I should be continually purposing of." In pursuance of this last, he writes : —

[1] Read Exodus, etc.: Prayed: Examined the children : read Descartes : read commentators, etc.: breakfasted : prepared sermon : took part in family prayer : heard pupils recite : read Salmon on medicine : dined : visited many friends : read various books : prepared sermon : heard pupils recite : meditated, etc. : prayed : supped : prepared sermon : took part in family prayer.

"While I was lying on my Couch in the Dusk of the Evening I extempore composed the following Hymn, which I then sang unto the Lord." A typical stanza runs:

> "I will not any Creature *Love*
> But in the *Love* of Thee Above . . .

"I designed rather pietie than poetrie in these lines."

He comments on them in three closely written pages.

He hit upon a device of fining himself for any misconduct: —

"Thus I Laid a penalty for some while upon myself, That if in Joining with the *prayers* of another, I did Lett more than one entire Sentence pass me, at any Time, without annexing some Ejaculation pertinent thereunto, I would forfeit a piece of money to be given unto the poor. And I found this effect of it, that in a Week or Two, I had Little occasion to Lay my *penalty;* for I found my Distractions in my Duties, which had been my plague, most wonderfully cured."

During an evening walk, when he

"had such a prospect of our Neighbourhood as gave mee to see that God had cast my Lot, in a place exceedingly *populous*, I found my Heart, after a more than ordinary manner melted in Desires after the Conversion and Salvation of the Souls in this place. And my soul was afterwards exceedingly Transported, in prayers for such a Mercy."

Praying over a friend critically ill,

"the good man felt, as it were, a Load or Cloud, beginning to Roll off his Spirits; and from that Instant, unto his own admiration, he began to Recover. . . . Oh! my Soul, why dost thou forgett such Benefits!" In July, "Overlooking the addresses of persons to join unto the church, I found over *Thirty Seals* of my ministry in this place. . . . From whence I may form a *probable computation* of many Scores, that have here and elsewhere been thereby helped in their acquaintance with the Lord. Blessed be God." At a young people's thanksgiving late in the year, "the Lord helped mee to preach unto them almost Three Hours (tho' I had Little more than One Hour's Time to prepare for it). . . . And a good Day it was !"

Two little incidents this year impressed him much. His father admiring his watch, he gave it to him; shortly afterwards a gentleman from whom he "had no reason to expect such a visit" gave him a better one: an experience which induced a resolution to stir up dutifulness to parents in himself and others. And a gentleman imported a seal for him, which was lost in a fire, but subsequently found in the ruins.

"I prayed herewithal," he writes, "That by no *Fire*, neither the *Fire* of *Lust* here, nor the *Fire* of *Hell* hereafter I might miss of the promise which the Blood of the Lord Jesus Christ hath sealed."

Far edifying as this year was, it was not without sorrows. His baby sister Katharine died. And in July comes a note that shows a more intimate trouble : —

"Using of sacred *meditations* (with mixed *Supplications*) at my waking minutes every morning in my *Bed*, and in this Course going over many portions of the *Scriptures* a *Verse* at a Time, the Thought of Isaac having his happy Consort brought unto him *when* and *where* he was engaged in his Holy Meditations, came sometimes into my mind, and I had sometimes a strange persuasion, That there would a Time come, when I should have my Bed Blessed with such a Consort given unto mee, as Isaac, the Servant of the Lord, was favoured withal."

In December he found Satan buffeting him with unclean temptations.

"Besides my . . . usual . . . Devotions," he writes, " I

did this Day write after this manner, That I may pluck out my Right Eye, and cutt off my Right Hand. . . . Oh! Blessed Saviour, Save me from the horrible pitt."

He prayed and fasted assiduously; but a month later the same "Sorrowful and Horrible Vexation" tormented him again. About the same time an elderly minister violated the Seventh Commandment: Cotton Mather fasted and prayed more than ever.

" I likewise carried the wounded minister in my prayers unto the Lord for all reasonable mercies."

At the very end of the year, he began to fear that he had carried his mortification of the flesh so far as to violate the Sixth Commandment: —

"'T is well, if I escape a Consumption. . . . What! Are my Duties now but Murders? Lord, pardon mee and pitty mee, for the sake of Jesus Christ!"

The record of the year closes with a long list of the ejaculatory prayers he accustomed himself to utter on all occasions: a typical one is this: —

"On the Gentlewoman that carv'd for the Guests: 'Lord, . . . Carve a rich Portion of thy Graces and Comforts to that Person!'" [1]

He was the grandson of John Cotton and Richard Mather, the son of Increase Mather, sprung from a race of the chosen vessels of God, himself a chosen vessel; and he was just twenty-one years old.

The diary for 1685 finds him approaching ordination. In April there was some trouble about it, which led him to pray that if his life were a real prejudice to

[1] S. Mather, Life, p. 107.

God, or a necessary occasion of strife and sin, he might be taken out of the world. But the "design of Satan" was frustrated by "a most uniting work of God upon the Spirits of the people." From the 22d of April to the 3d of May he was in a state of sustained ecstasy; on the 4th of May came reaction, and on that day he wrote and signed his formal covenant with God: —

"I renounce all the Vanities and Cursed Idols & Evil Courses of this World," it runs. "I engage That I will ever have the Great God my Best Good, my Last *End*, and my only *Lord*. That I will ever bee Rendering of Acknowledgments unto the Lord *Jesus Christ* in all the Relations which Hee bears unto mee. That I will ever bee studying what is my *Dutie* in these things; and wherein I find myself to fall short, I will ever make it my *grief*, my *Shame*, and for *pardon* betake myself unto the *Blood of the Everlasting Covenant*. Now, Humbly Imploring the *Grace* of the *Mediator*, to bee *Sufficient* for mee, I do as a further Solemnitie, hereunto *subscribe* my Name with both *Hand* and *Heart*."

His signature to this document is more than twice the usual size.

On the 13th of May he was finally ordained, in a frame of mind adequately expressed by his covenant. Sewall was present.

"Mr. Cotton Mather is ordained Pastor by his Father," he writes,[1] "who said, My son Cotton Mather, and in 's sermon spake of Aaron's Garments being put on Eleazar, intimating he knew not but that God might now call him out of the World. Mr. Eliot[2] gave the Right Hand of Fellowship, calling him a Lover of Jesus Christ."

[1] Diary, I. 76.
[2] The Apostle to the Indians. See Magnalia, III. III.

Samuel Mather adds a characteristic trait : —

" A truly primitive Ordination! which he never . . . scrupled the *Validity* of. After a curious Examination of most of the *Fathers* in the three first *Centuries*, he was verily perswaded that *every one* of them had been perverted and abused by designing Men to serve their own Ends, especially in the Instance of *Ordination*." [1]

Ten days later, Sewall notes a " private Fast," which gives a glimpse of the manners of the time : —

" The Magistrates . . . with their wives here. Mr. Eliot prayed, Mr. Willard preached. I am afraid of Thy judgments. — Text Mother gave. Mr. Allen prayed ; cessation half an hour. Mr. Cotton Mather prayed ; Mr. Mather preached, Ps. 79. 9.[2] Mr. Moodey prayed about an hour and half ; Sung the 79th Psalm from the 8th to the End ; distributed some Biskets, & Beer, Cider, Wine. The Lord hear in Heaven his dwelling place."

How busy Cotton Mather was this year appears from a note he made in December : —

" The Last Week of the month I *preached* on Lords-Day, Monday, Tuesday, Wednesday, Thursday in the same week Yea, several weeks I have in *one week* preached *five times;* and once I preached *five times* in *Two Days* which came together."

In the course of the year he preached above a hundred carefully written sermons. At the same time he was constantly engaged in parish visiting ; and, besides starting an elaborate method of Bible reading, and pursuing his studies, and devoting many days to prayer

[1] Life, p. 18.
[2] " Help us, O God of our salvation, for the glory of thy name : and deliver us, and purge away our sins, for thy name's sake."

and thanksgiving, he had a number of pupils. And not content with teaching these, he

"did successively use to send for them, *one by one*, into his Study, and there in the most moving, soft, obliging, and yet most solemn and lively manner discourse with them about their own *everlasting Interests ;* and he would then bestow some good Books on them to further the Work of GOD . . . upon their Spirits: And . . . in every Recitation he would . . . make an Occasion to let fall some Sentence, which might have a tendency to promote *the Fear of GOD* in their Souls." [1]

His private devotions meanwhile were more pro- longed and more ecstatic than ever; his emotional condition throughout the year was more and more overwrought. And for this there were several reasons : besides being constantly impressed with the solemnity of the ordination which made him at last a fully equipped minister of the Gospel, and an Overseer of Harvard College, he suffered, as did Massachusetts, from not a few buffets of Satan. In August, his sup- plications were

"especially to seek for the guidance and Blessing of God in what concerns the change of my condition in the world, from Single to married; whereto I have now many in- vitations."

In October, a similar state of mind recurred, slightly complicated by the fact that, like his father, he was quite willing to die for the salvation of any soul. Early in November, he was more concerned about matrimony than ever : he wanted to do God's will; if celibacy were God's will, he accepted it; but he vowed that,

[1] S. Mather, Life, p. 40.

if God would permit him to marry, he would always keep two annual thanksgivings with his wife. Late in January came another fast, very similar, more intense. Meanwhile the scope and variety of his good resolutions, of his thanksgivings, of his self-searching meditations, are bewildering. And he had not a few assurances of Divine presence with him.

The most remarkable of these was apparently connected in his mind with those public affairs which this year were so troublesome. Some of his records concern these. In May, when James II. was proclaimed, two friends happened in as he was busy with a private fast.

"I preached unto my Two Friends," he writes, "Three Sermons each of them about an Hour Long apeece, on a Text, which was the very first, that on the opening of my Bible for a subject of Meditation, came to sight: namely Psal. 109. 19. 20,[1] which proved wonderfully suitable."

All three resolved to do special services for Christ, if He would relieve His people from the distresses now upon them. In September, the "calamities & confusions of the English Nation" caused him to be called daily an hour earlier than usual, that he might "Retire for *Sighs*, and *prayers*, and *psalms*, to bee employed for the distressed churches of God": within a fortnight after tidings of the Lord's victory, he vowed he would keep a special day of thanksgiving, and ponder other acknowledgments. Late in January comes the following retrospective note: —

[1] "Let it be unto him as the garment which covereth him, and for a girdle wherewith he is girded continually. Let this be the reward of mine adversaries from the Lord, and of them that speak evil against my soul."

"The Glorious Assurances which I have enjoyed and
uttered, very many times, for now some years together,
about the Lords Appearing to deliver His people from
Impending Desolations are now answered. That monster
Kirk, who was coming to *N. England* with a Regiment of
Red Coats, to sacrifice the best Lives among us, is diverted
from coming hither, by the happy Death of that greater
Monster, K. *Charles* II. And with K. James II. Things
are operating towards such a Liberty for the *Dissenters* as
may for aught I know bring the *Resurrection of the Lord's
witnesses:* it being just three years and a half since their
Congregations were all Dissipated, and a *Thanksgiving* celebrated thro' a wicked nation for it. Wherefore Lett me
now procure as many *Dayes of praise* as I can among the
meetings with whom I have had so many *Dayes of prayer*
on these occasions."

This entry bears no date. The one before it, dated
January 27, relates a prolonged thanksgiving, which
closes with a consideration of what services Cotton
Mather shall render to the Lord for His mercies to
himself and to New England : in particular, he con-
cludes, he should "immediately procure some Testimony, against some Common and growing Evils, which
offend him in the land." A note of Sewall's throws
some light on this entry and the next : —

"Jan. 20th. . . Cousin Fissenden tells me there is a
Maid at Woburn who 't is feared is Possessed by an evil
Spirit."

On the 6th of February, 1685–86, Cotton Mather
wrote as follows : —

"It will cost mee very Bitter Toyle and paines yett perhaps I may bee very serviceable in it: If I procure to myself an Exact Account of those *Evil Humours*, which the

place is at any Time under the observeable Dominion of. And, whereas those *Divels* may bee *cast out* by *Fasting and prayer*, sett apart (first) a Day of *Secret prayers* with *Fasting* on the occasion of each of them : to *Deprecate* my own guiltiness therein, and *supplicate* for such Effusions of the Spirit from on High, as may Redress, Remove, and Banish such *Distempers from the place*."

We have seen enough of Cotton Mather now, I think, to understand at once the tremendous reality to him, and the bearing on what we have just read and on what is coming, of the record I shall copy next. It bears no date ; it is written on the inner side of the cover — the first leaf — of the diary for 1685 : —

"Res Mirabilis et Memoranda. Post Fusas, Maximis cum Ardoribus, Jejunisqu:, *Preces*, apparuit ANGELUS, qui *Vultum* habuit solis instar Meridiani micantem: Caetera *Humanum*, at prorsus *imberbem : Caput* magnificâ Tiarâ obvolutum : In Humeris, *Alas : Vestes* deinceps Candidas et Splendidas: *Togam* nempe Talarem : et *Zonam* circa Lumbos, Orientalium cingulis non absimilem. Dixitqu: hic *Angelus*, à Domino JESU, se missum, ut Responsa cujusdam Juvenis precibus, articulatim afferat, referatqu: Quamplurima retulit hic *Angelus*, quae hîc Scribere non fas est. Verum inter alia memoratu digna ; Futurum Hujusce Juvenis Fatum optime posse exprimi, asseruit in illis Vatis Ezekielis verbis. Ezek. 31 : 3, 4, 5, 7, and 9. *Behold hee was a Cedar in Lebanon, with fair branches, and with a Shadowing Shrowd and of an High Stature, and his Top was among the Thick Boughs. The waters made him great, the Deep Sett him up on High with her Rivers running about his plants. His Heighth was Exalted above all the Trees of the Field, and his Boughs were multiplied, and his Branches became Long, because of the Multitude of Waters when he shott forth. Thus was hee fair in his Greatness, in the Length of his Branches, for his*

*Root was by the Great Waters. Nor was any Tree in
the Garden of God like unto him in his Beauty. I have
made him fair by the multitude of his Branches, so that
all the Trees of Eden, that were in the Garden of God,
Envied him.* Atqu : particulariter clausulas de *Rationis*
ejus extendendis, exposuit hic *Angelus*, de *Libris* ab hoc
Juvene componendis, et non tantùm in *Americâ*, sed etiam
in Europâ, publicandis. Additqu : peculiares quasdam
praedictiones, et pro Tali ac Tanto peccatore, valdè mira-
biles, de *Operibus Insignibus*, quae pro Ecclesiâ Christi in
Revolutionibus jam Appropinquantibus, Hic Juvenis olim
facturus est. *Domine Jesu !* Quid sibi vult haec res tam
Extraordinaria ? A *Diabolicis Illusionibus*, obsecro te,
Servum Tuum Indignissimum, ut Liberes et Defendas ! "[1]

Thus we find him at the close of his twenty-third

[1] "A strange and memorable thing. After outpourings of
prayer, with the utmost fervour and fasting, there appeared an
Angel, whose face shone like the noonday sun. His features
were as those of a man, and beardless ; his head was encircled
by a splendid tiara ; on his shoulders were wings ; his garments were white and shining ; his robe reached to his ankles ;
and about his loins was a belt not unlike the girdles of the
peoples of the East. And this Angel said that he was sent
by the Lord Jesus to bear a clear answer to the prayers of
a certain youth, and to bear back his words in reply. Many
things this Angel said which it is not fit to set down here. But
among other things not to be forgotten he declared that the
fate of this youth should be to find full expression for what in
him was best : and this he said in the words of the prophet
Ezekiel, etc. . . . And in particular this Angel spoke of the influence his reason should have, and of the books this youth should
write and publish, not only in America, but in Europe. And
he added certain special prophecies of the great works this
youth should do for the Church of Christ in the revolutions that
are now at hand. Lord Jesus ! What is the meaning of this
marvel ? From the wiles of the Devil, I beseech thee, deliver
and defend Thy most unworthy servant."

year: the youth in whom Cotton and Mather have joined and shown themselves once more in life; a minister so busy that it is still a marvel how he found time for half the things he did; torn by emotions that he believed to come now from God, now from Satan, — never from anything less; bound by covenant to do great works for the God who had answered his prayers for New England; assured by a celestial visitant that his works shall be fruitful; and with his thoughts directed by a chance that might well seem providential to those visitations of the Devil — so strangely akin to his own visitations from heaven — that the doctors of his time called witchcraft. He was very anxious to be married, too; a fact which probably had more than he knew to do with his state of mind.

For the year 1686, troublous enough to New England, was a much more peaceful one for him. Almost his first note tells how he paid one of his first visits to a young gentlewoman, the daughter of worthy and pious parents in Charlestown, "unto an Acquaintance with whom the wonderful providence of God, in Answer to many prayers directed" him. This was Abigail, daughter of the Honourable Colonel Phillips. He writes at some length his notions of how godly his wooing ought to be. He notes how one Sunday he stayed at home from Charlestown, to preach, after the custom of the time, to a criminal,[1] who was to be executed during the week, and was formally brought into church to hear his last sermon; and how, as a re-

---

[1] James Morgan. See Sewall's Diary, I. 111, 124-126; Magnalia, VI. VI. App. (VII.).

ward, this sermon was published.   Cotton Mather never lost the passion for seeing himself in print ; and this was apparently the first book he acknowledged : it was reprinted, with an appendix containing an account of his talk with Morgan on the way to execution.   He notes later how he examined himself, and made sure that he really preferred Jesus to anything else, how he prayed for a comfortable habitation, how he refrained from asking the church to raise his salary, how older ministers asked him to join their prayer-meeting and met in his study.   Then he tells how a young minister has been disciplined for some fall from grace, and prays that, if similar treatment of him may do God good, he may be similarly treated : " Here I am," he writes, " Do with me as Thou wilt."   He notes how his heart goes out toward neighbours who have a low opinion of him ; he prays that he may not be a vessel of dishonour ; and that he may be very careful of other people's reputations.   In short, he shows himself as thoroughly in love as an honest Puritan could be.

The 4th of May was his wedding-day.   He got up early, to ponder ; but in spite of his pondering he reached Charlestown ahead of time.   So he repaired to the garden with his Bible, and read the second chapter of John,[1] fetching " one observation and one supplication out of every verse in that story."   Then the appointed time came, and " the good providence of God " caused his wedding " to be attended with many circumstances of respect and Honour, above most that have ever been in these parts of the world."

[1] The wedding at Cana.

Next Sunday he preached at Charlestown; the next, at
Boston, on Divine Delights, stoutly asserting that after
all the Bible was the most delightful thing in his
experience. This was on the very Sunday when Mr.
Willard "prayed not for the Governour"; [1] next day
Joseph Dudley assumed the Presidency.

For several months Cotton Mather lived with his
father-in-law, serene in mood and noting various promises in Scripture which we should remember daily.

"The methods of Religion," he writes, "which the
Spirit of the Lord has heretofore taught me, were the most
that now, for some considerable while, I contented myself
withal. And I wish that thro' my slothful and carnal Disposition, some of *these* also had not begun to wither with me."

At length he moved to Boston, where he took

"An *House* wherein my Father Lived in the years 1677
and 1681 and wherein my more *Childish Age* made many
Hundreds of prayers unto the God of Heaven. I could
not but observe the providence of God, in Ordering my
Comforts now, in those very Rooms where I had many
years before sought him with my prayers."

A year before, Mr. Shepard [2] of Charlestown, being
ill, had asked Cotton Mather to preach for him. "As
for you, Syr," he had said after church, "I beg the Lord
to bee with you unto the end of the world." That very
night, to the consternation of all his friends, Mr. Shepard had died. In September, 1686, Cotton Mather
had a startling dream: he dreamt he saw Mr. Shepard,
whom he knew to have been dead for above a year.

"On that account," he writes, "I was contriving to slip
out of the Room; whereupon he nimbly coming up with

[1] Cf. page 41.   [2] See Magnalia, IV. IX.

mee, took me by the Hand, and said, *Syr, you need not be so shie of mee, for you shall quickly be as I am, and where I am.*"

A short fit of illness followed, in which Cotton Mather felt "the Foretastes and Earnests of *Life Eternal*."

He recovered in a somewhat disturbed spiritual condition; he had an excessive ecstasy, which made him resolve to be particular about the spiritual welfare of his dear consort and her father. He started some Sunday evening prayer-meetings, which outgrew his house, and which, for want of a colleague, he had finally to give up by reason of their very success. His last note for the year tells of a thanksgiving: he went, he writes,

"from Room to Room in my house, Deliberately Looking upon the Distinct parcels of the Estate whereof I am now become the Owner, or as I would rather say, the Steward. And with a Ravished Soul, I gave Every Thing back to God, variously contriving and so Declaring How All that I have should bee made serviceable unto his glory."

He formed numerous good designs this day, too: one was to be kind to the French refugees, but to stir them up about Sabbath-keeping; another was to start certain gentlemen and certain religious families in prayer-meetings. And he recorded two distinct resolutions: —

"I. The *common-prayer worship* now being sett up in this country I would procure and assist the publication of a Discourse written by my Father that shall enlighten the Rising Generation in the unlawfulness of that Worship, and Antidote them against Apostasy from the principles of the

First Settlement. II. And I would prosecute the publication of the Like *Testimony* against several other
superstitions that are now creeping in upon the *Rising
generation*."

Sir Edmund was Governor now, Joseph Maylem was
making merry on Shrove Tuesday, and there were people abroad possessed of evil spirits. No one knew
quite what was coming. "And thus," closes the record, "the Good Hand of God brings mee to the end of
my Twenty Fourth year."

V

THE REVOLUTION OF 1689 AND THE NEW CHARTER

1686–1692

SIR EDMUND ANDROS, the new Governor, who came over vested with the absolute authority secured to James II by the vacating of the Charter, was a gentleman of Guernsey, whose youth had been passed in attendance on the King's aunt, the Queen of Bohemia. From 1666 to 1680 he had served in America, for the last six years of that period as Governor of New York. In this capacity he had come into collision with the authorities of Connecticut, who had disputed his claim to the country between the Connecticut River and the Hudson. And what happened then was enough to impress him and the people of New England with sentiments of mutual disgust. In point of fact, he seems to have been an honest gentleman, a good churchman, a man of the world, and a governor of no small ability.[1] But no temperament and no policy could have been much more foreign than his to the curious society, half theocratic, half democratic, that he came to govern with an authority more arbitrary than has ever been assumed in New England, before or since. It is no wonder that, to theocrats and democrats alike, he seemed the incarnation of

[1] See Andros Tracts, I. Memoir of Sir Edmund Andros.

political villany, that in common opposition to him the theocratic spirit and the democratic forgot for a while any differences of their own, and that the unanimous tradition of America has preserved his memory to the present day as that of a very bad man indeed.

His jurisdiction was not confined to Massachusetts, but comprised the whole of New England. Boston, to be sure, by far the most important town in America, was his capital; but here he exerted a power which extended from Canada to the Hudson. Putting aside the charges of extortion and corruption and treasonable plotting with Indians, — probably honestly made, but certainly insufficiently supported by any extant evidence, — we may perhaps reduce the grave phases of what is still called his tyranny to three : an effort to establish the Church of England ; the assumption of the power of taxation without the consent of the people ; and the laying down of the principle, that all titles to land had been vacated along with the Charter, and so that whoever wanted a sound title must get his claim confirmed by Sir Edmund, and pay for it. When certain people pleaded the privileges of Englishmen, they were told that these things would not follow them to the ends of the earth, and that they had no more privileges left them but that they were not bought and sold for slaves. And this I see no reason to doubt that Sir Edmund very honestly believed. " In short," says Cotton Mather,[1] " all was done that might be expected from a *Kirk*, Except the *Bloody Part*. But that was coming on."

In all probability, the Mathers, along with most good

[1] Parentator, XXIII.

people of New England, honestly thought their heads in danger. That they really were, there is no evidence at all. But it is no wonder that so complete an over-turn of the government set all manner of wild fancies afloat. Increase Mather opposed Andros in every possible way, and meantime betook himself to prayer for good tidings out of England.

"I sought unto GOD," he writes, early in 1687, "in se-cret with Tears that He would send Reviving News out of *England: And* I could not but Believe that He will do so."

He had not long to wait. In April, 1687, James II issued his Declaration of Indulgence.[1] Really de-signed, of course, to relieve the Catholics, this pro-claimed liberty of conscience, suspending all laws against non-conformity, and authorizing all British sub-jects to meet and serve God in their own way. How grateful it was to Dissenters, Cotton Mather's own words characteristically express : —

"*It brought them out of their Graves:* And if it as-sumed an Illegal Power of *Dispensing with Laws*, yet in Relation to *Them*, it only dispensed with the Execution of such Infamous *Laws* as were *ipso facto* Null and Void be-fore : *Laws* contrary to the *Laws* of GOD, and the *Rights* and *Claims* of Human Nature."

The ministers of New England were for a public thanksgiving, which Sir Edmund forbade, with threats of military force. On the motion of Increase Mather, the churches of New England drew up an address of

[1] See Sewall's Letter-Book, I. 52, note.

thanks to the King. This it was thought best to in-
trust to some "*Well-qualified Person*," who "might,
by the Help of such *Protestant Dissenters* as the King
began upon *Political Views* to cast a fair Aspect upon,
Obtain some Relief to the Growing Distresses of the
Country: and Mr. *Mather* was the Person that was
pitch'd upon." He referred the question of his going
to his church: "They that at another time would have
almost assoon parted with their Eyes as have parted
with him now were willing to it: *They Unanimously
Consented.*" Randolph made an effort to stop him by
bringing against him an action for libel, based on a
letter in which Mather had intimated a belief that
Randolph had forged the treasonable document signed
with his initials in 1683.[1] But Mather, having once
been released by a jury, avoided a second arrest by
slipping out of his house in disguise, and remaining
for a little while in hiding at Colonel Phillips's, in
Charlestown. On the 7th of April, 1688, he managed
to board a ship, well down the harbour, and so bore
away for England. On the 6th of May he landed at
Weymouth. His church was left in charge of his son
Cotton. Harvard College, of which he had been President since 1685, was left in the hands of Leverett and
Brattle, resident tutors, and Fellows of the Corporation.

The story of Increase Mather's mission in England
is told at length in the "Parentator," and has been
admirably illustrated by the "Andros Tracts." Taken
from the midst of the petty colonial society of whose
limits we should by this time have a pretty thorough
notion; placed in the midst of the turmoil, the bustle,

[1] Cf. page 46.

the intrigue, of a great capital and a corrupt court: taken from the post of an eminent leader in matters ecclesiastical and political alike ; placed where at best he was one of a multitude, struggling and plotting for the notice and the favour of the great, Increase Mather proved himself no common man.   Hitherto, at least in the " Parentator," on which I have chiefly relied for my impressions of him, he has appeared as an honest, godly Puritan minister, doing his best to maintain the principles that are already becoming traditions.   Now, without sacrificing a shade of his principle, without giving up those ecstatic prayers and afflations which whoever would understand the passionate enthusiasm of old Puritanism must always keep in mind, he shows himself able, in a rare degree, to conduct the affairs of men.   In brief, his task was to persuade a Catholic King, full of belief in the Divine authority of his absolute power, to restore, of his free will, the vacated Charter of Massachusetts.   On the 30th of May he presented the Addresses of Thanks to James II, thus for the first time fulfilling his mother's prophecy. [1]   Two days later he had another audience with the King, who listened kindly to his complaints of the conduct of Andros.   It was James's purpose, Cotton Mather thinks,[2] to set up the Roman Catholic religion in America.   It was Mather's purpose to secure a restoration of the theocratic democracy of the fathers, and incidentally to procure for Harvard College a royal charter which should permanently secure it to the Calvinistic dissenters who had founded and cherished it.   These

[1] Cf. page 17.   [2] Parentator, XXV.

purposes agreed in not being exactly those of poor Sir Edmund. James spoke kindly, but did nothing; Mather worked vigorously, using every influence he could command.

On the 22d of November, 1688, Sewall sailed from Boston, partly for the purpose of joining Mather in London. His notes of the voyage are pretty full.

" Friday, Dec. 21," runs one, " I lay a [wager] with Mr. Newgate that shall not see any part of Great Britain by next Saterday senight sunset. Stakes are in Dr. Clark's hand." He won his bet. Still at sea, on " Sabbath, Dec. 30th. Spake with a ship. Tells us he spake with an English Man from Galloway, last Friday, who said that the King was dead, and that the Prince of Aurang had taken England, Landing six weeks agoe in Tor Bay. Last night I dreamed of military matters."

A fortnight more the voyage lasted, and each vessel they spoke gave some new version of the great news. In point of fact, William had landed on the 5th of November, James had fled from London on the 23d of December; and on "Sabbath, Jan. 13th," when Sewall finally went ashore at Dover, to "hear 2 Sermons from Isaiah, 66. 9," [1] the Revolution was accomplished. Two weeks later, William and Mary were proclaimed.

On the 4th of April, 1689, a young man named John Winslow arrived in Boston from the island of Nevis, with a copy of the Declaration issued by the Prince of Orange on his landing in England. Sir Edmund, hear-

---

[1] "Shall I bring to the birth, and not cause to bring forth ? saith the Lord: Shall I cause to bring forth, and shut the womb ? saith thy God."

ing the news, sent for him, and tried to silence him
by threats and promises; failing, he committed him to
prison "for bringing traitorous and treasonable libels
and papers of news." But it was no use. The people
of Massachusetts were ripe for revolution. Palfrey tells
the story very graphically.[1] On the 18th of April,
Boston rose in arms, seized the chief magistrates, be-
sieged Sir Edmund in the Castle, dismantled the Rose
frigate, and took possession of the government in the
name of "His Highness" (the Prince of Orange) and
"the English Parliament." To appreciate the full
boldness of this bloodless revolution, we must remember that no rumor of the Prince's fortunes had reached
New England, and that every man of those who put
themselves at the head of the movement knew that,
if, as might well be, James had prevailed in England,
their action would probably cost them their heads.
For all this, the magistrates who had last served under
the vacated Charter resumed the power provisionally.
Samuel Mather[2] says that they did it lest inaction on
their part should result in bloody work by less prudent
leaders. It was their fortune to be justified by what
had happened abroad. On the 26th of May, a ship
arrived with orders to proclaim William and Mary;
on the 29th, they were proclaimed. And Sir Edmund, with Joseph Dudley and the rest of his crew,
as Cotton Mather called them, were fast prisoners in
Boston Castle. And absolute authority in New England had seen its last day.

[1] Book III. Chapter XV.
[2] Life of Cotton Mather, II. 2, 2. This passage is probably
the most valuable historically in the lifeless book.

The next service that Increase Mather [1] did for New England was — at least for his contemporaries — perhaps the most notable of all. On the accession of William and Mary, a circular letter was drawn up to all the Colonies, confirming the old governors until further order. Had this been sent to New England, it would have reinstated Sir Edmund; and how that hot-tempered gentleman might have conducted himself towards his enemies nobody knows. By some means, Mather succeeded in stopping it, and in leaving authority temporarily in the hands of the provisional government. In the end, Sir Edmund and his crew were shipped to England for trial. Far from condemnation, they were received there with favour. Sir Edmund was soon made Governor of Virginia; Joseph Dudley was made Chief Justice of New York, and later Lieutenant Governor of the Isle of Wight; later still he became a member of Parliament. But New England saw Sir Edmund no more: as for poor Randolph, all we hear further of him is that he died in Virginia, so miserably that only two or three negroes attended his funeral; [2] and Dudley for the moment had his hands agreeably full abroad. There is good reason, I think, to believe that this peaceable issue of what might have been a very tragic matter was due chiefly to Mather's diplomacy.

There were now high hopes in New England that the Charters would be restored. To prove their loyalty, the Colonies fitted out an expedition against Port

[1] For all facts about Increase Mather in the rest of this chapter, see Parentator, XXVI, XXVII.

[2] Parentator, XXIV.

Royal, and temporarily annexed to the British dominions the country that is now Nova Scotia. Encouraged by this, they followed it by a still more formida-
ble expedition against Quebec, under the command,
like the former, of the redoubtable Sir William Phipps.
But this armament came to grief in the St. Lawrence,
going far to unmake the favourable impression established by the previous success. And the country was
generally in a disturbed condition, doubtful as to what
form its government might take, harassed on its bor-
ders by French and Indians, and infested along the
coast by the pirates whose traditional hoards still excite the interest of credulous treasure-seekers. It is to
this epoch, though not precisely to this moment, that
we owe the fame of Captain Kidd.

In England, meanwhile, Increase Mather — preaching, praying, making the best of his way among what
Dissenters were in favour at court — was doing his utmost to secure the restoration of the Charters. He
waited on the King more than once, to be received with
marked, though guarded civility. He waited on the
Queen, when the King was gone to Holland, and,
pressing the claims of the New England Dissenters,
heard from her lips what Cotton Mather calls a "Divine
Sentence": "I wish all good men were of one mind;
however, in the mean time I would have them live
peaceably, and love one another." But all he could
do brought his business little further. William of
Orange was a good Calvinist, but no Republican: he
was willing enough to say civil things to New England,
but by no means disposed to make a prosperous part
of his dominions virtually independent. The longer

Mather waited, the clearer it became to him, if not to his colleagues in the mission, that the best he could do for Massachusetts was to secure for it the best Charter he could induce the King to sign. The old Charter was hopelessly lost.

Such was the state of affairs at the beginning of the year 1692, — the next for which Cotton Mather's diary is preserved.[1] What impressions I have of his personal career for these five years, then, I gather from outside sources. In the first place, we shall do well to remember the situation in which he found himself at the age of twenty-five. Full of traditional belief in the Divine authority of his professional work, he was left, by the absence of his father on the most important public business ever yet confided to a native of New England, in full charge of one of the greatest churches in America. There is no reason to doubt that, according to the standard of his time, he was a scholar unapproached by any one of his age : that is, he had read more books than anybody else, he was reading more day by day, and he was already launched in that career of authorship which made him at last the most voluminous of American writers. And the state of public affairs, bringing theocracy and democracy for the moment into complete accord, and throwing political as well as spiritual leadership once more — and for the last time — chiefly into the hands of the clergy, gave his words and actions such public authority as he never enjoyed again. All the while, too, there is every reason to

---

[1] In possession of the American Antiquarian Society. Occasional citations in print seem to show that some of the intermediate diaries may be preserved. But I have not come across them.

believe that his ecstatic prayers and fastings kept him in what he never doubted was direct communication with the angels of God.

Sewall's Diary gives a few glimpses of his public preaching, and of pastoral visits all the more notable for the fact that Sewall was a member, not of Mather's church, but of Mr. Willard's, the Old South. One of his sermons, in 1687, taught Sewall a practical lesson of which he made immediate use.

"Went to Roxbury," runs Sewall's note,[1] "and heard Mr. Cotton Mather preach from Colos. 4. 5, Redeeming the Time.[2] Shew'd that should improve Season for doing and receiving good whatsoever it cost us. His Excellency[3] was on the Neck, as came by, call'd Him in and gave Him a glass of Beer and Claret and deliver'd a Petition respecting the Narraganset Lands."

Three years later, Sewall heard another of his sermons with less satisfaction.

"March 19, 1690," he writes, "Mr. C. Mather preaches the lecture from Mat. 24, and appoint his portion with the Hypocrites.[4] In his proem said, *Totus mundus agit histrionem.*[5] Said one sign of a hypocrit was for a man to strain at a Gnat and swallow a Camel. Sign in 's Throat discovered him; To be zealous against an innocent fashion, taken up and used by the best of men; and yet make no

---

[1] Diary, I. 181.

[2] "Walk in wisdom towards them that are without, redeeming the time."

[3] Andros.

[4] Matt. 24. 51. "[The lord of that servant] shall cut him asunder, and appoint him his portion with the hypocrites: there shall be weeping and gnashing of teeth."

[5] Everybody plays a part.

Conscience of being guilty of great Immoralities. Tis supposed means wearing of Perriwigs: [1] said would deny themselves in any thing but parting with an oportunity to do God service; that so might not offend good Christians. Meaning, I suppose, was fain to wear a Perriwig for his health. I expected not to hear a vindication of Perriwigs in Boston Pulpit by Mr. Mather; however, not from that Text. The Lord give me a good heart and help to know, and not only to know but also to doe his Will; that my Heart and Head may be his."

Of Cotton Mather's domestic life, meanwhile, I find but two or three stray notes. Three daughters were born to him before 1693; and one of them died. In 1688, he was much excited by a case of witchcraft in Boston, and for a while had one of the possessed girls in his own house. The same year his brother Nathaniel died, — a very godly youth, who, if we may trust the account of him which Cotton Mather published,[2] systematically studied and worried himself to death. One of his notes, which Cotton Mather quotes, gives a curious insight into his character. He is lamenting, in terms which suggest all manner of misdeed, the sins of his boyhood.

"Of the manifold sins which then I was guilty of," he goes on, "none so sticks upon me as that, being very young, I was *whitling* on the Sabbath-day; and for fear of being seen, I did it behind the door. A great reproach of God! a specimen of that *atheism* that I brought into the world with me."

Samuel Mather[3] is the chief authority concerning the

---

[1] Cf. page 34. In his only existing portrait, Cotton Mather wears a remarkably full wig.

[2] Magnalia, IV. X.   [3] Life, II. 2. 2.

part Cotton Mather played in the Revolution of 1689.
Before the outbreak, he says, "the principal Gentlemen
of *Boston* met with Mr. Mather to consult what was best
to be done : and they all agreed, if possible, that they
would extinguish all Essays in our People to an *Insurrection.*" In case of an outbreak, however, they determined to prevent undue violence by putting themselves
at the head of it. "And a Declaration was prepared
accordingly." [1] At a public meeting of the inhabitants
of Boston, shortly before the outbreak, Cotton Mather
succeeded in calming the people by an "affectionate
and moving Speech . . . at which many fell into Tears
and the whole Body . . . present immediately united in
the Methods of Peace Mr. Mather proposed unto them."
In spite of this he was to have been committed to prison
for his politics on the very day when the insurrection
broke out : on that day and the exciting ones that
followed, he devoted all his energies, with success, to
hindering "the Peoples proceeding any further than
to reserve the Criminals for the Justice of the *English*
Parliament." On the whole, Samuel Mather's last
remark on this subject is the most notable.

"Upon Discoursing with him of the Affairs," it runs,
"he has told me that he always pressed *Peace* and *Love*
and *Submission* unto a legal Government, tho' he suffered
from some tumultuous People, by doing so; and upon the
whole, has asserted unto me his *Innocency* and Freedom
from all *known Iniquity* in that time, but declared his Resolution, from the View he had of the fickle Humors of the
Populace, that he would chuse to be concern'd with them
as little as possible for the future."

[1] See Andros Tracts, I. 20. This paper has been attributed
to Cotton Mather.

Apart from this, I get my chief impression of him during this interval from the list of his works in Sibley's "Harvard Graduates." Indeed, there are but two definite facts that I have noted from any other authority. One is, that on the 12th of June, 1690, he was elected a Fellow of Harvard College.[1] I doubt if the Corporation has ever had a younger member.[2] The other is, that in November of the same year, when there was a dispute between hot-tempered Sir William Phipps and his prisoner, M. de Meneval, the captured Governor of Port Royal, concerning certain moneys on which Sir William had laid hand, "Mr. Moody and Mr. Mather . . . had very sharp discourse ; Mr. Mather very angrily said that they who did such things as suffering Sir William to be corrected by Meneval were Frenchmen, or the people would say they were, etc."[3] Cotton Mather had a temper of his own, it seems, which sometimes got the better of him. But the more serious side of his personal life between 1687 and 1692 shows itself chiefly in his writings. From "Military Duties" — a sermon preached in September, 1686, but not published till the next year — to the "Midnight Cry," — the last of his publications during the period covered by this chapter, — Sibley mentions twenty-nine titles. Of these, one appeared in 1687, seven in 1689, ten in 1690, nine in 1691, and two in the beginning of 1692. Twenty of the twenty-nine were sermons, including some political sermons, and three funeral discourses, — two of which were enlarged into the biographies of Nathaniel Mather and of the

---

[1] Sewall's Diary, I. 322.   [2] 27 years, 4 months.
[3] Sewall's Diary, I. 339.

Apostle Eliot, which appeared again in the Magnalia;
two dealt with the Quakers; five concerned devotional
matters in general; and two — "Memorable Providences," first published in 1689, and "Late Memorable Providences," published in 1691 — concerned
witchcraft.[1] From the moment that his glorious assurances were justified by the news that King Charles was
dead and Kirk's coming averted in 1685, this matter
seems to have been much on his mind. He was
bound by covenant to do special work for the Lord,
and here was special work to be done.

So we come to that portion of his diary for 1692
which belongs in this chapter. Like the other volumes I have noted, this one is not the original, but an
abridged copy in his own hand of what portions he
deemed worth preserving. And it is certainly true that
the notes he has copied for this year are less specific
and fewer than usual. To those who hate his memory, and they are not few, this fact should count
against him; for my part, as I have said, the better I
grow to know him, the more honest I believe his intentions. I shall note very briefly all that I have found
in the earlier part of this manuscript volume.

"This year finds me," it begins, "in my public Ministry
handling the Miracles of our Lord Jesus Christ. . . .
Who can tell, what miraculous Things, I may see, before
this year bee out?"

The next thing he notes is, that he has induced a
meeting of ministers at Cambridge to vote that the
churches shall make catalogues of "such things as can

---

[1] Increase Mather's "Remarkable Providences" had appeared
in 1684.

indisputably bee found amiss among them," and then shall relentlessly put them down. Most of the churches paid little attention to this vote. But Mather himself drew up an instrument denouncing sixteen distinct common evils and transgressions of the covenant. He preached about this; he wove it into his prayers; and on the 2d of April it was adopted by a vote of the North Church. He had it printed, and conveyed the little book to every communicant. On the 29th of April, he held a day of secret humiliation and prayer. His prayers for the Holy Spirit were answered with assurances. He went on to recount the abasing circumstances of the land, to pray for the awakening of the churches, particularly by himself; therefore he prayed above all for the smiles of God on his "Midnight Cry," "which was just then coming out of the press." He obtained of God an assurance that

"Hee will make use of me, as of a John, to bee an Herald of the Lord's Kingdom now approaching. . . . But my prayers," he goes on, "did especially insist upon the horrible Enchantments and possessions broke forth upon Salem Village, — things of a most prodigious Aspect. A good issue to these things and my own Direction and protection thereabout I did especially petition for."

His next note, undated, tells that his health is "lamentably broken, . . . partly by my Excessive Toyle in the public and private Exercises of my Calling, but chiefly, I fear, by my Sins against the God of my Health." In spite of this, and of preaching when he "had been fitter to have been in my bed," he has had great assistances in the pulpit; "and come easier out of the pulpit than I went into it." Whoever has had crazy nerves knows what that means.

"But now," he goes on, " Illnesse and Vapours, with an Aguish Indisposition, grows upon me at such a rate that indeed I Live in Exceeding Misery: and I can see nothing but a *Speedy Death* approaching. *Blessed be God, that I can Dy !* "

"But the time for Favour was now come !" runs the next note I have copied, " the Sett Time was Come ! I am now to Receive the answer of so many prayers as had been employed for my absent parent ; and for the Deliverance and settlement of my poor Countrey, for which hee had been Employed in so long an Agencie. We have not the former Charter, but wee have a Better in the Room of it : one which much better suits our Circumstances. And instead of my being made a Sacrifice to Wicked Rulers, all the councellours of the province are of my own Father's Nomination."

Among them were his father-in-law and several brethren of his church. And the Governor was Sir William Phipps, one whom he himself had baptized, in March, 1690.[1]

In fact, the four years' work of Increase Mather had reached a successful issue in October, 1691. Convinced that nothing could revive the old Charter, he had done all he could to make the new one as good as possible. The appointment of the Governor, and the final power of veto, were left with the King ; the franchise was made a matter no longer of church-membership, but of freeholds : but the people were to elect the Governor's Council ; and above all, the power of taxation was vested in the bodies they elected. Mather's colleagues refused to accept the inevitable : they came back to New England, ready to stir up feel-

[1] See Magnalia, Life of Sir William Phipps.

ing against him. And Sewall notes that as early as February 8, 1691–2, when the first copy of the new Charter reached Boston, there was much discourse. But Mather's diplomatic tact had actually enabled him to name the chief officers who were to put the government into operation; and the good man came home to his good son with the full conviction that now at last good people were to have their way in New England.

"May 14th, 1692," writes Sewall, "Sir William arrives in the Nonsuch Frigat: Candles are lighted before he gets into Town-house. Eight companies wait on Him to his house, and then on Mr. [Increase] Mather to his. Made no volleys because 't was Satterday night."

Next day, though ill and unprepared, Cotton Mather preached on "the Lord's passing over the water," with much assistance from Heaven.

"Monday, May 16," writes Sewall, 'Eight Companies and two from Charlestown guard Sir William and his Councillours to the Townhouse, where the Comissions were read and Oaths taken. I waited on the Dept. Governour to Town, and there was met by Brother Short . . . who informed me of the dangerous illness of my father, so . . . I was not present at the Solemnity: found my father much better. At Ipswich,[1] as we were going, saw a Rainbow just about Sunset."

"Thus," writes Cotton Mather the same day, "have I seen the wonderful effects of prayer and Faith; and now I will call upon the Lord as Long as I Live."

[1] The elder Sewall lived at Newbury.

VI

WITCHCRAFT

1692–1693

WHAT happened in the next two years was of less consequence to New England than the matters we have been considering. To Cotton Mather, however, and to the cause which throughout his life he had most at heart, — the preservation, the restoration, of the pure polity of the fathers, — these two years were fatal. It was the great tragedy of witchcraft, I think, that finally broke the power of theocracy: it was almost surely the part Cotton Mather played in it that made his life, for the five and thirty years that were left him, a life — at least publicly — of constant, crescent failure. Tragic even if we join with those who read in the records left us no more worthy story than that of frustrated ambition, his career takes an aspect of rare tragic dignity if in his endless, undiscouraged efforts to do God's work we can honestly see what he tells us was there, — an all-mastering faith that the fathers were divinely right, that all which tended away from their teaching was eternally wrong, and that his own failure meant nothing less than the failure of the kingdom of Christ in a land whither Christ's servants had come with high hopes that here, as nowhere else on earth, Christ's kingdom should prevail.

Sir William Phipps, the new Governor, is in certain aspects a most romantic figure. The obscure son of a settler in the wilds of Maine, he was first an apprentice to a ship-carpenter: coming to Boston early in manhood, he learned there to read and write, and soon married a widow of position and fortune decidedly above his own. Prospering for a while as a shipbuilder, he soon took to the sea; and by the year 1684 he had so distinguished himself that he was put in command of a frigate, in which he sailed to the West Indies in search of a wrecked Spanish treasure-ship. After various adventures and mutinies, he actually discovered the wreck. He brought back to England treasure to the amount of three hundred thousand pounds, in return for which feat he was knighted by James II. And in Sir Edmund Andros's time he came home to Boston with a comfortable fortune of his own and the office of High Sheriff of New England. By no means in sympathy with the Governor, he soon went back to England for a while, where he had more or less to do with Increase Mather. In 1690 he was again in Boston, where, as we have seen before, he took command of the successful expedition against Port Royal. The first real rebuff in the career of this archetype of self-made Yankees was the failure of the expedition which, too late in the same year, he led against Quebec. Undiscouraged, he went back to England with plans for a fresh expedition against the French. This came to nothing; but Increase Mather, who saw much of him in London, pitched on him, and obtained the approval of King William for him, as the man of men to be the first Governor of the royal Province of Massachusetts.

It would have been hard to find a governor who should promise more for the polity to which the Mathers gave every energy of their lives. A man of the people, conspicuous above any one else of his time for just that kind of material success which most touches the popular imagination, Sir William, though hotheaded and full of the pompous tyranny of the quarterdeck, seems to have had one of those big, hearty, human natures which command liking even where one cannot approve. He might be expected at once to command the sympathy of the people, who would see in him an example of what any one of them might become, and to be very firm in his determination to have his own way. If such a man be on the right course, he will carry things farther than any other kind. And, like most self-made Yankees, Sir William was on exactly the right course, from the point of view of the clergy. As a class, self-made men to this day grow up with a rather blind faith in the superiority to other men of ministers of the Gospel: in worldly moments they may smile at their spiritual advisers as impractical; but they go to church, and when it comes to spending their money they are very apt to spend it as the minister tells them to. And more than most self-made men Sir William looked up to the clergy, and most of all the clergy to the Mathers. It was Increase Mather's sermon on "The day of trouble is near," in 1674,[1] that first made him sensible of his sins; it was by Cotton Mather, just before the expedition to Port

[1] Cf. page 26.

Royal, in 1690, that he was baptized and received into the communion of the faithful; it was to Increase Mather that he owed the office which crowned his worldly ambition. Clearly such a man as this might be trusted, if anybody might, to do the will of God as the Mathers expounded it. And the Mathers meant to expound it in the good old orthodox way; and the new Charter gave the Governor more power than he had ever had under the old; so there was never a moment when the hopes of Christ's kingdom looked brighter.

To understand what followed, we may well recall some things at which we have glanced already. In the view of the Puritans, the continent of America, whither they came to live in accordance with no laws but those of Scripture, had been until their coming the special territory of the Devil. Here he had ruled for centuries, unmolested by the opposing power of the Gospel: whoever doubted this had only to look at the degradation of his miserable subjects, the native Indians, to be pretty well convinced. The landing of the Puritans was a direct invasion of his territories. He fought it in all manner of ways, — material and spiritual. The physical hardship of the earlier years of the settlement was largely his work; so were the disturbances raised within the Colonies by heretics and malcontents; so, more palpably still, were the Indian wars in which his subjects rose in arms against the servants of Christ; so, too, were certain phenomena that every one at the present day would instantly recognize as natural: more than once Cotton Mather remarks as clearly diabolical the fact that the steeples of churches are oftener

struck by lightning than any other structures. And from
the very earliest days of the settlement the Devil had
waged his unholy war in a more subtle way still: appearing in person, or in the person of direct emissaries
from the invisible world, to more than a few hapless
Christians, he had constantly striven with bribes and
threats to seduce them to his service. Whoever yielded
to him was rewarded by the possession of supernatural
power, which was secretly exerted for all manner of
malicious purposes; these were the witches: whoever
withstood him was tortured in mind and body almost
beyond the power of men to bear; these were the
bewitched. There was no phase of the Devil's warfare
so insidious, so impalpable, so dangerous, as this: in
the very heart of the churches, in the pulpits themselves, witches might lurk. Their crime was the dark-
est of all, — deliberate treason to the Lord; but it was
the hardest of all to detect and to prove, — the most
horrible, both in its nature and in its possibility of evil-
doing. Mysterious, horrible, inevitable, it demanded
every effort of Christians to withstand its subtle power.

To the Mathers, I believe, all this was very real. In
1684 Increase Mather had written a book against
witchcraft. Two years later, as we have seen, Cotton
Mather had had what he might well have believed a
special message from Heaven that his chief mission for
the moment was to fight the witches. The sins of the
Colonists had brought on them the most terrible of
their misfortunes: the Charter was gone, and Kirke was
coming with his red-coats; and, in the deep agony of
secret prayer, Cotton Mather was beseeching God to
show mercy to New England, and promising, when such

mercy came, what special services the Lord might see
fit to demand. The good news came, at a moment
when the Lord was rewarding his prayers by visions
of a white-robed angel from whose lips he heard assurances of Divine favour. King Charles was dead,
Kirk was coming no longer. His prayers had availed
to save New England from the worst of her dangers.
What should he do for the Lord? At that very moment, as we have seen, witchcraft was abroad. It was
his duty to collect testimony against it, to denounce it,
to fight it with all his might. From that moment, apparently, he began. And the more he studied it, the
more real and terrible he found it. In 1688 there was
a sad outbreak of it in Boston: Cotton Mather took
into his own house one of the afflicted children, whose
behaviour as he relates it was in all respects such as to
increase his belief both in the reality of the Devil's
work, and in the divine sanction of his own efforts
against it. And now, in 1692, when the prayers of
New England for a righteous charter had been granted,
when the best of governors was come, ready to put
into execution the best of policies, when at last the material prospects of Christ's kingdom were fairer than for
years before, the Devil began such a spiritual assault on
New England as had never before been approached.

The story of Salem Witchcraft has been told by
Upham with a fulness and a fairness that leave nothing
to be added. But he fails, I think, sympathetically to
understand a fact which he emphasizes with characteristic honesty, — the tremendous influence on human
beings of that profound realizing sense of the mysteries
that surround us, to which those who do not share it
give the name superstition.

At various periods of history epidemics of superstition have appeared, sometimes in madly tragic forms, sometimes, as in modern spiritualism, in grotesquely comic ones. These are generally classed as pure delusions, based on no external facts. But for my part, though I may claim none of the authority which would come from special study of the subject, I am strongly inclined to believe that from the earliest recorded times a certain pretty definite group of mysterious phenomena has, under various names, really shown itself throughout human society. Oracles, magic, witchcraft, animal magnetism, spiritualism, — call the phenomena what you will, — seem to me a fact. Certain phases of it are beginning to be understood under the name of hypnotism. Other phases, after the best study that has been given them, seem to be little else than deliberate fraud and falsehood; but they are fraud and falsehood, if this be all they are, of a specific kind, unchanged for centuries. The evidence at the trial of the Maréchal de Rais, a soldier of Joan of Arc and the original of the tale of Blue-Beard, relates phenomena that anybody can see to-day by paying a dollar to a "materializing medium." And some of them are very like what are related in the trials of the Salem witches. So specific is the fraud, if only fraud it be, that it may well be regarded, I think, as a distinct mental, or perhaps rather moral disorder.

With no sort of pretension to scientific knowledge, I have found that a guess I made in talk some years ago throws what may be a little light on many of the mysterious phenomena that in Cotton Mather's time were deemed indisputably diabolical. I shall venture, then,

to state it here, to be taken for no more than a layman's guess may be worth. If, as modern science
tends to show, human beings are the result of a process of evolution from lower forms of life, there must
have been in our ancestral history a period when the
intelligence of our progenitors was as different from the
modern human mind — the only form of intelligence
familiar to our experience or preserved in the records
of our race — as were their remote aquatic bodies from
the human form we know to-day. To-day we can perceive with any approach to distinctness only what re-
veals itself to us through the medium of our five senses;
but we have only to look at the intricate wheelings of
a flock of birds, at the flight of a carrier pigeon, at the
course of a dog who runs straight home over a hundred
miles of strange country, to see more than a probability
that animals not remote from us physically have per-
ceptions to which we are strangers. It seems wholly
conceivable, then, that in the remote psychologic past
of our race there may have been in our ancestors certain powers of perception which countless centuries of
disuse have made so rudimentary that in our normal
condition we are not conscious of them. But if such
there were, it would not be strange that, in abnormal
states, the rudimentary vestiges of these disused powers
of perception might sometimes be revived. If this
were the case, we might naturally expect two phenomena to accompany such a revival : in the first place, as
such powers of perception, from my very hypothesis,
belong normally to a period in the development of our
race when human society and what we call moral law
have not yet appeared, we should expect them to be

intimately connected with a state of emotion that
ignores what we call the moral sense, and so to be
accompanied by various forms of misconduct; in the
second place, as our chief modern means of communication — articulate language — belongs to a period
when human intelligence has assumed its present form,
we should expect to find it inadequate for the expression of facts which it never professed to cover, and
so we should expect such phenomena as we are considering to be accompanied by an erratic, impotent
inaccuracy of statement, which would soon shade into
something indistinguishable from deliberate falsehood.
In other words, such phenomena would naturally in-
volve in whoever abandons himself to them a mental
and moral degeneracy which any one who believes in a
personal devil would not hesitate to ascribe to the direct
intervention of Satan.

Now what disposes me, scientifically a layman I
must repeat, to think that my guess may have something in it is that mental and moral degeneracy —
credulity and fraud — seem almost invariably so to
entangle themselves with occult phenomena that many
cool-headed people are disposed to assert the whole
thing a lie.   To me, as I have shown, it does not seem
so simple.   I am much disposed to think that necro-
mancers, witches, mediums, — what not, — actually do
perceive in the infinite realities about us things that
are imperceptible to normal human beings; but that
they perceive them only at a sacrifice of their higher
faculties — mental and moral — not inaptly symbolized
in the old tales of those who sell their souls.

If this be true, witchcraft is not a delusion: it is a

thing more subtly dangerous still. Such an epidemic of it as came to New England in 1692 is as diabolical a fact as human beings can know: unchecked, it can really work mischief unspeakable. I have said enough, I think, to show why I heartily sympathize with those who in 1692 did their utmost to suppress it; to show, too, why the fatally tragic phase of the witch trials seems to me, not the fact that there was no crime to condemn, but the fact that the evidence on which certain wretched people were executed proves, on scrutiny, utterly insufficient. It was little better than to-day would be the ravings of a clairvoyant against one accused of theft. And yet, if there be anything in my guess, this too is just what we might expect. Not knowing what they did, the judges would strain every nerve — just as in their rapt ecstasies the Mathers strained every nerve, along with their Puritan fellows, and the saints of every faith — to awaken from the lethargy of countless ages those rudimentary powers which can be awakened only at the expense of what we think the higher ones that have supplanted them. The motive may make a difference: he who strives to serve God may end as he began, a better man than he who consents to serve the Devil. But, for all that, bewitched and judges alike, the startled ministers to whom the judges turned for counsel, and perhaps not a few of the witches too, who may well have believed in themselves, vie with one another in a devil's race, harking back to mental and moral depths from which humanity has taken countless centuries to rise.

Whoever cares to know in detail the story of 1692 may read it in Upham, or in Palfrey. In brief, the

children of Mr. Parris, minister of Salem Village, were
seized early in the year with disorders which seemed
of no earthly origin. They accused certain neighbours
of bewitching them; the neighbours were arrested. The
troubles and the accusations spread with the speed
of any panic. By the time Sir William assumed the
government, the whole region was in an agony of superstitious terror; and whoever raised his voice against
the matter fell under suspicion of league with the Devil.
At that moment, as the old judicial system had fallen
with the Charter, there were no regular courts. Within
a few weeks, Sir William, full of the gravity of the
situation, and probably under the direct advice of the
Mathers, appointed a special Court of Oyer and Terminer to try the witches. William Stoughton, the
Deputy Governor, was made Chief Justice: his six
associates were gentlemen of the highest station and
character in the Province: among them was Samuel Sewall, whose Diary I have so often quoted. On
the 2d of June this court condemned one Bridget
Bishop: on the 10th she was executed for witchcraft.
Before proceeding further, the court consulted the
ministers of Boston and the neighbourhood. The answer
of the ministers is said to have been drawn up by
Cotton Mather: in general terms it urged "the importance of caution and circumspection in the methods
of examination," but "earnestly recommended that the
proceedings should be vigorously carried on." [1]

It is largely on this document that the charge against
Cotton Mather rests: he is believed by many deliberately to have urged the judicial murder of innocent

[1] Upham, II. 268.

people for the simple purpose of establishing and maintaining his own ascendency in the state. To me, and what I have written already should show why, the paper seems the only possible thing for an honest, superstitious man — himself in direct communication with the blessed part of the invisible world — to have written. Witchcraft was to him the most terrible of realities; not to proceed against it would have been to betray the cause of Christ; but the Devil stood ready to beguile the courts themselves; the evidence must be carefully scrutinized, or who could tell what mischief might come?

Thus encouraged, the Court proceeded. How many wretched people were committed can never be quite known: Upham thinks several hundreds.[1] Nineteen were hanged; one was pressed to death for refusing to plead to his indictment; at least two died in jail. By the end of September, a revulsion of popular feeling had come. The accusations had spread too far: the evidence on which the witches were executed was beginning to seem too flimsy. On the 22d of September came the last executions. In January, 1693,[2] the special Court of Oyer and Terminer was supplanted by a regular Superior Court, consisting of much the same men. It threw out "spectral evidence," — that is, it declined to consider the ravings of the bewitched: only three out of fifty indicted for witchcraft were condemned, and none of these was executed. In May, 1693, the panic was over. By proclamation, Sir William Phipps discharged all the accused. "Such a jail delivery," says Hutchinson, "has never been known in New England."

[1] Upham, II. 351.   [2] Ibid., II. 349.

In all this matter Increase Mather seems to have played no conspicuous part. Four years of diplomacy in the capital of the British empire had perhaps taught him practical lessons of prudence not to be learned in any less arduous school. But while these were learning, his son, not yet thirty years old, had been surrounded by influences diametrically different. In the provincial Boston, which was at once the greatest city in America and the only home he ever knew, Cotton Mather had found himself, at an age when most men are still passed by as young, among the chiefs of the leaders. And then, as later, it had been his lot to meet hardly anybody whom he could honestly deem by his own standards superior to himself. As we shall see by and by, his later career was marked by what has often seemed, particularly when we remember his constant failure to achieve the public ends he strove for, a ridiculous and overweening vanity. But I think that few can rise from a careful study of his diary without feeling that this vanity was no blind self-approval; but at most a conviction, in his happier moments, that, far as he was from the attainment of his ideals, there were none about him who were any nearer the attainment of theirs, and that there were many — and year by year more — who were falling away from the ancestral traditions that he never gave up. In 1692 he was still in the flush of youth and of success. No one was more active in fighting the Devil's works as revealed in witchcraft. No one, for well on to two centuries, has borne so much of the odium of what was done as he.

We have seen how his books and his conduct in 1688 tended to stir up public feeling against the

6 21 2

witches; we have seen how the letter of the ministers which he drew up encouraged the puzzled Court of Oyer and Terminer to proceed with its deadly work. On the 19th of August, 1692, the most eminent of the victims of the proceedings was hanged; this was the Rev. George Burroughs, a graduate of Harvard College, and for something like twenty years a minister of the Gospel. Four others died with him. One of Sewall's very few notes of this period describes this day.

" A very great number of Spectators . . . present. Mr. Cotton Mather was there. . . . All of them said they were innocent. . . . Mr. Mather says they all died by a Righteous sentence. Mr. Burroughs, by his Speech, Prayer, protestation of his Innocence, did much move unthinking persons, which occasions their speaking hardly concerning his being executed." In the margin Sewall has written " Dolefull Witchcraft ! " [1]

Calef, of whom we shall hear more by and by, gives a fuller account of the scene : —

" When [Mr. Burroughs] was upon the ladder, he made a speech for the clearing of his innocency, with such solemn and serious expressions, as were to the admiration of all present : his prayer (which he concluded by repeating the Lord's prayer [2]) was so well worded, and uttered with such composedness, and such (at least seeming) fervency of spirit, as was very affecting, and drew tears from many, so that it seemed to some that the spectators would hinder the execution. The accusers [3] said the black man stood and dictated to him. As soon as he was turned off, Mr.

[1] Diary, I. 363.

[2] It was believed that no witch could repeat the Lord's prayer without error.

[3] The bewitched : a capital example of spectral evidence.

Cotton Mather, being mounted upon a horse, addressed himself to the people, partly to declare that . . . [Burroughs] was no ordained minister, and partly to possess the people of his guilt, saying that the devil has often been transformed into an angel of light; and this somewhat appeased the people, and the executions went on. When he was cut down, he was dragged by the halter to a hole . . . between the rocks, about two feet deep, his shirt and breeches being pulled off, and an old pair of trowsers of one executed put on his lower parts ; he was so put in . . . that one of his hands and his chin . . . were left uncovered." [1]

Just a month later, Giles Corey was pressed to death for refusing to plead to his indictment, — the solitary instance in America of this terrible barbarity of the old English criminal law.

"Sept. 20," writes Sewall, " Now I hear from Salem that about 18 years agoe he was suspected to have stamped and press'd a man to death, but was cleared. Twas not remembered till Ane Putnam was told of it by said Corey's Spectre the Sabbath-day night before the Execution." [2]

On this very day, the 20th of September, two days before the last of the executions, Cotton Mather wrote to Stephen Sewall, clerk of the court at Salem, a letter which Upham deems conclusive of his artful dishonesty.[3]

" That I may bee the more capable to assist, in lifting up a standard against the Infernal Enemy," it runs, " I must

---

[1] Page 213.

[2] Diary, I. 364. Upham, II. 341, *seq.*, shows the charge against Corey to have been groundless. There is no more notable example of the popular infatuation.

[3] Upham, II. 487, *seq.* Cf. Sibley, III. 11.

Renew my most IMPORTUNATE REQUEST, that you would please quickly to perform, what you kindly promised, of giving me a Narrative of the Evidences given in at the Trials of half a dozen, or if you please a dozen, of the principal Witches, that have been condemned. . . . I am willing that when you write, you should imagine me as obstinate a Sadducee and Witch-advocate as any among us: address mee as one that Believ'd Nothing Reasonable; and when you have so knocked mee down, in a spectre so unlike mee, you will enable mee, to box it about, among my Neighbs, till it come, I know not where, at last."

Two days later, on that very 22d of September when the last witches were hanging, Sewall notes that " William Stoughton, Esqr., John Hathorne, Esqr., Mr. Cotton Mather, and Capt. John Higginson, with my brother St., were at our house, speaking about publishing some Trials of Witches." [1] The result of this letter and conference seems to have been Cotton Mather's well known " Wonders of the Invisible World," published the next year both in Boston and in London.

A few of Sewall's notes show the course of popular feeling meanwhile. On the 15th of October he went to Cambridge to discourse with Mr. Danforth about witchcraft: Mr. Danforth

" thinks there cañot be a procedure in the Court except there be some better consent of Ministers and People." On the 26th, " A Bill is sent in about calling a Fast, and Convocation of Ministers, that may be led in the right way as to the Witchcrafts. The reason and mañer of doing it,

---

[1] Diary, I. 365. Stoughton, Hathorne, and Sewall were judges of the Court of Oyer and Terminer; Stephen Sewall, clerk of the Court, was the man to whom Cotton Mather had written on September 20.

is such, that the Court of Oyer and Terminer count themselves thereby dismissed. 29 Nos and 33 yeas to the Bill."
On the 28th, Sewall, "as had done several times before,
desired to have the advice of the Governour and Council
as to the sitting of the Court of Oyer and Terminer next
week : said should move it no more; great silence, as if
should say, do not go." Next day, " Mr. Russell asked
whether the Court of Oyer and Terminer should sit, ex-
pressing some fear of Inconvenience by its fall. Governour
said it must fall. Lieut.-Governour [1] not in Town."

It was nearly a year later, in September, 1693, that
Cotton Mather, in Upham's phrase,[2] "succeeded in
getting up" the case of witchcraft that cost him dearest. One Margaret Rule, a young woman of Boston
whose character seems to have been none of the best,
was seized with all the symptoms of possession. One
symptom, mentioned I think only in her case, throws
considerable light on her disorder : the devils prevented her from eating, but permitted her occasionally
to swallow a little rum. Both of the Mathers visited
her, surrounded by her startled and credulous friends;
they listened with full faith to her tales of black spirits
and white who haunted her; they examined her person with what in less holy men might have savoured
of indiscretion; they prayed with her and for her.
And finally, the discouraged devils fled away; and she,
returning perfectly to herself, though extremely weak
and faint and overwhelmed with vapours, most affec-
tionately gave thanks to God for her deliverance.[3]
This case, portending such a diabolical descent on Boston as had passed over Salem, attracted the attention

---

[1] Stoughton.   [2] Upham, II. 489.   [3] Calef, p. 34.

among others, of one Robert Calef, a merchant of the town. He visited Margaret Rule when the Mathers were with her. A perfect matter-of-fact man, thoroughly honest and equally devoid of imagination, he saw in her sufferings only a vulgar cheat, and in the conduct of the Mathers something which seems to have impressed him as deliberate and not wholly decent connivance in her imposture. He made notes of what he had seen, and submitted them to Cotton Mather. The controversy that followed, which has been admirably summarized by Sibley,[1] lasted in one form or another for six years. In 1700, Calef's book on the subject was published in London, and soon found its way to Boston.[2]

Calef's temper was that of the rational Eighteenth Century: the Mathers belonged rather to the Sixteenth, — the age of passionate religious enthusiasm. To me, both sides seem equally honest; and the difference between them seems chiefly due to the fact that, as in a thousand other cases in human history, a man of the future can rarely so rise above himself as to understand men of the past. In such a controversy, it is the man of the future that the future holds right. In the time that has passed since the Mathers and Calef have lain in their graves, the world has seen an age of reason, and not of imaginative emotion. And most of those who have concerned themselves about these dead men have deemed Calef all in the right, and the Mathers foolish, if not worse. But did Calef see all? Is there, after all, in a great epidemic of superstition nothing

---

[1] Harvard Graduates, III. 12–18.
[2] Cf. pages 150, 186.

beyond what those who escape the contagion perceive?
Are we not to-day beginning to guess that there may be
in heaven and earth more things than are yet dreamt
of in your philosophy?   If there be, it may in the
end prove the verdict of men that neither honest Calef
nor the honest Mathers saw all that passed before
their eyes; but that each in his own way caught a
glimpse of truth, and that each believed that all the
truth was comprised in the bit he saw.

But we are come now to a point where we must turn
to Cotton Mather himself; where we must look to the
diaries he has left us, and to the works he wrote later,
for an account of what these critical years meant to
him.   The substance of his later writings seems to me
adequately represented by the passages about witchcraft in the "Magnalia" and the "Parentator."   A few
words of these, and we will pass to his diaries for 1692 [1]
and 1693.[2]

The substance of his final view of the case, as shown
in his published works, seems to have been this:
The witchcraft was a real attack of the Devil, permitted perhaps as a punishment for dabblings in sor-
cery and magical tricks which people had begun to
allow themselves.[8]   The afflictions of the possessed,
which he details in all their petty absurdities, that
seem nowadays as monstrously trivial, were really
diabolical.

"Flashy people may burlesque these things, but when
hundreds of the most sober people in a country where they

---

[1] In possession of the American Antiquarian Society.
[2] In possession of the Massachusetts Historical Society.
[8] Parentator, XXVIII.

have as much *mother-wit* certainly as the rest of mankind, know them to be *true*, nothing but the absurd and froward Spirit of Sadducism can question them." [1]

The only doubtful question was whether the Devil had the power of assuming before the eyes of his victims the shape of innocent persons. The assumption on the part of the judges that he had no such power led to the conviction on spectral evidence of not a few victims of the court. The abandonment of this assumption led to the cessation of the prosecutions, and to the jail delivery of 1693. Mather asserts in substance that he always opposed spectral evidence; and it is certain that Increase Mather's "Cases of Conscience," published in 1694, clearly condemns it. It is certain, too, that Cotton Mather's letter to John Richards, dated May 31, 1692,[2] warns the judge in the most specific terms against the dangers of spectral evidence. Cotton Mather's own position, as he finally states it, then, seems to have been a persistent belief in witchcraft, a persistent determination to keep the public alive to all the horrors of the crime, and to oppose it by every means in his power, but a growing doubt as to how far so mysterious and terrible an evil can be dealt with by so material an engine as the criminal law. On the whole he inclines more and more to reliance on fasting and prayer. This was undoubtedly the view taken, when the panic was once over, by even the most strenuous advocates of the reality of witchcraft, and Cotton Mather undeniably takes to himself the credit of having held and urged it all along.

---

[1] Magnalia, II. App. § 16.
[2] Mather Papers, 392, *seq.* See page 110.

The part of the "Magnalia" in which these facts appear is the Life of Sir William Phipps, first published separately and anonymously in 1697. On the fact that this book was anonymous, Calef bases much of his charge that Mather wrote it dishonestly to praise himself, and to delude people into believing him free from the responsibility of having urged on the prosecutions. On this fact, on the feebleness of the caution addressed by the ministers to the Court of Oyer and Terminer, and on the letter to Stephen Sewall, rests most of the charge of dishonesty from which Mather's name has never been cleared to the satisfaction of his opponents. It seems to me that the anonymous publication — by no means the only example of it in Mather's voluminous works [1] — may well have been due to no worse motive than a wish for a fair hearing, which might not have been accorded to a name which was held up to public execration. It seems to me, too, that the letter of the ministers may be taken for just what it purports to be, — an honest warning of a danger, in spite of which the Court has no moral right to hesitate in the performance of its official duty. And in the letter to Stephen Sewall I can see nothing inconsistent with the conclusion that what Cotton Mather wished to maintain unshaken was not the fatal penalty of the law, but that belief in the reality of witchcraft which he certainly never abandoned. Calef and posterity seem to me to have confused two distinct things, — this belief in the reality of witchcraft, and insistence on the validity of spectral evidence. But, when all

[1] What is more, he acknowledged the book in 1702, when the "Magnalia" was published.

is said, I think two facts against Mather remain: his conduct and his words had as much as any one man's could have to do with the raising of the panic; and in his final presentation of the matter, both in his diaries and in his published works, he never grants or meets the full strength of the case against him.

But before we agree with those who believe him to have been deliberately dishonest, it will be only fair to read what his diaries tell us of these troubled years; and to read it, too, with certain facts in mind that seem to me too little considered. In the first place, as we have seen, Cotton Mather had for years been a religious enthusiast whose constant ecstasies brought him into such direct communication with Heaven as he believed the witches to maintain with Hell; in other words, he had for years been, what he remained all his life, a constant victim of a mental or moral disorder whose normal tendency is towards the growth of unwitting credulity and fraud. In the second place, I grow to believe more and more that the ceaseless activity of mind and body, of thought, of emotion, of action, into which he never ceased to lash himself, — the activity which produced in actual words and deeds a life-work whose bulk to-day seems almost incredible, — never permitted him, in any act or word, to be really deliberate at all. Striving with all his might to do the Lord's work, believing that the Lord's will forbade him for a moment to relax a particle of his energy, he went through this world from beginning to end in a state of emotional exaltation, of passionate afflation and reaction, which left him in all the sixty years of his conscious life hardly an hour of that cool thoughtfulness without which any deliberation is impossible. It has been his fate — a man whose whole career was a storm of passion — to be judged, in the seclusion of libraries, by unimaginative, unimpassioned posterity. So cool sympathizers with old Calvinism who have sought to defend him, and cooler Protestants who have constantly condemned him, have alike failed to understand.

They have failed, too, adequately to emphasize what seems to me the most notable piece of contemporary evidence. On May 31st, 1692, we have seen, — three days before Bridget Bishop, the first victim of the Court, was sentenced, — Cotton Mather wrote to John Richards, one of the judges, a letter in which he takes, with the utmost decision, exactly the ground he occupied to the end of his life.

"Do not lay more stress upon pure Spectre evidence than it will bear," he writes. . . . "It is very certain that the divells have sometimes represented the shapes of persons not only innocent, but also very vertuous."

There should be confession, or unmistakable signs: he believes in witch-marks, to be sure, and in the water-ordeal. But at the very end he adds this caution : —

"It is worth considering whether there be a necessity alwayes by Extirpačons by Halter or fagott [to punish] every wretched creature that shall be hooked into some degrees of Witchcraft. What if some of the lesser Criminalls, be only scourged with lesser punishments, and also put upon some solemn, . . . Publike . . . renunciation of the Divel? I am apt to thinke that the Divels would then cease afflicting the Neighbourhood."

So we come back to the diary for 1692.[1] As I have said already, this is far more abridged and less specific than most of his diaries. But I do not believe it untrue. The last entry I quoted was made in May, when his father had just returned, and the new Charter was just passing into operation. "And now," he wrote, " I will call upon the Lord as long as I live."

The rest of his entries for the year bear no date. He notes briefly that he has preached against temporal persecution of heresy; " And I hope the Lord will own me with a more Singular Success in the suppression of Haeresy by Endeavours more Spiritual and Evangelical." He notes that in his public ministry he has been largely handling the Day of Judgment, from texts in the 25th chapter of Matthew. Then comes a long note beginning, " The Rest of the Summer was a very doleful Time unto the whole Countrey." He tells how devils possessed many people, how witches were accused in the visions of the afflicted, how he himself testified both publicly and privately against the dangers of spectral evidence, and how it was he who drew up the letter from the ministers to the Court of Oyer and Terminer.

"Nevertheless," he goes on,[2] "I saw in most of the Judges a most charming Instance of prudence and patience, and I knew their exemplary pietie, and the Anguish of Soul with which they sought the Direction of Heaven: above most other people, whom I generally saw enchanted

[1] In possession of the American Antiquarian Society.

[2] This passage, and indeed the diaries concerning this matter in general, have been studied and cited by Peabody: Sparks's American Biographies, Vol. VI.

into a Raging, Railing, Scandalous and unreasonable disposition as the distress increased upon us. For this cause,
though I would not allow the Principles, that some of the
Judges had espoused, yet I could not but speak honourably
of their Persons, on all occasions: and my Compassion
upon the Sight of their Difficulties Raised by my Journeys
to Salem, the Chief Seat of these Diabolical Vexations,
caused me yett more to do so. And merely, as far as I
can Learn, for this Reason, the mad people thro' the Countrey under a fascination on their Spirits equal to what the
Energumens had on their Bodies, Reviled *mee*, as if I had
been the Doer of all the Hard Things that were done in the
prosecution of the Witchcraft."

He goes on to note how he offered to provide in his
own family for six of the possessed, that he might try
whether prayer and fasting " would not putt an End to
their Heavy Trials "; how throughout the summer he
prayed and fasted weekly for this heavy affliction to the
country; how he visited witches in prison and preached
to them; and how he wrote his " Wonders of the Invisible World."   And at the end of this passage is a note
in brackets, apparently made at some later time : —

"[Upon the severest Examination, and the Solemnest
Supplication, I still think, that for the main, I have *Written
Right*.] "

Later come less coherent notes. One remarks that
the spectres brought books in which they urged the
possessed to sign away their souls. Now, as Cotton
Mather worked for God largely by writing books, this
looked as if " this Assault of the Evil Angels upon the
Countrey was intended by Hell as a particular Defiance
unto *my* poor Endeavours to bring the Souls of men
unto Heaven."   Whereupon, he wrote " Awakenings

for the Unregenerate," which he resolved, if he lived, to give away at the rate of two a week for two years. In the margin he notes that the evil angels, through a possessed young woman, reproached him for never having preached on Rev. 13. 8.[1] "I to oppose them," he goes on, "and yett not follow them, chose to preach on Rev. 20. 15."[2] Later he makes a memorandum: as the devils bid Energumens sign books, he will sign the best of books. On the fly-leaves of his favourite Bibles he wrote professions and confessions of his faith: for example, "Received as the Book of God and of Life by Cotton Mather."

"The Hearty Wishes of Cotton Mather," come next. "I have ever now and then gone to the good God with the most Solemn Addresses *That I may be altogether delivered from* Enchantments: *that no* Enchantment on my *mind may hinder mee from seeing or doing any thing for the glory of God, or dispose mee to anything whereat God may be displeased.* The Reason of this Wish is Because I beleeve, that a Real and proper *Enchantment* of the Divels do's blind and move the minds of the most of men: even in Instances of every sort. But I remember, That much Fasting as well as prayer is necessary to obtain a Rescue from Enchantments."

The last entry I have noted for the year, when I remember all the circumstances of the man's life, has for me real pathos: he would carefully avoid personal quarrels,

[1] "And all that dwell upon the earth shall worship him [the beast], whose names are not written in the book of life of the Lamb slain from the foundation of the world."

[2] "And whosoever was not found written in the book of life was cast into the lake of fire."

" Because no man can manage a personal Quarrel against
another without Losing abundance of precious Time. . . .
And one Likely to Live, so little a *Time*, as I, had need
throw away, as Little of his Time, as ever he can."

The diary for 1693[1] is a little more full than that
for 1692 ; but, like that, is an abridgement of the original, and omits most of the dates. On his birthday, he
preached from the text, " O my God, take me not away
in the midst of my days." Then he set to preaching over the whole Epistle of Jude,[2] " intermingled
with occasional texts." A little later he notes that a
young woman possessed of devils has been delivered
after he has held three fasts for her. He holds a
thanksgiving accordingly ; but, her possession being
renewed, falls again to fasting and prayer : —

" And unto my amazement, when I had kept my *Third
Day* for her, shee was finally and forever delivered from the
hands of the *Evil Angels :* and I had afterwards the satisfaction of seeing, not only *Her* so brought home unto the
Lord that she was admitted into the *Church*, but also many
others, even some scores, of young people Awakened by
the picture of *Hell* exhibited in *her* Sufferings, *to flee from
the wrath to come.*"

The next note I have copied tells more than any
other I have found of Cotton Mather's pastoral
methods : —

" The church having hitherto extended a *Church Watch*
unto none but Communicants, and confined *Baptism* unto
Them and *Their Children*, I was desirous to bring the

---

[1] In possession of the Massachusetts Historical Society.
[2] A most minatory scripture.

church into a posture more Agreeable unto the Advice of the *Synod,* in the year, 1662." So he preached on the subject, and, allowing no disputation, proceeded to circulate among the brethren of the church "an instrument containing my Sentiments and purposes." The brethren "generally signed a Desire and Address unto myself thereto annexed that I would act accordingly. As for the few . . . who were Disaffected unto my proceedings, I carried it so peaceably, and obligingly, and yett resolutely, towards them, that they patiently Lett me take my way: and some of them told mee, they thought I did well to *do* as I did: tho' they could not yett come to *see* as I did. . . . Thus was the church quietly brought unto a point, which heretofore cost no Little Difficulty. But my Charge of such as now submitt themselves to my *Ecclesiastical Watch* was exceedingly increased. — Lord, LETT THY GRACE BEE SUFFICIENT FOR ME."

He notes that during the spring his days of fast and humiliation were so frequent that he lost record of them; that he kept, too, one or two days of Thanksgiving in his study. On one of these days, he goes on, —

"My Special Errand unto the Lord was this: That whereas His Good *Angels,* did by *His Order,* many good offices for His people, Hee would please to grant unto mee the Enjoyment of all those *Angelical Kindnesses,* which are to bee done by *His Order,* for His *Chosen Servants* . . . in a manner and measure more *Transcendent,* than what the great *Corruptions* of the generalty of *Good Men,* permitted them to be made partakers of. Now that I might bee *Qualify'd* for this Favour, I . . . Entreated that I *may* not, and Engaged that I *will* not, on the Score of any *Angelical Communications,* forsake the Conduct of the Lord's *Written Word.*"

He goes on to state certain lines of conduct which he proposes to follow, with the hope of making his behaviour as agreeable to that of angels as he can. And his closing purpose is this : —

" To *Conceal* with all prudent Secrecy whatever *Extraordinary Things* I may perceive done for mee, by the *Angels*, who love *Secrecy* in their Administrations. ☞ I do now believe," he adds, " That some Great Things are to be done for mee by the *Angels* of God."

On the 28th of March his first son was born. The child had a malformation beyond the reach of contemporary surgery. On the 1st of April it died unbaptized. It was buried beneath the epitaph, " Reserved for a glorious Resurrection."

" I had great reason," writes the bereaved father, " to suspect a *Witchcraft*, in this præternatural Accident; because my Wife, a few weeks before her Deliverance, was affrighted with an horrible *Spectre*, in the porch, which fright caused her Bowels to Turn within her ; and the *Spectres* which both before and after, Tormented a young woman in the Neighbourhood, brag'd of their giving my Wife that Fright, in hopes, they said, of doing mischief unto her *Infant*, at Least, if not unto the *Mother :* and besides all this the child was no sooner Born but a suspected Woman sent unto my Father a Letter full of Railing against myself, wherein shee told him *Hee little knew what might quickly befall some of his posterity.* However, I made little *Use* of, and laid little *Stress* on, this Conjecture : desiring to submitt unto the will of my Heavenly Father without which, *Not a sparrow falls unto the Ground.*"

He notes how during the summer he testified against the sin of uncleanness, on the occasion of the execution of two young women for child murder.

"I accompanied the wretches to their execution," he writes, "but extremely fear all the Labours were lost upon them: however sanctify'd unto many others." He notes how his preaching at Reading started a revival there; how he conceived the idea of writing the Church History which, under the name of "Magnalia Christi Americana," remains by far the most notable of his publications; how in July a fleet arrived, and he started down the harbour to preach to it, but fell so ill that he had to go home; and how he recovered in the afternoon to find that there was yellow-fever aboard the ships, and to be convinced that an Angel of the Lord had upset his stomach for the purpose of preserving him from infection. He notes how he has prayed and preached against vices which are bringing judgments on the community, "and such of these vices as called for the Correction of the Magistrates, I hope, I did effectually stir up some of the Justices to prosecute." Then, very ecstatically, he notes how in these dying times he feels himself quite ready for death: yellow-fever was abroad now. He notes a resolution to visit widows and the fatherless: he tells how he wrote a "True and Brief Representation of the Country," which was transmitted "with all the Secrecy desirable, unto the KING's own hand: who Read it with much Satisfaction, and I hope, formed from thence, in His own Royal Mind, those Characters of the Countrey whereof we shall reap the good Effects for many a day." He notes how he wrote a book called "Winter Meditations," which when winter came on was published; and how towards the end of the summer he began his great commentary on the Bible, — a collection of every scrap of learning he can discover which has any bearing on Scripture. He worked at this for twenty years: it still remains in manuscript, under the name of "Biblia Americana."[1]

Early in September, he went to preach at Salem, where he sought "Furniture" for his Church History, and endeavoured "that the complete *History* of the Late *Witchcrafts and Possessions* might not be Lost." The notes from which he intended to preach were stolen "with such Circumstances, that I am . . . satisfy'd, the Spectres, or Agents in the *Invisible World*, were the Robbers." But he preached from memory, "so the Divel gott nothing." He had an interview with a pious woman, lately visited by shining spirits. Along with some things "to be kept secret," she prophesied a new "Storm of Witchcraft . . . to chastise the Iniquity that was used in the wilful Smothering . . . of the Last." On his return home, he found Margaret Rule down.

"To avoid gratifying of the *Evil Angels*, . . . I did . . . concern myself to *use*, and *gett* as much *prayer* as I could for the afflicted Young Woman; and at the same time, to forbid, either her from *Accusing* any of the Neighbours, or others from *Enquiring* anything of her.[2] Nevertheless, a Wicked Man wrote a most Lying Libel to revile my Conduct in these Matters, which drove me to the Blessed God with my supplications. . . . I did at first, it may bee, too much Resent the Injuries of that Libel; but God brought *good* out of it: it occasioned the multiplication of my *prayers* before Him; it very much promoted the works of *Humiliation* and *Mortification* in my Soul."

---

[1] In possession of the Massachusetts Historical Society.
[2] In Calef himself I find nothing to contradict this.

He resisted the temptation to desert, in consequence of the libel, the lecture at the Old Meeting-House. As for his missing notes, he adds, the spectres bragged to the possessed girl that they had stolen them, but confessed that they could not keep them. Sure enough,

" On the fifth of October following Every Leaf of my Notes, . . . tho' they were in eighteen separate . . . sheets, . . . were found drop't here and there about the Streets of Lyn ; but how they came to bee so Dropt I cannot Imagine, and I as much wonder at the Exactness of their preservation."

On the 3d of October, his little daughter Mary[1] was ill. He prayed for her

" With such Rapturous Assurances of the Divine Love unto *mee* and *mine*, as would richly have *made Amends for the Death of more Children, if God had then called for them.* I was Unaccountably Assured, not only that *this child* shall be Happy forever, but that I never should have *any Child*, except what should bee an everlasting Temple to the Spirit of God : Yea, *That I and Mine should bee together in the Kingdome of God, World without End.*"

On the 6th, the child died : next day she was buried : her epitaph was " Gone but not Lost." On the 8th, in spite of his bereavement, he administered the sacrament ;

" And, I hope, that I now so exemplify'd such a Behaviour as not only to embolden my Approaches to the Supper of the Lord, but also to direct and instruct my Neighbourhood, with what frame to encounter their Afflictions."

On the 10th, a military training day, he prayed and fasted, particularly for a possessed girl,— doubtless Mar-

[1] Born in 1691.

garet Rule. A white spirit appeared to her, with word
that God had made Cotton Mather her father, and
thereupon she was delivered.

He notes in detail how he drew up a plan for a
Negro meeting, in which he carefully attended both to
the spiritual welfare of the Africans and to their temporal duties in the station of slavery to which it had
pleased God to call them; and how he prayed and
preached at the almshouse. He tells then how he
was himself accused of witchcraft: the tormentors of
a possessed young woman made

"my Image to appear before her, and they made themselves Masters of her tongue so far, that she began in her
Fits to complain that I Threatened her, . . . tho' when shee
came out of them, shee owned that They could not so
much as make my *Dead Shape* do her any Harm. . . . Her
greatest outcries when shee was *herself*, were for my poor
prayers."

Aware of the terrible danger to his influence, if these
rumours should gain credence,

" I was putt," he writes, " upon . . . Agonies, and Singular . . . Efforts of Soul, in the *Resignation* of my *Name*
unto the Lord; content that if Hee had no further Service
for my *Name*, it should bee torn to pieces. . . . But I cried
unto the Lord as for the Deliverance of my *Name* from the
Malice of Hell, so for the Deliverance of the Young Woman
whom the powers of Hell had seized upon. And behold !
. . . the possessed person . . . was Delivered . . . on the *very
same day;* and the whole *plott of the Divel* to Reproach a
poor Servant of the Lord Jesus Christ was Defeated."

In January, his only surviving child, Katharine, was
very ill; praying for her, he was assured that she should

recover, and presently she did. His last note for the
year tells how he offered to give up a part of his salary
to some members of his church who lived at a distance,
and were for starting a new meeting nearer home : but
nothing came of it.

Meanwhile he had published nine works : two, — a
volume of sermons, and some meditations on the last
judgment, — in 1692 ; and seven, — a preface to Mos-
ten's " Spirit of Man," two volumes of sermons, his
warnings against uncleanness, his " Winter Meditations," a letter on Witchcraft, and his "Wonders of
the Invisible World," which was printed both at home
and abroad, — in 1693.

I have cited with perhaps tedious detail his account
of himself during these years that proved the most
critical of his life, because I have not found it much
noticed elsewhere, and without it he cannot, I think,
be fairly judged. I have told enough, I hope, to enable
whoever cares, to pass honest judgment on him. There
remain two or three facts, without which our notion of
the great tragedy of witchcraft would be incomplete.

Sewall, it will be remembered, was one of the judges
who accepted spectral evidence. In the years that
followed, he suffered many afflictions. In his diary for
January, 1696–7, is this note : —

" Copy of the Bill I put up on the Fast day ; giving
it to Mr. Willard as he pass'd by, and standing up at
the reading of it, and bowing when finished ; in the
Afternoon.

" Samuel Sewall, sensible of the reiterated strokes of God
upon himself and family ; and being sensible, that as to the
Guilt contracted upon the opening of the late Comission

of Oyer and Terminer at Salem (to which the order for this Day relates) he is, upon many accounts, more concerned than any that he knows of, Desires to take the Blame and shame of it, Asking pardon of men, And especially desiring prayers that God, who has an Unlimited Authority, would pardon that sin and all other his sins ; personal and Relative : And according to his infinite Benignity, and Sovereignty, Not Visit the sin of him, or of any other, upon himself or any of his, nor upon the Land : But that He would powerfully defend him against all Temptations to Sin, for the future ; and vouchsafe him the efficacious, saving Conduct of his Word and Spirit."

It is said that when Stoughton, the Chief Justice of the Court of Oyer and Terminer, heard what Sewall had done, he declared that he had no such confession to make, having acted according to the best light God had given him.[1]

In Cotton Mather's diaries for later years[2] are two entries that belong here. The first was made at this very time, January 15th, 1696–7.

" Being afflicted last Night," it runs, " with Discouraging Thoughts as if unavoidable *marks* of the *Divine Displeasure* must overtake my Family, for my not appearing with *vigour* enough to stop the proceedings of the Judges, when the Inextricable Storm from the *Invisible World* assaulted the Countrey, I did this morning in prayer with my Family, putt my Family into the merciful Hands of the Lord. And with Tears I Received Assurance of the Lord that *marks* of His Indignation should not follow my Family, but that having the *Righteousness* of the Lord Jesus Christ pleading for us, *Goodness and Mercy* should follow us and Signal Salvation of the Lord."

[1] Sewall's Diary, I. 446, note.
[2] Both diaries are in possession of the American Antiquarian Society.

The other entry comes years later. On the night between the 15th and 16th of April, 1713, he held a vigil: in it he prayed that many books which he had published might do the good in the hope of which he had written them; and finally, in the troubled perplexity of spirit that had been growing during these long years, when his public influence and the public power of the church had been constantly waning, he wrote these words: —

"I also entreated of the Lord, that I might understand the meaning of the Descent from the Invisible World, which nineteen years ago produced in a Sermon from me, a good part of what is now published."

VII

THE END OF SIR WILLIAM PHIPPS

1692–1695

THE importance to the Mathers of the tragedy of witchcraft has warranted me, I think, in treating the matter by itself. Before we proceed, however, we must glance at certain other matters that were in progress at the same time. It was not witchcraft alone, perhaps hardly witchcraft at all, which in 1694 brought to a close the administration of Sir William Phipps, and with it the control of the Mathers in affairs of state.

Witchcraft was by no means the only thing that bothered poor Sir William. There were French and Indian wars, Canada way, which he managed rather clumsily. And there was a great deal of political trouble at home. The new Charter was not popular. The people had been used to electing their own governors: what privileges Increase Mather had secured for them failed, in the popular imagination, to balance the fact that their chief executive officer was a nominee of the King, and that he proved, after all, by no means the sort of man they would have chosen. Honest enough, everybody knew, this hot-headed, uneducated, self-made, self-willed Sir William was in nobody's opinion a man of much administrative ability. The democratic spirit declared itself more and more vigorously against him ;

not a few ministers took that side. And the old theocracy, represented by the Mathers, found itself at last quite divorced from the popular party; and at most a power behind the throne of the royal Governor. From this time on, in fact, the politics of Massachusetts was not a question of theocracy and democracy, but was rather a struggle, which culminated in the American Revolution, between the royal power and the rights of the people.

The chief figure in the opposition was Elisha Cooke, a gentleman who had been associated with Increase Mather in the mission to England, and who had bitterly opposed the acceptance of the new Charter. A few of Sewall's notes show how matters ran in Boston. In November, 1692, Cooke came home; and on the 15th he kept a day of thanksgiving for his safe arrival. Most of the Boston worthies joined him in the festival; but Sewall notes: "Mr. Mather not there, nor Mr. Cotton Mather. The good Lord unite us in his Fear, and Remove our Animosities." The next May, in the teeth of an election sermon preached by Increase Mather on the great benefit of primitive counsellors,[1] Cooke was elected a member of the Governor's Council, along with certain other opponents of the government. On the 1st of June, Sir William used his privilege to veto the election of Cooke. "June 8," notes Sewall, "Mr. Danforth labours to bring Mr. Mather and Mr. Cook together, but I think in vain. Is great wrath about Mr. Cook's being refused, and 'tis supposed Mr. Mather is the cause." We begin to see more of what poor Cotton Mather

[1] See Quincy, I. 73.

meant by resolving not to waste precious time in
personal quarrels towards the end of 1692. On the
11th of July, Sewall notes, Cotton Mather prayed at
the opening of the Council; he prayed there again
on the 15th; and in the afternoon of that day the
Governor dissolved the assembly, being "much dis-
gusted . . . about the not passing of the Bill to regu-
lat the house of Representatives."

The bill in question was passed on the 25th of November. To all appearances a mere political device
for strengthening the power of the government at a
given moment, it has proved perhaps the most mischievous measure in the whole madcap history of
American legislation. So far as the Mathers were responsible for it, they did their utmost to weaken the
character of legislative bodies throughout this continent. As a matter of fact, in 1693, the opposition to
the government was far stronger in Boston than in the
country: chiefly, if not wholly, to weaken the opposition in the legislature, this bill provided that a representative must reside in the place he represented. It
has been followed in practice throughout America: as
a consequence no American constituency is able to-
day to elect a competent representative unless, by the
blessing of providence, a competent person happens to
reside among them. And as, in the nature of things,
the most able men generally congregate in large cities,
the greater part of every American legislature is composed of men personally insignificant.

But even this device proved of little use. In addition to his other troubles, Sir William was always getting into hot water on his own account. Early in

his administration, he had a difficulty with the collector of the port of Boston, which culminated in a hand-to-hand fight. In January, 1693, another difficulty with the captain of a royal frigate brought upon the captain a caning at the hands of Sir William in the streets of Boston. It was chiefly for this, apparently, that he was summoned to England to explain his conduct. After all, the godly, self-made adventurer had not proved the Governor the Mathers hoped for: he was not one to make friends for the new Charter.

A few of Sewall's notes for November, 1694, give the most vivid pictures of his last days in New England.

"Nov. 1. . . . Capt. Dobbins refusing to give Bail, the Sheriff was taking him to Prison, and Sir William Phips rescued him, and told the Sheriff He would send him, the Sheriff, to prison, if he touch'd him, which occasioned very warm discourse between Him and the Lieut. Governour."—"Nov. 3. . . . Governour adjourns the General Court. . . . Several of the Council desired a dissolution, lest some Emergency should require the Calling of an Assembly, and this adjournment bind our hands: but the Governour would not hearken to it. . . . Said, This Court is dissolved to such a time; being put in mind of his mistake, said I mean Adjourn'd."—"Nov. 9. . . . Lieut. Governour and Council dine at James Meers's: The Treat was intended for the Governour; but is so offended at Capt. Dobbins Imprisonment, that He comes not, nor Mr. Mather the Father, nor Son . . .; so chair at the uper end of the Table stands empty. Note. Mr. Cotton Mather was sick of a grievous pain in his face, else He had been there, as he told me afterward."—"Seventh-day, Nov. 17th. . . . Just about Sunset or a little after, the Governour goes from his House to the Salutation Stairs, and there goes on board his

Yatcht; Lieut. Governour, many of the Council, Mr. Cotton Mather, Capts. of Frigatts, Justices and many other
Gentlemen accompanying him. 'Twas six oclock by that
time I got home, and I only staid to see them come to sail.
Guns at the Castle were fired about seven : Governour
had his Flagg in main top. Note. Twas of a seventh day
in the even when the Governour came to Town, and so tis
at his going off, both in darkness : and uncomfortable,
because of the Sabbath."

Stoughton, the Lieutenant Governor, was left at the
head of affairs for several years. In March, Cooke
was elected to the Council, where he served annually
till Joseph Dudley's time.

Two or three more notes of Sewall's tell a little of
Cotton Mather, and all the rest there is to tell of poor
blundering Sir William.

" Monday, April 29, 1695. . . . About 2 P. M. a very
extraordinary Storm of Hail, so that the ground was made
white with it, as with the blossoms when fallen. . . . Mr.
Cotton Mather dined with us, and was with me in the new
Kitchen when this was; He had just been mentioning that
more Ministers Houses than others proportionably had
been smitten with Lightening ; enquiring what the meaning
of God should be in it. Many Hail Stones broke throw
the Glass and flew to the middle of the Room. . . . I got
Mr. Mather to pray with us after this awfull Providence ;
He told God He had broken the brittle part of our house,
and pray'd that we might be ready for the time when our
Clay-Tabernacles should be broken. . . . I mentioned to
Mr. Mather that Monmouth made his descent into England
about the time of the Hail in '85, . . . that much cracked
our South-west windows."

Whether Sewall thought this storm equally portentous
does not appear. But on

"May 5, 1695. About 3 hours News comes to Town of the death of Sir William Phipps, Feb. 18th, at which people are generally sad. Lay sick about a week of the new Fever as 'tis called." — "May 6th. . . . Mourning Guns are fired at the Castle and Town for the Death of our Governour." — "May 8, 1695. I visit my Lady, who takes on heavily for the death of Sir William. Thinks the Lieutenant and Council were not so kind to him as they should have been."

9

VIII

HARVARD COLLEGE

1636–1701

FROM this time on, the history of Massachusetts takes a course of less interest to us. Stoughton, the Lieutenant Governor, remained at the head of affairs until 1699, when Lord Bellomont, who had been appointed Governor some time before, came to Boston. Two years later Bellomont died. In 1702 Joseph Dudley, who had been virtually an exile from Massachusetts since he was shipped to England with Andros, was appointed Governor. There is reason to believe that his appointment was much advanced by a letter from Cotton Mather, which Dudley showed the King, stating that "there was not one minister nor one of the Assembly but were impatient for his coming." [1]

The chief public affairs in Stoughton's time were connected with the French and Indian wars in Maine. In Bellomont's time, the legislature established a judiciary in a form which ultimately led to trouble with England, and began the series of squabbles with the Governor about his salary which lasted well through Cotton Mather's day. Bellomont's most notable act was perhaps the suppression of piracy: it was he who brought Captain Kidd to justice. In brief, the political history

[1] Palfrey, III. 183.

of Massachusetts up to the time of Joseph Dudley may
be said to have been a slowly strengthening opposition
in the legislature — and so among the people — to the
power of the Governor and the Crown.

With all this the Mathers had far less to do than
with the politics of earlier times. It is very typical of
their history, and of the history of the theocratic party
in Massachusetts, that, from this time on, their most
notable public activity concerns not the Province,
but Harvard College. It will be worth our while, then,
hastily to glance at the history of this institution.

This has been very thoroughly written by President
Quincy. In 1636, only seven years after the arrival of
Governor Winthrop with the first Charter of the Colony,
the General Court voted four hundred pounds "towards
a School or College." Two years later, the Rev. John
Harvard, a young graduate of Cambridge who had emi-
grated to Charlestown, died, leaving half of his estate
and his whole library to the new College. With this
encouragement, the College was immediately opened,
and, in honour of its first benefactor, received the name
of Harvard. In 1642 a Board of Overseers was established, consisting of the Governor and Deputy Governor, all the magistrates, and the teaching elders of the
six adjoining towns. In 1650, a charter was granted
by the General Court, placing the government of the
College in the hands of a Corporation, consisting of
the President, the Treasurer, and five Fellows named
in the act, and empowered, with the counsel and consent of the Overseers, to perpetuate themselves. Under this charter, after various vicissitudes and some
very radical changes in the nature of the Board of

Overseers,—who are now elected by the alumni,— the College is governed at the present day.

Amid the utmost poverty and privation the College began its work, which was chiefly to educate the more promising youth of the Colony to a point which should render them efficient ministers of the Gospel in the inevitable days when the emigrant ministers should be no more. What manner of men it turned out we should know by this time : both Increase and Cotton Mather were graduates of Harvard; and Sibley's [1] amazingly careful biographies of those who graduated before 1689 prove the Mathers to have been typical men. It is curiously characteristic of Harvard, however, that the first two Presidents—if we except, as the records do, a rather disreputable person who was for a little while made master of the school—were decidedly inclined to heresy in the matter of baptism. Earnest, devoted, learned, ill paid, half starved, they gave every energy to the College; and before Chauncy, the second President, died, he began to see the gifts to the College come in, which have continued to the present time. The third President, Leonard Hoar, came from England to take office. For some obscure reason he was unpopular : there were intrigues against him, which encouraged the students — in the words of Cotton Mather [2]— to turn " cud-weeds, and, with great violations of the fifth Commandment, set themselves to *travestie* whatever he *did* and *said*." He resigned, and is believed to have died of a broken heart. His successor, Urian Oakes, seems to have been the leader of the intrigues against him : he seems

---

[1] Harvard Graduates, 3 vols.
[2] Magnalia, IV. I. § 5.

to have been orthodox, however, if we may credit the words in which, as we have seen, he addressed young Cotton Mather in 1678.[1] When he died, in 1681, Increase Mather was chosen his successor. He declined, and so did another reverend gentleman; but John Rogers, who became the fifth President of the College, survived his inauguration less than a year; and in 1685 Increase Mather finally accepted the office. He took it on condition that he should not reside at Cambridge, but should be permitted to continue, at the same time, his pastoral work at the Second Church in Boston. He held it throughout his mission to England: he retained it throughout the administrations of Phipps, Stoughton, and Bellomont, under circumstances which we shall have to consider in some detail.

For what reason no man knows, the acts of the General Court which founded and moulded the College contained no phrases which could fairly bind it to any sectarian policy. In 1642, *piety* is the only term used that connects the College with any distinct religious principle; in 1650, there appears no more stringent term than *godliness;* and the first seal of the College, adopted on the 27th of December, 1643, bears only the word "Veritas." [2] It was not until Increase Mather's time, in all probability, that affairs led to the adoption of the other, and far less characteristic, motto still in use, — " Christo et Ecclesiæ." [8] Whether, as President Quincy inclined to think, this apparently studied religious liberality was real, may perhaps be doubted: there is, I think, about as much reason for

[1] Cf. page 37.　　　　　　[2] Truth.
[8] For Christ and the Church.

supposing that, at the time the charter was granted
and the seal adopted, piety, godliness, and truth meant
to the men who used these terms nothing more or less
than orthodox Calvinism; that to have defined this
further would have seemed to them a waste of words.
But, whatever the reason, as the political power of the
clergy began to weaken, it became evident that there
was a dangerous flaw in the construction of their in-
nermost stronghold. To the defence of this, then, the
Mathers devoted their utmost energy.

In 1686 — the year after Increase Mather had accepted the presidency — came, as we have seen, the final
news of the vacating of the Charter of the Colony.
With this, of course, fell all the minor rights that the
Colonial authorities had granted under it, and among
others the charter of Harvard College. For twenty-
one years, until, in December, 1707, the old charter of
1650 was not too regularly revived, the College had
no settled government. Throughout this period the
Mathers, with whomever they could get to follow them,
fought, and worked, and prayed for a charter which
should permanently commit the College to the care
of men whose chief thought should be to preserve
uncontaminated the traditions of the fathers. They
hopelessly failed; the College they longed to see the
perpetual breeder of a priesthood has grown to be perhaps the most potent nurse of every shade of liberal
protestantism and toleration in the English-speaking
world. So those there who remember the Mathers at
all nowadays either scoff at their memory or abuse it.
But I think we shall grow to feel, as we read their
story, that, whatever their errors, they fought their ear-

nest fight with all their hearts, with all their souls, with all their might.

During Increase Mather's stay in England, he was constantly endeavouring to get a royal charter for the College. In an interview with James II., on the 2d of July, 1688, he asked the King directly to grant a charter for the non-conformist institution.

" ' Certainly, Syr,' " he said; " ' they may think it hard that the College built by Non-Conformists, should be taken from them and put into the Hands of Conformists.' The King replied, ' It is Unreasonable, and it shall not be.' " — " What ? " notes Cotton Mather in the margin, " King James himself declare so! "[1]

But before long poor King James was where he could grant no more charters, and Increase Mather paying court to William and Mary. He had his last interview with the king on the 3d of January, 1691–2.

" ' We have in *New England*,' " he said, as he took his leave, " ' a COLLEGE where many an Excellent Protestant Divine has had his Education.' The KING said, ' I know it.' He thereupon added, ' If Your Majesty will cast a favourable Aspect on that Society, it will yet Flourish more than ever.' The KING returned, ' I shall willingly do it.' — And so *Ended* the *Final Conference*." [2]

Home again, he busied himself at once to obtain a new charter for the College. On the 27th of June, 1692, the very month when the first of the Salem witches was hanged, Sir William Phipps signed one. This charter vested absolute power in a Corporation of ten persons, every one of whom was selected by Increase

---

[1] Parentator, XXV.   [2] Parentator, XXVIII.

Mather; and it made no provision for any kind of visiting board.   It was immediately sent to England for royal
approval.   Meantime the new Corporation assembled
as if the new charter had been thoroughly sanctioned,
and among their first acts conferred the first honorary
degrees.   They made Increase Mather Doctor of Divinity: Leverett and Brattle, who had managed the
College in his absence, were at the same time made
Bachelors of Divinity.   There is something significant
in this very fact: Leverett and Brattle were men of far
more liberal sentiment than Mather; Brattle is believed to have given Calef much assistance in the
preparation of his book against witchcraft;[1] and the
two Bachelors of Divinity proved leaders in the movement that finally drove the Reverend Doctor from
power.

In 1693, Increase Mather published his Election Sermon on the benefit of primitive counsellors.[2]   " Bene
agere et male audire regium est," [3] was its motto; and
in his preface he tells how he had been warned in England that he should find New England ungrateful for
his public services; and how he had replied, that he
would go to New England and see, and that if he
found their prognostications true he should see his
call clear to return to England again.   In spite of this
warning, the General Court, far from sending him to
England again, passed a vote that the President of
Harvard College ought to reside at Cambridge.   Mather,
who had no notion of resigning his church, offered his
resignation of the presidency to the Corporation; they

[1] Sibley, III. 17, 18.   [2] Cf. page 125.
[3] " It is the lot of kings to do good and to hear evil."

refused it, and requested him to go on in the old way. Here matters stood in July, 1696, when word came from England that the King had vetoed the Charter of 1692, for the reason that it provided no visiting board. The effect of this news on Increase Mather was the renewal of a special assurance, which persisted for years, that he should once more be permitted to do work for the Lord in England.[1]

A note in Sewall relates what next happened.

" Oct. 12. [1696.] Lt. Governour goes to Cambridge. . . . Complemented the Pressedent etc., for all the respect to him, acknowledg'd his obligation and promis'd his Interposition for them as become such an Alumnus to such an Alma Mater : directed and desired the Presdt and fellows to go on : directed and enjoined the students to obedience. Had a good diñer. . . . Mr. Cotton Mather took off Mr. Chauncy and Oakes's Epitaphs as I read them to him."

A vivid little note I find this : Mather the father succeeding for the time in somehow continuing his power over the nursery of the old faith ; Mather the son busy meantime in gathering material for the great Church History which remains its most notable literary monument.

It is Sewall, too, who gives the most vivid account of what came next. On the 17th of December, 1696, the Council passed a new charter.

" Dec. 18," writes Sewall, " Mr. Mather, Allen, Willard, C. Mather give in a paper subscribed by them, shewing their dislike of our draught for the Colledge charter, and desiring that their Names might not be entered therein.

[1] Quincy, I. App. IX.

One chief reason was their apointing the Govr. and
Council for Visitor.[1] . . . I doe not know that I ever saw
the Council run upon with such a height of Rage before.
The Lord prepare for the Issue. . . . The Ministers will
go to England for a Charter, except we exclude the Council
from the Visitation."

In 1697 Increase Mather drew up a new charter,
which was somehow fought through the legislature.
And the first public indications of the troubles that
were brewing within the College appeared in the dropping of Leverett's name from the Corporation. "How
the Deputies will resent it," writes Sewall,[2] "I know
not." And there was a petition of some ministers that
Increase Mather be sent to England to push the charter; and the General Court refused it; and Mather
threatened to resign. Late in the same year, Sewall
gives another glimpse of the poor man's troubles: —

"Nov. 20. Mr. Willard[3] told me of the falling out between the President and him about Chusing Fellows last
Monday. Mr. Mather has sent him word, He will never
come to his House more till he give him satisfaction."

Next January came another petition that Mather be
sent to England, likewise rejected. And at the end of
1698, the General Court renewed the vote that President Mather "remove to the College, and take up his
residence there."

Two accounts are extant of the interview that followed, on the 8th of December, between Mather and

[1] I. e. Lay overseers threatened the predominance of the clergy.
[2] Diary, I. 450.
[3] Minister of the Old South. The year before, Willard and
Mather had joined in protesting against the charter of 1696.

the representatives of the General Court who brought him this order.

" I told them," writes Increase Mather himself,[1] " that I was discouraged. . . . Col. Byfield said . . . every one in the House desired that I should be the President, etc. I objected that I was not willing to leave my preaching work. Mr. Sewall's reply was, I might preach to the scholars by expositions every day. I told them, I could not go till the church spared me." — " Oh," he writes two days later, "that God would accept of service for me in England according to my faith ! "

Sewall's account of the interview runs thus : —

"'Twas near 7 in the even before we got thither. I began, and ask'd excuse for our being so late. The reason was, most of us were come from a Wedding : However, I hop'd it was a good omen, that we were all coming to a Wedding. . . . We urged his going all we could; I told him of his Birth and education here ; that he look'd at work rather than Wages,[2] all met in desiring him, and should hardly agree so well in any other. Mr. Speaker, in behalf of the House, earnestly desired him. Objected want of a House, Bill for Corporation not pass'd ; Church ; [his attachment to it] Must needs preach once every week, which he prefered before the Gold and Silver of the West Indies. I told him would preach twice aday to the students. He said that . . . was nothing like preaching."

All of which Mather repeated formally in a letter to Stoughton on December 18.[3] And putting the question of leave of absence to his church a few weeks later, he had the satisfaction of being refused. In April,

---

[1] Quincy, I. 480, 481.
[2] Among other troubles was a dispute about salary.
[3] Sewall's Diary, I. 493, 494.

1699, came news that the King would not approve the charter of 1697.

The next month Lord Bellomont, the new Governor, arrived. In his message to the General Court, on the 2d of June, he expressed a wish to promote a charter for the College. A few days later, Cotton Mather had a spiritual experience perhaps worth recording here. On the 7th of June, 1699,[1] one of his children was very ill. He had had a particular faith that she should recover ; but as she grew worse, " being in distress lest my particular Faith should prove but a Fancy, and a Folly, and end in Confusion," he held a special fast ; and the child mended forthwith.

" God has ordered this Matter," he goes on, " for my Encouragement about several greater points of my particular Faith not yett accomplished. . . . This day as I was, (may I not say ?) in *the Spirit*, it was in a powerful manner assured me from Heaven, That my Father shall one Day be carried into England: and that he shall there glorify the Lord Jesus Christ: And that the *particular Faith* which has Introduced it, shall be at last made a matter of wonderful glory and Service unto the Lord. And thou, O Mather the Younger, shalt Live to see this Accomplished. And thy Son [2] too shall glorify the Lord Jesus Christ, after thou also hast followed thy Father into the Kingdom of God."

On the 7th of July,[3] the Mathers and six other ministers addressed to the General Court a request that in the new charter

" our holy religion may be secured to us and unto our posterity, by a provision, that no person shall be chosen

[1] The diary for 1699 is in possession of the American Antiquarian Society.

[2] Cf. pages 175–177.   [3] Quincy, I. 99.

President, or Fellow, of the College, but such as declare their adherence unto the principles of reformation, which were espoused and intended by those who first settled the country and founded the College, and have hitherto been the general profession of New England."

Such a provision was inserted in the charter passed on the 13th of July; none of the previous charters had contained anything of the kind. On the 16th, Cotton Mather had another ecstatic assurance that all should be well. On the 18th, Lord Bellomont objected to the religious proviso in the new charter, which he probably deemed a direct attack on the Church of England. This charter, then, and the fervent particular faiths of the Mathers came to nothing.

Meantime another matter had been growing that sorely troubled the Mathers. Quincy tells the story clearly. We have seen already that Leverett and Brattle had begun to show a tendency to heterodoxy. In 1697, Cotton Mather published a Life of Jonathan Mitchel, Minister of Cambridge.[1] To this Increase Mather prefixed a dedicatory letter to the church in Cambridge and the students in the College there. The substance of this long assertion of the pristine principles of New England is, that " to admit persons to partake of the Lord's Supper, without any examination of the work of grace in the heart, would be a real apostacy and degeneracy from the churches of New England "; and he warns the tutors of the College not to become " degenerate plants or prove themselves apostate." This was a direct attack on Leverett, Brattle, and their friends. They were not slow in retorting

---

[1] Reprinted in the Magnalia, IV. IV.

At the beginning of 1698, they organized a new church in Boston on new principles, expressly rejecting " the imposition of any public relation of experiences " as the condition of admission to the Lord's Supper.[1]   In November, 1699, the Rev. Benjamin Colman arrived to take charge of the new church ; an accomplished young man, graduated at Harvard College seven years before, and since that time resident in England, where under William of Orange clever Dissenters had been having a very comfortable time. A few notes from Cotton Mather's diary and from Sewall's [2] will tell the rest of the story.

"7th, 10th m. [1699]," writes Cotton Mather, " A company of headstrong men in the town, the chief of whom are full of malignity to the holy ways of our churches, have built in the town another meeting-house. . . . And without the advice or knowledge of the ministers in the vicinity, they have published, under the title of a *manifesto*, certain articles that utterly subvert our churches. . . . This drives the ministers that would be faithful unto the Lord Jesus Christ, and his interest in the churches, unto a necessity of appearing for their defence. No little part of these actions most unavoidably fall to my share."

Two days later Colman called on Sewall, who talked at some length about the startling manifesto.

" At his going away," writes Sewall, " I told him, If God should please by them to hold forth any Light that had not been seen or entertained before ; I should be so far from

[1] Quincy, I. 130, 131. For a somewhat fuller account of their principles, see Palfrey, III. 170, *seq*.

[2] All these are cited in the Appendix to the first volume of Quincy.

envying it, that I should rejoice in it: which he was much affected with."

On the 5th of January, 1699–1700, poor Cotton Mather's mood was far from placid.

"I see Satan," he writes, "beginning a terrible Shake unto the Churches of New England, and the *Innovators* that have sett up a New Church in Boston, (a *New* one indeed!) have made a Day of Temptation among us. The men are Ignorant, Arrogant, Obstinate, and full of malice and slander, and they fill the Land with Lyes, in the misrepresentations whereof I am a very singular sufferer. Wherefore I set apart this day again for prayer in my study, to cry mightily unto God."

But by the 21st of January, he had so far controlled himself as to be able to draw up a proposal of terms on which the old party and the new might agree. Sewall tells the rest of the story for the moment.

"Jany. 24th. The Lt. Govr. calls me with him to Mr. Willards, where out of two papers[1] Mr. Wm. Brattle drew up a third for an Accomodation to bring on an Agreement between the New-Church and our Ministers; Mr. Coleman got his Brethren to subscribe to it. — Jany. 25th. Mr. I. Mather, Mr. C. Mather [and others] wait on the Lt. Govr. ... to confer about the writing drawn up the evening before. Was some heat; but grew calmer, and after Lecture agreed to be present at the Fast which is to be observed Jany. 31. — Jany. 31. Fast at the New Church. Mr. Coleman reads the Writing agreed on. . . . Mr. I. Mather preaches, Mr. Cotton Mather prays. . . . Mr. Mather gives the Blessing. His text was, Follow peace with all men and

---

[1] This phrase seems to me to dispose of Quincy's charge that Cotton Mather falsely claimed the authorship of the agreement. One of the "two papers" was doubtless his. See Quincy, I. 237.

Holiness. Doct. must follow peace as far as it consists with Holiness. . . . C. Mather pray'd excellently and pathetically for Mr. Colman and his Flock. Twas a close dark day."

The next May, Lord Bellomont in his address to the General Court advised that "the settlement of the College will best be obtained . . . by addressing the King for his royal charter of privileges." Accordingly the General Court prepared an address to his Majesty, humbly soliciting his approval of a charter they prepared in form. The influence of the Mathers appears in the fact that neither Leverett, nor either of the Brattles, the Rev. William, and Thomas, the Treasurer, was named in this charter. How matters now appeared to Cotton Mather, his diary tells.[1] On the 16th of June, 1700, he writes in much detail of his particular faiths about the College : he was holding a day of fasting and special prayer.

"I beg'd of the Lord," he goes on, "that if my *particular Faith* about my Father's voyage to *England,* were not a Delusion, He would please to Renew it upon mee. All the while my Heart had the Coldness of a Stone upon it, and the Straitness that is to be expected from the bare Exercise of Reason. But now all on the sudden, I felt an inexpressible Force to fall on my Mind, an *Afflatus* that cannot be described in words ; *None knows it, but he that has it ;* If an *Angel* from Heaven had spoken it Articulately, the communication would not have been more powerful. It was told me that the Lord Jesus Christ Loved my Father, and Loved mee, and that Hee took Delight in

[1] The whole passage from which I make selections is printed in Quincy, I. 484-486. The diary for 1700 is in possession of the Massachusetts Historical Society.

us as in Two of His Faithful Servants: and that Hee had
not permitted us to be Deceived in our *particular Faiths*,
but that my Father should be carried into *England*, and
there glorify the Lord Jesus Christ before his passing into
Glory: . . . and that I shall also live to see it; and that
a Sentence of *Death* shall be written on . . . our *particular Faith*, but the Lord Jesus Christ, who *Raises the
Dead*, and is *the Resurrection and the Life* shall give a
New Life unto it! Hee will do it! Hee will do it!—
Having Left a Flood of Tears fetched from me by these
Rayes[1] from the *Invisible World* on my study-floor, I
Rose and went unto my chair. There I took up my Bible,
and the First place that I opened was at Act 27. 23. 24.
25,[2] 'There stood by me an angel of God, whose I am, and
whom I serve, saying, Fear not, thou must be brought before Cæsar.' . . . A New Flood of Tears immediately
gush'd from my flowing Eyes, and I broke out into these
Expressions: 'What! Shall my Father yett appear before
Cæsar? Has an *Angel* from Heaven told me so? And
must I believe what has been told me? Well then, It
shall be so! It shall be so!'"—"And now," runs the
next entry, "what shall I say? When the affair of my
Father's agency . . . came to a turning point . . . some
of the Tories so wrought upon the Governour that he
deserted[3] it. The Lieutenant Governour . . . appeared
with all the Little Tricks imaginable to confound it. It
had, for all this, been carried, had not some of the Council
been inconveniently called off. . . . The whole affair of
the College, was left unto the management of the Earl of
Bellomont. So that all expectation of a Voyage for my

[1] Not *rages*, as Quincy read.

[2] Like most of Cotton Mather's quotations, this is not quite
accurate in detail. It is characteristic of his eternal hurry, that,
while he rarely misses the spirit of a quotation, he is apt, even
when citing Scripture, to make verbal slips.

[3] Not *deferred*, as Quincy read.

Father unto *England* on any such occasion, is utterly at an end. What shall I make of this Wonderful matter. Wait! Wait!"

Before he had waited a month, his particular faith had a worse buffet still. On the 10th of July, the General Court, far from bidding Increase Mather go stand before Cæsar, voted more decidedly than ever that the President of Harvard College ought to reside there; and that Increase Mather should "repair to Cambridge as soon as may be." Sewall visited him the same day,

"at three in the afternoon. I told him the Honor of Athanasius, *Maluit sedem quam Fidei syllabam mutare :*[1] Worthies of N. E. left their Houses in England, and came hither where there were none to preserve [2] Religion in its Purity. Put him in mind how often God had renewed his Call to the work which was to be consider'd. That were 19 in the Council: and had every vote."

But poor Increase Mather, who had stood before three Cæsars, had no mind to "leave preaching to 1500 souls . . . only to expound to 40 or 50 Children, few of them capable of Edification by such Exercises."[3] At least he must get the consent of his church, the official representative of the 1500 souls. To his grief, they gave their consent. A note of Cotton Mather's early in July tells the story.

"There was a coincidence of many things," he writes, "to incline the Church unto such a Vote; but the chief

---

[1] "He would rather change his home than a jot of his faith."
[2] May not this be a misprint for *persecute ?*
[3] I. Mather to Stoughton, 16 December, 1698. Sewall's Diary, I. 493.

was, The Ferment and the Tumult of the Countrey, about
the State of the too-corrupted College, and the Danger of
its falling into Ill Hands, if my Father should not have answered the Cry of the publick about it. And it was the
apprehension of his best Friends, that if my Father had
now declined going to Cambridge, the Clamour and Reproach of all the Land against him, would have been insupportable; he must have Died with Infamy. My Father
upon the vote of the Church immediately (the next week)
hastens away to Reside at Cambridge. But I am now
plunged into Distresses of two sorts. First, The Strangely
melancholy and Disconsolate Condition of Mind which my
Father has carried with him to *Cambridge*, (the place, which
of all under Heaven, was most Abominable to him) fills me
with Fear, what may be the Event. If he would be cheerful, all would be easy; but his Spirit is prodigiously un-
framed, unhing'd and broken; and if the Lord be not very
merciful to Him, the Name of the Lord Jesus Christ will
suffer more Dishonour from his Uneasiness than I am willing to see. Lord, Rate off, and Chain up, the Tempter,
that falls upon my poor Father with such molestation.
Secondly, I am now Left alone in the care of a Vast congregation, the largest in all these parts of the world. I am
afraid, lest now they grow foolish and froward, and lest the
Devices of Satan may some way or other prevail to scatter
them, or Lest some Distemper arise among them. And, I
am feeble; and in this Town I have many Enemies: indeed, all the Enemies of the Evangelical Interests are
mine. I need a more than ordinary prudence and patience,
and the Defence of Heaven."

For all this time there were other troubles entangled
with those directly concerning the College. The dis-
sensions with the Brattle Street people had broken out
afresh. Before the reconciliation of January, 1700,
the two Mathers had, " with many prayers and studies,

and with humble resignation of our names unto the Lord, prepared a faithful antidote for our churches against the infection of the example, which we feared this company had given them."[1] The reconciliation stopped the publication of this antidote : but in March, the Mathers published it, — a book entitled the "Order of the Gospel." It was a direct, violent attack, in general terms, on the innovations that were creeping into the churches of New England. Some notes from Cotton Mather's diary for 1700 tell how this matter showed itself to him. On the 1st of March, the day the book came out, he writes,

"The Venome of that malignant Company who have lately built a New Church in Boston disposes them to add unto the Storm of my present persecution; for it may bee never had any men more of that Character of *Grievous Revolters*, To bee *walking with Slanders*, than too many of that poor people have."

On the 14th of April, he comforted himself with the reflection that as Christ was persecuted on earth, so would naturally be His faithful servants : he ought, then, to be thankful for his sufferings.

"It was powerfully sett home upon my heart," he adds, "that I have in this Disposition an *Infallible Symptome*, That my Lord Jesus Christ will ere Long fetch me away to *Heavenly Glory*, and that he will *glorify* me with Himself world without End." On the 11th of May, he had an assurance "That something shall befall the Disorderly Society of Innovators (now causing much Temptation and

[1] Cotton Mather's Diary, 21 January, 1700, quoted from Quincy, I. 487. For all this matter of the Brattle Street Church, see Quincy, Chap. VII.

Iniquity in the place) that shall confirm these Churches in the Right Ways of the Lord."

In spite of this assurance, " sundry ministers of New England " published the " Gospel Order Revived," [1] — a vigorous reply to the Mathers' " Order of the Gospel." On the 4th of July, less than a week before his ecstatic assurance, so dreadfully disappointed, that his father should be carried into England, Cotton Mather writes that there are hardly any but his father and himself

" to appear with any strength of Argument or Fortitude in Defence of the invaded *Churches*. Wherefore I thought I must cry mightily unto the Lord that He would mercifully Direct me . . . in all my feeble, but faithful Endeavours to serve Him . . . and preserve me from all the Devices of Satan . . . to blast me with Reproaches that may . . . Incapacitate me for Eminent Serviceableness. I also thought, that if it be the purpose of Heaven that the Apostasy should go on, they that will vigourously . . . stand in the way of that *Apostasy* may be in danger of a Stroke from the *Angel of Death*, that so a *way may be made for the Anger of God*. But then I resolved . . . I will oppose it, tho' it cost me my *Life*. Hereupon the Lord sent into my Spirit a Sweet Meditation, That my Life which I am thus willing to venture, shall the rather be prolonged ; and my Name, which I thus cast overboard, shall be the more precious in the Churches of the Lord."

On the 2d of September, when poor Increase Mather was at work expounding to his " 40 or 50 children " at Cambridge, Cotton Mather writes,

" Observing how powerfully the *Devices of Satan* are operating to bring on *Apostasies* and *Innovations* upon the

[1] For a curious contemporary comment on this controversy, see Sewall's Letter-Book, I. 255.

Churches, and particularly, a Minister of some Note in the Churches for his piety[1] having published a Book of Wretched Novelties, which, tho' it be offensive to the generalty of Good Men, yett is Entertained with Gladness by a carnal, Giddy Rising generation, I thought it my duty to defend the Churches."

So he wrote a "Defence of the Evangelical Churches," "whereto my Father joined with me, in setting his Name." This was apparently the pamphlet full of passionate vituperation which is described by President Quincy.

At the same time, another attack, and a more direct one, was making on the Mathers. We have already seen[2] how profoundly unimaginative Robert Calef was stirred by what seemed to him the deliberately monstrous conduct of the Mathers in the matter of witchcraft. In the intervening years he had put together his book on the subject, for which, Sibley says,[3] "he was furnished with materials . . . by Mr. [Wm.] Brattle of Cambridge and his brother of Boston, gentlemen who were opposed to the Salem proceedings." Likewise gentlemen, I may add, who started the Brattle Street Church, and in College matters were leaders of the opposition to the Mathers.[4] An honest book, I have said, it seems to me; a sensible one, if it be good sense to have no glimmer of imagination; but about as appreciative of what the Mathers really were as a good, practical Yankee of to-day might be of Cardinal Newman. It was printed in England: it arrived in Boston in November, 1700. Increase Mather had it publicly

[1] Colman, I believe.
[2] See page 105.
[3] Harvard Graduates, III. 17, 18.
[4] See page 144.

burned in Harvard Yard, thereby doubtless increasing its vogue. Just at this moment no blow could have hit the Mathers harder.

"First Calef's Book," writes Cotton Mather on the 28th of December, "and then Coleman's do sett the people in a mighty Ferment. All the Adversaries of the Churches Lay their Hands together as if by Blasting of us they hoped utterly to blow up all."

So this day he prayed and fasted. His devotions consisted largely of the singing of psalms. His psalm-book, he remarked with some surprise, opened of itself at places

"the most agreeable perhaps of any that I could have chosen. This observation may easily be abused unto superstition: but yett sometimes there is an Angelical Agency in these occurrences."

But the losing fight was almost over. On the 17th of October, 1700, Increase Mather, professing ill-health, had returned from Cambridge, desiring in a letter to Stoughton that another President be thought of. In February, 1701, Samuel Willard, Minister of the Old South, was made Vice President. On the 5th of March, Lord Bellomont died in New York, leaving the administration once more in the hands of Lieutenant Governor Stoughton. On the 4th of July, Sewall visited him, confined to his bed, with a committee of the General Court, who wished to arrange an adjournment.

"He agreed to it," writes Sewall, "very freely. I said the Court was afflicted with the sense of his Honors indisposition; at which he rais'd himself up on his Couch. When coming away, he reach'd out his hand; I gave him mine, and kiss'd his. He said before, Pray for me! This was the last time I ever saw his Honor."

Three days later the grim old Puritan was dead: he had been one of the crew of Andros; with the favour of the Mathers he had retained office in the time of Phipps; with the best light God had given him, he had done to death the Salem witches; and all that is left of him now is the forbidding portrait in Memorial Hall, with the stiff open hand that tells how he was the first native benefactor who built a hall for Harvard College.

The executive authority now vested in the Council. On the 6th of September, 1701, the General Court voted that Increase Mather, who had meanwhile gone back to Cambridge and again returned to Boston, be replaced by Mr. Samuel Willard, who promised to reside at the College one or two days and nights in a week. And so the "good President" who had stood before Cæsar, who had won for Massachusetts the Charter under which she flourished for more than eighty years, who had given every energy of his life to the defence of the old theocracy of the fathers, was left at sixty-two just what he had been at twenty-five, and what he remained all the rest of his life, — nothing but the Minister of the Second Church in Boston.

Twenty-three years later, when Cotton Mather wrote his father's life, he could speak thus: —

"His abdication was after all brought about, I will but *Softly* say, *Not so fairly as it should have been*. I think, there are Thanks due to me, for my forbearing to *Tell the Story*."[1]

[1] Parentator, XXIX. See pages 183–185.

At the time he was not so calm. It is probable that, almost at this moment, he had the sagacity to make his last forlorn attempt to master the government, by writing to Joseph Dudley the letter which clinched his appointment to the governorship.[1] Dudley might be grateful; things might still go better. But how he took it at the moment appears most vividly in a note of Sewall's.

"Oct. 20 [1701]. Mr. Cotton Mather came to Mr. Wilkins's shop, and there talked very sharply against me[2] as if I had used his father worse than a Neger; spake so loud that the people in the street might hear him."

Later notes of Sewall's show that some kind of reconciliation soon followed. So does a letter in Sewall's Letter-Book.[3] But to one who has learned from Sewall's artless record how close the good old man's fists were, the most startling of all his notes — a note that shows how, after all, his conscience smote him — is this: —

"Octr. 9. I sent Mr. Increase Mather a Hanch of very good Venison: I hope in that I did not treat him as a Negro."[4]

---

[1] Cf. page 130.
[2] Sewall was of the Council that finally dismissed President Mather.
[3] Cf. pages 183–185.   [4] Diary, II. 44.

IX

COTTON MATHER'S PRIVATE LIFE UNTIL THE DEATH OF HIS WIFE

1696–1702

IT is during the years we have just been considering, and the two that immediately follow, that Cotton
Mather's diaries give us the most continuous view of
his private life. The revised copies of his diaries
from 1696 to 1705 are preserved. The story of Increase Mather's presidency seemed important enough
to be considered by itself. In this chapter I purpose
telling what I have found concerning Cotton Mather's
personal career until the death of his wife in 1702.

In 1694, Sibley tells us, he published two books:
a treatise of Early Religion, and a lecture on the History of New England. In this year, too, his fifth
child, Abigail, was born. In 1695, he published seven
distinct books: four volumes of sermons, a book
against the Devil, a volume of biographies of eminent
emigrant ministers, and a Life of Queen Mary, who
was just dead. In this year, I take it, was born his
sixth child, Mehitabel. These were the years, we
shall remember, when Sir William Phipps came to
grief and died, and when Increase Mather's first
charter for Harvard College was still in the hands
of the King.

The next year, 1696, was that in which news came of the royal disapproval of the College charter; in which, as we have seen, Stoughton authorized Increase Mather to continue his presidency on the day when Cotton Mather was copying the epitaphs of Chauncy and Oakes; the year in which the objections of the Mathers killed the first College charter drawn by the Council; the year whose close brought the fast at which Sewall put up his confession of penitence for his share in the witch trials, and Cotton Mather put his family into the hands of God.

His diary[1] shows that he began the year in a state of depression, and closed it with more or less satisfactory assurances that his work was grateful to the Lord. The entries, which occur about once a week, are mostly in general terms: perhaps the most notable thing they show is an increasing interest in foreign affairs, concerning which he had occasional prophetic assurances. Early in the year he wrote his Life of Phipps, which Lady Phipps sent abroad for publication. I have found only two or three entries which seem worth noting in detail.[2]

The first is for the 22d of February, a day on which he fasted, with abasement and depression, and was rewarded by assurances that something should come of his prayers for England, Ireland, and Scotland.

" After this Day," he goes on, " I continued full of such Dejected and Abasing Thoughts of my own extraordinary Vileness as did fill mee in the Day itself. Oh ! the Lord is laying of me Low ! . . . So I wrote: and so it must

[1] In possession of the American Antiquarian Society.
[2] For another, see Sparks's American Biographies, VI. 261.

Come to pass. For 28. 12.[1] Early this morning my
daughter Mehitabel dyed suddenly in its Nurse's Arms:
not known to be dying till it was dead of some sudden
stoppage by wind: *The wind passed over the Flower,
and it was presently gone.*"

Next day the child was buried: its epitaph was, "In
Faith of the Resurrection your Bones shall flourish like
an Herb." In the margin he notes that he " Forgot to
pray for M. that morning": reproaching himself, he
found that the child was dead at the time. "Alas,"
he adds, "the child was overlaid by the Nurse."

The only other notes I have copied for this year
come in the following January. One I have already
quoted,[2] in which, on the occasion of the fast, he
commends his family to God. The other, for the 23d
of January, 1696–7, gives a little glimpse of fact:—

"So extremely cold was the weather that in a Warm
Room on a great Fire the Juices forced out at the end of
short billets of wood by the Heat of the Flame on which
they were laid, yett froze into Ice on their coming out."
[So he gave up a projected fast], "because I saw it impossible to serve the Lord without such Distraction as
was Inconvenient."

On the 29th, the weather seems to have moderated:
at all events, he had an assurance that his consort
should have easy travail. The next day she was out
of order; his servant was ill; and little Nibby[3] fell
into the fire, happily without much hurt.

This year he published five books: four volumes of
sermons, and an account of memorable experiences
of those captured by Indians.

---

[1] 12 = February. Mather begins his years with March.
[2] See page 122.   [3] Abigail.

The next year, 1697, was that in which Increase
Mather drew up his second charter for the College, in
which the first application for his agency to England
was refused, in which he threatened to resign, and fell
out with Mr. Willard about the choosing of Fellows.

Cotton Mather's diary for this year[1] is more interesting than the last. One of its mottoes is characteristic:
"Tully, in his Second Book, De Natura Deorum, says,
'*Nemo Vir Magnus sine aliquo Afflatu Divino unquam
fuit*.'"[2] He began the year by an ecstatic birthday.
A week later, he was writing to Connecticut for relief
for famine-stricken Massachusetts. A few days later,
prayer and fasting were rewarded by an assurance that
he should "ere long bee with the Innumerable company of Holy Angels," and that his offspring should
want for no good thing. And on the 27th of February
another fast, ending with assurances of a speedy revolution in England and France, led him to resolve on
daily prayers, like Daniel's, for the emancipation of the
Church from captivity, and later to start a prayer-
meeting for the coming revolution and reformation.
The close of this note is a good example of his manner of recording his afflations in general: —

"In the close of the Day, when I lay prostrate on my
Floor, in the Dust, before the Lord, I obtained Fresh and
Sweet Assurances from Him, That altho' I have been the
most Loathsome Creature in the World, yett His *Holy
Spirit*, would with Sovereign and Glorious Grace, Take
possession of me, and Accept mee, and employ mee, to glorify His Name exceedingly. And I successfully Renewed

[1] In possession of the Massachusetts Historical Society.
[2] "No man was ever great without some afflation from God."

my Cries unto the Lord, that Hee would visit *France*, and *Great Britain*, speedily, with a mighty *Revolution*."

A little later, his seventh child, Hannah, was born.

A note of Sewall's for the 8th of April gives a characteristic glimpse of Mather: —

" Mr. Cotton Mather gives notice that the Lecture hereafter is to begin at Eleven, . . . an hour sooner than formerly. Reprov'd the Towns people that attended no better; fear'd twould be an omen of our not enjoying the Lecture long, if did not amend."

But it is not till August that I find in Mather's own diary anything else noteworthy. On the 20th, he held a private thanksgiving for his life, his health, his speech freed from impediment, his library, his dwelling-house, his consort, his children, his unblemished reputation, "and such deliverances granted unto the Countrey that my opportunities to be serviceable have not been overwhelmed in the Ruines of it." That evening he went into his empty church, where he had much ecstasy. In the midst of a thousand other works he had finished his " Magnalia," his great Church History of New England.

Though several years passed before this most notable of his works was published, we may perhaps best consider it here, at the moment of its completion. Its scope and purpose are well expressed, I think, in a few words from the General Introduction : —

" It may be, 't is not possible for me to do a greater service unto the Churches on the *best Island* of the universe, than to give a distinct relation of these great examples which have been occurring among Churches of *exiles*, that were driven out of that Island, into an horrible wilderness,

merely for their being well-wishers unto the Reformation.
. . . 'Tis possible that our Lord Jesus Christ carried some
thousands of Reformers into the retirements of an American
desart, on purpose that, with an opportunity granted unto
many of his faithful servants, to enjoy the precious *liberty*
of their Ministry, though in the midst of many temptations
all their days, He might there, *to* them first, and then *by*
them, give a *specimen* of many good things, which He
would have His Churches elsewhere aspire and arise
unto; and *this* being done, he knows not[1] whether there
be not *all done* that New England was planted for; and
whether the Plantation may not, soon after this, *come to
nothing.*"

He has written nothing but truth, he says : —

"I have not commended any person, but when I have
really judged, not only that he *deserved* it, but also that it
would be a benefit unto posterity to know wherein he deserved it; . . . yett I have left unmentioned some censurable occurrences in the story of our Colonies, as things no
less unuseful than improper to be raised out of the grave,
wherein Oblivion hath now buried them."

That defines the whole book, I think ; it seems to me
an honest effort, at a moment when the old order was
changing, to preserve and emphasize all the best things
that in the olden time had been thought, and said,
and done. If the sons could but be brought to emulate
the virtues of the fathers, all might still go well. And
those old days were glorious days that filled Cotton
Mather with enthusiasm ; and their sins and errors
might best be tenderly forgotten. He had conceived
the book, we have seen,[2] in 1693. Meanwhile he had

---

[1] Should not this rather be " I know not "?
[2] See page 117.

been incredibly busy with all sorts of other matters: his pastoral duties, politics, the College, his incessant private devotions, his many other writings, including the great "Biblia Americana," on which he worked for twenty years.

"All the time I have had for my Church History," he writes, "hath been . . . chiefly that which I might have taken else for less profitable recreations; and it hath all been done by *snatches*. . . . I wish I could have enjoyed, entirely for this work, one quarter of the little more than two years [1] which have rolled away since I began it."

The "Magnalia" bears throughout traces of the crowded haste with which it was written. It is flung together, not composed at all. There are seven chief divisions, or books: the first recounts the history of the Colonies; the second contains the lives of governors and magistrates, closing with that of Sir William Phipps; the third contains the lives of some sixty emigrant ministers; the fourth tells the history of Harvard College, and contains the lives of ten eminent ministers graduated there; the fifth gives an account of the orthodox creed and discipline of the New England churches; the sixth contains a record of many remarkable providences, judgments, and the like, that have been experienced in New England; the seventh tells of the "Wars of the Lord," or the various disturbances that have attacked the churches and the people there. Along with

[1] According to his own diaries, the book was begun at the end of 1693, and finished in the middle of 1697. This inaccuracy is characteristic, — palpable, unimportant. Anyway, before the "Magnalia" was published, he revised it and inserted new matter.

much new matter, these books contain reprints of at least fifteen volumes published separately: ten before the end of 1697, five after. Just as these volumes were naturally independent, so are all the chapters in the whole work. And there is no question that it is full of superstitions now incredible, and of hasty errors of date and the like.

For all this, the "Magnalia" has merits which dispose me to rate it among the great works of English literature in the Seventeenth Century. The style, in the first place, seems to me remarkably good. Any one can detect its faults at a glance: it is prolix, often overloaded with pedantic quotation, now and then fantastic in its conceits. But these were faults of Mather's time. And he has two merits peculiarly his own: in the whole book I have not found a line that is not perfectly lucid, nor many paragraphs that, considering the frequent dulness of his subject, I could honestly call tiresome. In the second place, admitting once for all every charge of inaccurate detail, I am inclined to think the veracity of spirit that pervades the book of very high order. Somehow, as no one else can, Cotton Mather makes you by and by feel what the Puritan ideal was: if he does not tell just what men were, he does tell just what they wanted to be, and what loyal posterity longed to believe them. In the third place, not even the sustained monotony of his style and temper can prevent one who reads with care from recognizing the marked individuality of his separate portraits. It was my conviction of this that made me, in my account of his grandfathers, tell their story as nearly as might be in his own words. A glance back at what I have

11

said about John Cotton and Richard Mather[1] will show
as clearly as need be the strength and the weakness
of the "Magnalia." I have known the book for eleven
years; and the better I know it, the more I value it.
Whatever else Cotton Mather may have been, the
"Magnalia" alone, I think, proves him to have been
a notable man of letters.

But to return to the diary for 1697. A few days
after his ecstasy in the empty church, he notes, as a
serious matter, a week's journey to Salem and Ipswich.
I believe he never went much farther from home.
On the 18th of September, he held a fast, rewarded by
assurances from Heaven, "in a manner which I may
not utter." This probably means that a visible angel
appeared; for the next day he writes: —

"The Spirit of the Lord came near unto mee; Doubtless,
the angel of the Lord made mee sensible of his Approaches.
I was wondrously Irradiated. My Lord Jesus Christ shall
yett be more known in the vast Regions of *America;* and
by the means of poor, vile, sinful mee he shall be so."
And Great Britain shall undergo a reformation, and France
shall feel a mighty impression from the hand of Christ,
and Cotton Mather shall be concerned in these matters.
"Nor was this all, that was then told mee from Heaven;
but I forbear the rest."

His next note shows a phase of him rarely seen in
his diary. He was reputed, they say, good company:
here, for once, he gives us a bit of his conversation.
On the 24th of September,

---

[1] See pages 7–16. For an admirable example of Mather's best
work, see his account of the last days of Theophilus Eaton,
Magnalia, II. IX. §§ 9, 10.

" Discoursing with a worthy minister who lay . . . sick,
I said unto him, To *praise Christ*, in the midst of Myriads
of *Angels* in *Heaven*, may in some respects bee as good
as to *preach Christ*, in the midst of Hundreds of *Mortals*
on Earth. Hee replied, *It's true.* I added (for our Discourse was managed with a certain serious and sacred
Hilaritie), But, Syr, have you . . . thought what to say
when you arrive among the Blessed *Angels ?* Hee replied:
Why, pray what do you intend to say ? I answered, I 'l
say, *Behold, o ye Holy Spirits, the most . . . Loathsome
Sinner that ever arrived among you; but it is the Glorious Christ that hath brought me hither. . . . I have as good
a Righteousness as any of you.* I 'l say, *Oh ! you Illustrious Angels, if you don't wonderfully glorifie the Grace
of the Lord Jesus Christ in fetching so vile a Sinner into
these mansions, you 'l never do it.*"

Just how vile the man really felt himself is hard to
tell. One thing is certain, however : the fate that six
days later befell his uncle, John Cotton, minister of
Plymouth, affected him very profoundly. Sewall tells
the story [1]: A Council of ministers " advised the
Church to dismiss [Mr. Cotton] with as much Charity
as the Rule would admit of. . . . This was for his
Notorious Breaches of the Seventh Com̄andmt." A
few days later, Sewall notes that Increase Mather " de-
clar'd among the Ministers . . . that they had dealt
too favourably with Mr. Cotton." On the 9th of
October, and again on the 16th, Cotton Mather, full of
agony for his " fallen uncle," and full of self-abhor-
rence and of fear lest his own sins should likewise be
condemned, prostrated himself before the Lord, and
enjoyed assurances from Heaven.

[1] Diary, I. 460. 30 Sept., 1697.

The next notable entry shows him in a character as yet new to us. His daughter Katharine was getting old enough to take life seriously: she was past her fifth birthday. On November 7th, a Lord's Day, he writes: —

" I took my little daughter, *Katy*, into my Study, and there I told my child That I am to *Dy* Shortly and Shee must, when I am *Dead*, Remember every Thing, that I now said unto her. I sett before her, the sinful . . . condition of her Nature, and I charged her to *pray in secret places* every day, . . . That God for the sake of Jesus Christ, would give her a *New Heart*. . . . I gave her to understand that when I am taken from her, shee must look to meet with more Humbling *Afflictions*, than she does, now she has a . . . Tender *Father* to provide for her. . . . I signified unto her, That the people of God would much observe how shee carried herself, and that I had written a Book, about *Ungodly Children*, in the conclusion whereof I say, that this Book will bee a forcible Witness against my own children, if any of them should not bee *godly*. At Length, with many Tears, both on my part and hers, I told my child, that God had from Heaven satisfied me, . . . *That shee shall be brought Home unto the Lord Jesus Christ.* . . . I . . . made the child kneel down by me; and I poured out my cries unto the Lord, That Hee would . . . Bless her, and Save her, and make her a *Temple* of His Glory. It will bee so! It will bee so! I write this, the more particularly, that the child may hereafter have the Benefit of Reading it."

This curious note shows but one side of his domestic discipline, however. And perhaps here, as well as anywhere, I may mention his son Samuel's account of how Cotton Mather treated his children.[1] He would

[1] S. Mather, Life, I. 4. 7.

constantly tell them delightful stories, especially at table; "and he would ever conclude with some lessons of piety." He would constantly "put them upon doing . . . Kindnesses . . . for other Children," and "would applaud them when he saw them delight in it." As soon as possible, he made them learn to write and copy "profitable Things."

"He incessantly endeavoured, that his Children might betimes be acted by Principles of *Reason* and *Honour*. . . . The *first Chastisement* he would inflict for any ordinary Fault, was *to let the Child see and hear him in an Astonishment* . . . that the Child could do so *base* a Thing. . . . To be *chased for a while out of his Presence*, he would make to be look'd upon as the sorest Punishment in his Family. . . . The *Slavish* way of *Education*, carried on with *Raving, and Kicking, and Scourging*, . . . he looked upon as a dreadful Judgment of GOD on the World; . . . and express'd a mortal Aversion to it. . . . He would often tell them of the *good Angels*, who love them; . . . who likewise take a very diligent Notice of them, and ought not in any measure to be disobliged. He would not say so much to them of the *evil Angels*, because he would not have them entertain any frightful Fancies about the Apparitions of *Devils:* But yet, he would briefly let them know, that there are *Devils*, who tempt them to Wickedness, who are glad when they do wickedly, and who may get leave of GOD to kill them for it."

And there is every reason to think that all his children loved him dearly.

But in 1697, only Katy was old enough for much discipline. We must back to the diary, in which there is little more to concern us. The rest of the notes refer chiefly to his devotions: he had fasts, and

thanksgivings, and ecstasies. A case of adultery in his
church caused him special humiliation. He preached
on peace, and forthwith ships arrived with news of
peace. A note of Sewall's on December 10th gives
another glimpse of him : —

"Mr. Cotton Mather was at the Townhouse Chamber
pretty merry and pleasant: but was made sad by Col.
Hutchinsons telling him of the death of his Unkle Mr. N.
Mather. . . . Visited the President in the evening. He is
sorrowful."

That very day Cotton Mather's Life of Phipps had
come from England. In January he was laid up with
an epidemic influenza. On his first Sunday out he enjoyed angelic help to such a degree that he was seized
next day with a " cholic "; but angels interfered again,
and by Thursday he was well enough to preach the
lecture. The volume closes with two closely written
pages of texts he preached from during the year.

In this year (1697) he published nine books: his
Lives of Mitchell, Phipps, and Moodey; three devotional works; another book about captivity among
the Indians; a volume of sermons; and a volume of
hymns.

The next year, 1698, was that in which the second
application for Increase Mather's agency was refused;
and at the close of which the General Court renewed
its request that the President remove to Cambridge,
and the church refused consent. It was the year,
too, when the Brattle Street Church was founded.

The mottoes in the diary for 1698 [1] are the queerest
of all.

[1] In possession of the Massachusetts Historical Society.

"Ego Sic semper et ubique Vixi," runs the first, "tanquam ultimam Diem, numquam redituram, Consumerem.[1] EUMORP. C. M. Can't say so!" Then come three other Latin phrases, with the notes, "C. M. would say so!" Lett C. M. . . . take the Caution!" and "C. M. heartily subscribes to This!"

The first month of the year shows him extremely ecstatic. On the 4th of March, in a secret fast, he put his Church History and another book into the hands of Christ; and it was told him from Heaven

"that they shall bee carried safe to *England,* and there employed for the Service of my glorious Lord."—"The . . . Beginning of this month," he goes on, "brought with it little that was Remarkable, besides multiplied Experiences of Strange *Dejections* and sad *Buffetings* upon my mind, just when I have been going to do some *special service* for the Lord Jesus Christ in my public ministry, and then a more than *Assistance* and *Enlargement* in the service itself."

Later he notes that a gentleman has remarked that good men speak well of Cotton Mather, and bad men ill. On the 7th of April, a lecture day,

"The Lord having Helped me beyond my expectation in preparing a Discourse for the Lecture,[2] Hee yett more gloriously *Helped* mee, in uttering of it, unto a vast Assembly of His people. I first Laid my Sinful mouth, in the Dust on my Study-floor before the Lord, where I cast myself, in my supplications for His Assistance and Acceptance, as utterly unworthy thereof. But the Lord made my sinful mouth to become this Day, the Trumpet of His

---

[1] "I have always and everywhere lived as if each day were my very last."

[2] This was the "Bostonian Ebenezer," reprinted as an appendix to the first book of the "Magnalia."

glory; and the Hearts of the Inhabitants of the Town were strangely moved by what was Delivered among them."

Immediately afterwards he fell ill of a fever, from which he recovered in a duly thankful mood.

He eagerly renewed his prayers and fasts. On the 13th of May two of his special subjects were the College and the scandals in his church; on the 20th his particular subject was one of his flock, to be censured for adultery, — " and one whom I had formerly, with many Cries to Heaven, rescued from the Hands of Evil Angels, which had a Bodily possession of her." On this occasion he humbled himself as a very vile sinner; and when the time came for pronouncing the censure, he enjoyed an extraordinary presence of the Lord. On the 29th comes a long note, in which he recapitulates the astonishing verifications of some of his particular faiths about public affairs, and goes on to assert his faith that certain prophesies point to a speedy completion at the end of one hundred and eighty years, of the " Half Reformation " of 1517 : " Make mee a very Holy, prayerful, watchful, and prudent man," he writes, " that I may bee fitt for my master's use." The next note, written on the 10th of June, is in Latin: he confesses to the Lord " peccatorum meorum aggrava-tionem " ;[1] he prays that the blood of Christ may wash him clean, and he enjoys an assurance that he shall actually see angels once more. The close of the note is worth quoting : —

" Latiné haec scribo, ne chara mea Conjux, has chartas aliquando inspiciens, intelligat." [2]

[1] " A heavy addition to my sins."
[2] " I write this in Latin, lest my dear wife, sometime looking over these papers, should understand it."

The next note is a very long one about Calef, a man "who makes little conscience of Lying," and who is attacking Mather for "public Asserting of such Truths as the Scripture has taught us about the existence and Influence of the *Invisible World.*" This man's book was about to be sent to England for publication. Cotton Mather prays that the Lord

"Forgive him, and do him Good even as to my own Soul." — "But then," he goes on, "I could not but cry unto the Lord that Hee would Rescue my *opportunities* of serving my Lord Jesus Christ from the Attempts of this man to damnify them. . . . So I putt over my Calumnious Adversary into the Hands of the *Righteous God.* . . . And I now Beleeve, That the *Holy Angels* of my Lord Jesus Christ, whose operation this Impious man denies (which is one great cause of his enmity against mee!) will do a *wonderful Thing* on this occasion."

Immediately afterwards, he remarks that pressure of work has caused him to give up the practice of taking notes as he listens to sermons : his attention is consequently flagging ; he must take notes again.

A month of ecstatic afflations and reactions followed. Towards the end of July,

"my Mind Being . . . Easy, and Ready to Dy, I . . . besought of the Lord, nevertheless, that Hee would yett spare my life, to work for Him, a Little more, among His people." And one Lord's Day in August, he writes thus : "Whereas one of the Last Times I was at the *Lords-Table,* I made my particular Application unto the Lord Jesus Christ in the way of *Sacramental Communion,* to obtain from Him, the Cure of that One Distemper, *An Heart Wandering with Impertinent Thoughts in Religious Exercises,* I must now Record that I have seen an Extraordinary Success of my Faiths making those Applications. On the *Lords-day* particularly I know not that one sentence passed mee, in all the Five prayers made by Father, or One Head or Text of all the Long Sermon preached by him, in the Forenoon, but what my Heart accompanied with some Agreeable *Ejaculation*. And my own Services in the Afternoon were under the Special Operation of Heaven."

On the 5th of September, he went to Salem for five days. Two of his notes during this considerable journey are worth recording. The first is this : —

" Finding, That whenever I go abroad, the *curiosity* and *vanity* of the people discovers itself in their *great Flocking* to hear me . . . causes me . . . exceedingly to *Humble* myself before the Lord, and cry from the *Dust* unto Him that the *fond expression* of the people, may not be chastised upon myself, in His Leaving of *mee* to any Inconvenience. By this Method, I not only am in a Comfortable Measure kept from the Foolish Taste of *popular Applause* in my own Heart, but also from the Humbling Dispensations from Heaven, whereto the Fondness of the people might otherwise Expose mee."

The other is this : —

" One Day, while I was at Salem, I Retired into the Burying place, and att the Grave of my dear Younger Brother[1] there, I could not but fall down on my knees before the Lord ; with praises to His Name, for granting the *Life* of my dead Brother to be writt, and spread, and Read among His people, and bee very serviceable; and for sparing me, a barren wretch, to survive these many years upon the Earth, to Serve His people, in Several parts of the World. I then considered, What if I were speedily to bee called away by *Death*, after my *younger Brother?* I found my Spirit, Gloriously

---

[1] Nathaniel, ob. 1688. Cf. page 81.

Triumphing in the Thought of going by Death, to bee with the Lord Jesus Christ, and among his *Angels*. But when I further Thought of *Staying* to Glorify Him, in the midst of *many Temptations*, among his people here, I did, at present, because of my *Age*, prefer *This;* and Request it of the Lord."

Some three weeks later, he went to Reading. On the way,

"riding over a Bridge, one of *the Rotten poles* upon it Broke: and my Horse broke thro' and broke in, and *sank down* his very *Breast*. I chose rather to keep the *Saddle*, than go off into the *River;* and the *Horse*, to the Astonishment of my Company *Rose* again (tearing off a *Shooe* in his Rising) and Leap'd over, with mee safe upon him. How happily do the *creatures* all serve us, while wee are serving their and our Lord, the Blessed Jesus."

In the middle of October came inspiring news from Medfield. A deaf old woman there had been greatly stirred by reading a book of Cotton Mather's, and had presently recovered her hearing; she remained piously afraid "that shee is not thankful enough unto the Lord Jesus Christ for so great a mercy." The same month Cotton Mather preached at the execution of a young woman for child-murder.[1]

In this October, too, Cotton Mather took his final leave of his fallen uncle, John Cotton. Some months before Sewall had seen the disgraced man at Plymouth.

"March 10," . . . he writes, " Had large discourse in the even with Mrs. Cotton, Mr. Cotton, Mr. Rowland.[2] I

---

[1] Sarah Threeneedles. Sewall's account of her is vivid: Diary, I. 486.

[2] Their son.

told Mr. Cotton, a free confession was the best way; spake
of Davids roaring all the day long and bones waxing old
whilest he kept silence. . . . When ready to come away,
March 11 I said his danger was lest catching at shadows,
he should neglect the cords thrown out to him by Christ
and so be drown'd. Some of my last words to him was
Kisse the Son, lest he be angry! This was in the house
between him and me alone. Just as was mounting, He
desired me to pray for him till I heard he was dead."

John Cotton was now called to take charge of a
church in South Carolina. He came to take leave of
his nephew. They prayed together with heartfelt pathos. And the broken man's last words were a solemn
denial of "the most and worst of the charges against
him."

The remaining months of the year passed amid
Cotton Mather's habitual ecstasies and activity. In
November he preached at the execution of some mur-
derers, where the assembly was so vast that he had to
climb into the pulpit over the heads of the people. In
January, little Nancy[1] fell into the fire, without permanent injury. But her father took the matter very
seriously.

"The fire that hath wounded the child," he writes,
"hath added a strong fire to the zeal of my prayer for her;
and God has now raised my prayer for her to this degree
of a particular Faith in her behalf. If this Writing of her
poor Father ever come to bee Readd by her, Lett her give
Thanks to God, that ever Hee cast her into a *Fire* which
thus enflamed the supplications of her Father for her."

He resolved that he would be more attentive to his
family duties, and finally determined to "see whether

---

[1] His daughter Hannah, born early in 1697.

there be nothing further that I may do, to save the *Children* of my flock from falling into the unquench-able *Fire* of the Wrath of God."

About this time, too, " a few Leisure minutes in the evening of Every Day, in about a Fortnight or Three weeks Time, so accomplished me I could write very good Spanish." So he composed a body of Prot-estant religion for the conversion of Spanish America. Later in the year he fell ill again, and was much de-pressed with fear of premature old age. The record closes with four pages of texts from which he has preached in his public ministry during the year.

In 1698 he published six works: two discourses, and a preface to a third; a history of the Non-Con-formists; a devotional volume; and a pastoral letter to English Captives in Barbary.

The next year, 1699, was that in which news came that the College charter of 1697 was disapproved, and in which, under Bellomont's advice, the new charter was drawn that contained the religious proviso which made Bellomont disapprove it. It was the year, too, in which Coleman arrived and published his manifesto, and the Brattle Street Church was finally opened, and the Mathers prayed and preached there. We have already seen what Cotton Mather wrote in his diary about these public matters.[1]

His diary for 1699 [2] shows his personal and pastoral experiences going on just as before. Two or three notes are perhaps worth remembering. He sent his Spanish book to a Jew who turned up in Boston; he

---

[1] See pages 140, 142, 143.

[2] In possession of the American Antiquarian Society.

translated some of the Psalms into French verse; he
heard of bears on the Ipswich road; he was much disturbed by an impostor named May, who pretended to
be a minister and made trouble, but ultimately ran
away, having been detected in very unministerial over-
tures to the ewes of his flock;[1] and when in Cotton
Mather's opinion the Church of England was conspir-
ing against him, he sent the conspirators a message,

"That tho' I am every way Little, yett I hope, thro' the
Help of Christ, I may Live to do for them the same kindness that Sampson did for their philistine Brethren, and
pull down their Temple about their Ears."

But what makes this year notable, besides its public
history, is what happened in his family. His relations
with his father were growing more and more intimate
and tender; at every turn he sustained and comforted
the worried old President; he shared and encouraged
his particular faith that he should by and by do great
works for Christ in England. The other family matters he tells of I shall mention in detail.

Towards the end of February, little Katy's head-
dress caught fire, and the child was severely burned.
As she lay in a fever, her father was assured that this

"Blessed Affliction . . . shall prove the salvation of my
child. It shall bee so! It shall bee so! Lord, How much
ought I to *Love* Thee, when Thou dost *Rebuke and Chasten me*."

The same day Mrs. Mather's mother died.

"I count it a Singular Favour of God unto mee," writes
Cotton Mather, "(and it might bee so unto *her!*) that tho'

[1] The curious may find a pretty full account of May in the
Magnalia, VII. VI. § 9.

shee was Delirious the First Night of her Illness, yett shee had the Free Use of *Reason* all the Rest of the Little Time : and hereby I enjoyed an opportunity *for Two Dayes* together, to *Talk* with her, and *pray* with her, and Do all that it was possible for mee to Do, in assisting her, about the *Great Acts* of Resigning her Spirit unto the Lord. She was a pious Woman, and one full of *prayers* and *Alms ;* and tho' shee were of a very *Fearful Temper,* and was particularly in her Life-Time under some Slavish Fear of *Death,* yett as her Death approached, shee comfortably gott over it."

In June, little Nancy fell ill. Reading in the Book of Job, her father broke off to pray that, like Job, he might retain three daughters.

"I purposed," he writes, "that I would grow yett more Fruitful in my Conversation with my Little Birds, and Feed them with more frequent and charming Lessons of Religion."

And he resolved to start schools, to make more pastoral visits, to give away more copies of his book about a " Family Well-Ordered," to write a book for the Indians. " Lord, pitty mee," he begs, " Assist mee, Accept mee ! "

The child did not mend ; but his Bible, opening by chance at Mark 10. 13–16,[1] assured him that she should live. Then he prayed for her again, and had fresh assurances, and she grew better ; and, as we have seen,[2] he took this for an omen of good concerning his particular faith about the College.

This particular faith, we may remember, was accompanied by an assurance that his son should glorify the Lord Jesus Christ after he himself had followed his

---

[1] " Suffer the little children to come unto me," etc.
[2] See page 140.

father into the kingdom of God. At the moment he
had no son; he had had none but the malformed child
whose fate he attributed to witchcraft.[1]　But his wife
was again near her time, and on the 8th of July showed
symptoms of travail; so he made a fast to obtain mercy
for his family and his ministry.

"In the Evening of this Day," he goes on, "near eleven
o'clock my Consort fell into her Travail. Just before this,
the Text with a meditation whereon I chose to entertain
my Family at our evening-prayers was that in Joh. 16. 21.
A woman when shee is in Travail hath sorrow, because her
Hour is Come; but as soon as shee is delivered of the
Child, shee Remembreth no more the Anguish, for Joy
that a Man is born into the World. After I had commended my Consort unto the Lord, I Laid mee down to
sleep, after midnight, that I might be fit for the Services of
the Day Ensuing. But after one a clock in the morning I
awoke, with a concern upon my Spirit, which oblig'd mee
to Rise, and Retire into my Study. There I cast myself
on my knees before the Lord, confessing my Sins that rendered mee unworthy of His Mercy, but imploring His
Mercy to my Consort, in the Distress now upon her. While
my Faith was pleading that the Saviour who was Born
of woman would send His good Angel to Releeve my
Consort, the people ran to my Study-Door, with Tidings
That a Son was Born unto mee. I continued then on my
knees, praising the Lord; and I received a wonderful Advice from Heaven, That this my Son, shall bee a Servant
of my Lord Jesus Christ throughout eternal Ages. Hee
was Born about three Quarters of an Hour past One, in the
morning of the (Lords-Day) 9d. 5m.[2] — an Hearty, and
Lusty, and comely Infant. . . . In the Afternoon, I Bap-
tised my Son, and in Honour to my Parent, I called him,

---

[1] See page 116.　　　[2] July 9, 1699.

INCREASE. After which, Retiring to my Study, it was again assured mee from Heaven, That this Child shall glorify my Lord Jesus Christ, and bee with Him, to Behold His Glory."

In October came sad news from Carolina. The plague had broken out in Charleston, and poor Uncle John Cotton had been stricken down at the beginning of his pastoral work there. In the diary is a brief note about him. But the letter which Cotton Mather wrote the same day to his uncle's faithful widow, who had been waiting at Plymouth for a chance to rejoin her husband, is more touching. I will quote a little from that, then.

"In their confusion, they tell us not the precise Time of his Death ; nor do they relate any Circumstances of it, only that hee lay sick Two Days, and hee Dy'd the Third, which is the period, wherein the sick of that pestilential Distemper use to dy. That circumstance will make you think of *Lazarus*, and you'l join with mee in hopes That my uncle was *one whom the Lord loved*. I need not say unto you, how near the Death of so beloved a Friend goes to the Hearts of his Relatives, . . . and in a special manner to mine. I had not many Friends on Earth like him. But in the midst of our sorrowes, . . . wee have a peculiar satisfaction in the Lord's accepting my uncle to Dy with Honour in the service of the Gospel and kingdom. — As it was no great mercy (I beleeve) unto Plymouth, for their Laborious, and good-spirited, and well-tempered Pastor to be driven from them, so it was a great Mercy unto my uncle to bee employed in gathering a church for the Lord Jesus Christ in a Countrey that had never seen such a Thing, from the Beginning of the world." [1]

[1] Mather Papers, 403. To Mrs. Joanna Cotton, 23 October, 1699.

In this year, 1699, Cotton Mather published nine separate works : a history of the Indian wars ; a statement of the orthodox faith of New England ; the " Family Well-Ordered " ; his Spanish book, of which part was reprinted separately ; an account of religious impostors ; a book for sailors ; and a book called the " Serious Christian." He also edited a collection of Cases of Conscience, made at a meeting of ministers at Cambridge.

The next year, 1700, as we have seen, was very troublous. Increase Mather, disappointed of his agency, deceived in his particular faith, was finally forced to Cambridge ; the Brattle Street controversy broke out again, and waxed fierce ; and Calef's book arrived. What Cotton Mather wrote about these matters we have read already.[1]

The other notes in the diary for 1700[2] show few new traits. His children were ill : little Increase had a terrible time with convulsions ; Nibby's head-dress caught fire, as Katy's had the year before ; and Nancy had a serious disorder. In the course of the year his ninth child, and third son, Samuel, was born.

A few of his notes, however, are worth remembering. In April,

" A Gentleman came to mee with a Desire that I would write a Sheet upon the horrid Evils of Debauching the Indians by Selling Drink unto them : a crime committed by too many in the country ; a crime fruitful in wickedness and confusion."

So he wrote the book : it would do good, he thought. A little later, on a lecture day, he writes of

[1] See pages 145–151.
[2] In possession of the Massachusetts Historical Society.

"Torturing pains in my Head, which have diverse days molested mee; (such as I have so often found præludious unto my doing some special service for my Lord Jesus Christ, that I cannot but have particular Thoughts about the Original of them.)" In spite of them he prepared his lecture. "And now, When I came to my public Services, I felt a Wonderful Force from Heaven, Strengthening, and Assisting, and Enlarging of mee. . . . The Vast Assembly, which was come together, saw That the Lord was with mee of a Truth — Now, o my Soul, Feed, Feed upon these Experiences."

In June he held a special fast.

"I this day putt up my Church History," he writes, "and pen down directions about the publishing of it. It . . . has lain by me, diverse years, for want of a fit opportunity to send it. A Gentleman, just now sailing for England, undertakes the Care of it; . . . and by his Hand I send it for London. O my Lord Jesus Christ, lett thy good Angels accompany it."

In October, he had doubts whether his habit of giving away good books was not too expensive; and indeed his son Samuel says[1] that he sometimes gave away a thousand volumes a year. But he rebuked his doubts, and looking for a sign soon found one: calling, for "pure religion," on a widowed gentlewoman, he was offered as many books as he chose to take from the late President Chauncy's library; he took about forty, which raised his own library to something near three thousand volumes. It was a sore trial to him a little later, though, when Calef's book arrived, and his own Church History had not even gone to press. A

[1] Life, II. 1. 16.

number of pious friends joined him in more than one day of prayer about this.

Another note of this year has a charm of its own.

" There was an old man," it runs, " (called Ferdinando Turyl) scarce known to me. . . . On a Saturday night [28d. 7m.] I was very strongly accosted in my sleep, with a Dream, of this importance. That this old man was brought into my Sight and that it was (I know not how) said unto me, *Take Notice of this Old Man. . . . Speak to him. Do for him.* On the Day following, I saw the Old Man, at our public sermons, very attentive: (where I suppose he had rarely attended.) On the Day after this, I mett the Old Man in the Street, and I Lett fall some such words as these unto him: *How d'ye do, Old Man. I am glad to see you still in this World: I pray God, prepare you for another; I suppose it won't be long before you are called away: Can I do you no service?* And so I turned from him. On the Day after that the old man came to me at my House: and I then Instructed him, how to prepare for Death: and I gave him a Little Book (of Grace Triumphant) further to assist him in it: Adding a peece of money to Encourage him. Afterwards he came to me several times: but in about seven weeks, after our first Interview, he Dyed suddenly. Going to his Funeral, I was told (from some who did not understand how much I had been concerned for him) and afterwards . . . from people of the House where the old man Lived, That he had been a poor Carnal Sorry old man until near seven weeks, before he dyed: but in his Last Six or Seven Weeks, they had observed a Wonderful Change upon him: he spent his whole Time in praying and Reading, and the Little Book (of *Grace Triumphant*) was his continual companion Day and Night. They never saw a man so altered; and they are verily persuaded he dyed a *Regenerate Man.* — Truly I have several Times observed That God hath strangely stirred up my Heart sometimes to visit persons, that were Strangers to me, and employ my particular methods, to excite and assist their giving themselves to Him. . . . And they have presently after dyed with great symptoms of Regeneration upon them."

On the 18th of January, Cotton Mather mentioned to his wife and his father a matter that troubled him deeply. In spite of many prayers, he could not feel a faith that his baby Samuel would serve the Lord in his churches. So, though the child was "lusty and heavy," he feared it would die in infancy. On the 7th of February comes this note : —

" *The Evil that I feared is come upon me.* On Tuesday night this week, my little son Samuel, was taken with very sad Convulsions. They continued all Wednesday incurable, and we were all that day in continual expectation of his expiration. But he lived all *Thursday*, too, and outlived more than a hundred very terrible Fitts. The Convulsions of my own mind, were all the while, happily composed and quieted; and with much Composure of Mind, I often and often in prayer Resigned the Child unto the Lord. Preaching the lecture, on *Thursday*, while we were every minute Looking for the Death of the Child, I chose to insist on that Joh. 19. 25., *I know, that my Redeemer Lives;* as a matter of satisfaction to us, at the Sight of our Dying Friends. On Thursday, about midnight, an odd thing fell out. The child, coming out of One of its worst Fitts most unaccountably fell a Laughing, and this held for diverse minutes; unto the amazement of the Spectators, who indeed were so amazed, that they could hardly keep from Swooning. After This, it had no more such Fitts as before; but Lingered along, till about ten a'clock this morning, when one of its fitts carried it off."

Cotton Mather preached as usual on Sunday, the 9th. On Monday, the child was buried. Its epitaph was, "Not as they that have no Hope."

The last note in the volume tells how friends have insisted on publishing a vindication of the Mathers from the attack of Calef, — a "laudable example of a people appearing to vindicate their injured pastors when a storm of persecution is raised against them." There are six pages, too, of an address to an assembly of ministers concerning an "offensive book about Churches"; and four pages of notes of texts preached from. On the back cover is a memorandum through which a pen has been very lightly drawn : —

"Ab Amico Satis Adulatore[1]

ON COTTON MATHER.

"For *Grace* and *Art* and an Illustrious *Fame*
Who would not look from such an Ominous Name?
Where *Two Great Names* their Sanctuary take,
And in a *Third* combined, a *Greater* make.

"Too Gross flattery for me to transcribe; (tho' the poetry be good.) "

In 1700, Cotton Mather published eighteen distinct works : five devotional books; three sermons; four monitory letters, including that about selling drink to Indians and one to Indians themselves in their own tongue; a pamphlet against balls and dances; an exposure of religious impostors; two books for young people and children; a Defence of Evangelical Churches; and another statement of the old Principles of New England.

[1] "By a sufficiently flattering friend."— This verse is a palpable imitation of Dryden's lines on Milton:

"Three poets in three distant ages born," etc.

The next year, 1701, was that in which Bellomont died, and Stoughton ; in which Willard was made Vice President of the College, and in which, amid all the heat of the Brattle Street controversy and Calef's attack, Increase Mather was excluded from the presidency.

It is notable that Cotton Mather's diary contains very little about these terribly grave matters. In fact, as I have read his diaries, nothing has impressed me more than his resolute abstinence from evil speaking. He had a hot temper and a quick tongue. But he did his best not to leave behind him written records that should defame any man. It would be hard, I think, to find another diary so long and so free from scandal. To get a clear notion of how he really felt at this moment, then, we must turn to Sewall again.

In the last chapter, I cited two of Sewall's notes.[1] Here are a few more : —

"Oct. 20. Mr. Cotton Mather . . . went and told Sam,[2] That one pleaded much for Negroes,[3] and he had used his father worse than a Negro, and told him that was his Father. I had read in the morn Mr. Dod's saying; Sanctified Afflictions are good Promotions. I found it now a cordial. And this caus'd me the rather to set under my Father and Mother's Epitaph, — Psal. 27. 10.[4] It may be it would be arrogance for me to think that I, as one of Christ's Witnesses, am slain, or ly dead in the street. — October 22. 1701. I . . . speak with Mr. Cotton Mather at Mr. Wilkins's. I expostulated with him from I Tim.

[1] See page 153.   [2] Sewall's son.
[3] Sewall had published a tract against slavery.
[4] "When my father and my mother forsake me, then the Lord will take me up."

5. 1. Rebuke not an elder. He said he had considered that: I told him of his book of the Law of Kindness for the Tongue, whether this were correspondent with that. Whether correspondent with Christ's Rule: He said, having spoken to me before there was no need to speak to me again; and so justified his reviling me behind my back. Charg'd the Council with Lying, Hypocrisy, Tricks, and I know not what all. I ask'd him if it were done with that Meekness as it should: answer'd, yes. Charg'd the Council in general, and then shew'd my share, which was my speech in Council: viz. If Mr. Mather should goe to Cambridge again to reside there with a Resolution not to read the Scriptures, and expound in the Hall: I fear the example of it will do more hurt than his going thither will doe good. This speech I owned. Said Mr. Corwin at Reading, upbraided him, saying, This is the man you dedicat your books to! I ask'd him If I should supose he had done something amiss in his Church as an Officer; whether it would be well for me to exclaim against him in the street for it. (Mr. Wilkin would fain have had him gon into the iñer room, but he would not.) I told him I conceiv'd he had done much unbecoming a Minister of the Gospel, and being call'd . . . to the Council, . . . I went thither. . . . 2 Tim. 2. 24. 25.[1] — Sign'd Mr. Mather's order for £25. Hañer'd out an Order for a Day of Thanksgiving. — Oct. 23. Mr. Increase Mather said at Mr. Wilkins's, If I am a Servant of Jesus Christ, some great Judgment will fall on Capt. Sewall, or his family. — Oct. 24. Rainy day. . . . I got Mr. Moody to copy out my Speech, and gave it to Mr. Wilkins that all might see what was the ground of Mr. Mather's Anger. . . . Mr. Wilkins carried [it] to Mr. Mathers; They seem to grow calm."

[1] "And the servant of the Lord must not strive; but be gentle unto all men, apt to teach, patient; in meekness instructing those that oppose themselves; if God peradventure will give them repentance to the acknowledging of the truth."

On the 30th of November, Sewall writes : —

" I spent this Sabbath at Mr. Coleman's [church], partly
out of dislike to Mr. Josiah Willard's cutting off his Hair,
and wearing a Wigg: . . . Partly to give an example of
my holding Comunion with that Church who renounce the
Cross in Baptisme, Humane Holy days etc. as other New-
english Churches doe. And I had spent a Sabbath at the
Old Church, and at Mr. Mathers." [1]

In Sewall's Letter-Book we find how the quarrel
ended. On December 31, 1701, he wrote to Cotton
Mather thus : —

" Sir, — I once intended an Answer to yours of the 30th
of Octobr. last, principally as to some matters of fact therein recited. But since you were pleased to sit with me last
Tuesday was fortnight, and to honour my Pue, with publishing there the very acceptable News of Liberty again
granted to our dear Brethren of the Palatinat, I do now
Remise, Release and forever quit claim, as to any personal
Controversy we were lately managing at Mr. Wilkins's. It
has been my thought ever since, and the consideration of
this being the last day of the year, suffers me to delay it
no longer. And at the same time I assure you that I am
your truly loving friend and humble Servant S. S."

In Sewall's Letter-Book for this year is one other
document worth remembering. On October 6th, he
and Isaac Addington wrote a long letter of advice to
the gentlemen who were about to start a new college

---

[1] The Old Church was the First; Mr. Mather's, the Second;
Mr. Willard's, the Old South, the Third; Mr. Colman's, the
Brattle Street, the Fourth. There were as yet no other Congre-
gational churches in Boston; and Sewall was doing his best to
make the brethren dwell together in unity. — And concerning
Willard's wig, cf. pages 34, 80.

in Connecticut.   They enclosed hints for an act of
incorporation; and went on,

"We should be very glad to hear of flourishing Schools
and College at Conecticut, and it would be some relief to
us against the Sorrow we have conceived for the decay
of them in this Province."

Sewall and the Mathers agreed in feeling that Harvard was lost to orthodoxy; and no three men hailed
with more prayerful enthusiasm the rising star of Yale.

Cotton Mather's diary for 1701 [1] shows the general
condition of his activity, his enthusiasm, and his affections unchanged.   In the beginning of the year, he was
much excited by Calef's book.

"One Vile Tool," he writes on the 5th of April, "namely
R. Calef,[2] . . . employed by [the Enemies of the Churches]
to go on with his Filthy Scribbles to hurt my precious
opportunities of glorifying my Lord Jesus Christ," — disposes him to special fast and prayer.   And on the 11th,
"because I would *bespeak the Lord thrice*," he summoned
six friends, for the third time, to pray with him that "the
Lord would send his Angel to stop the Adversary in the
Course of his Wickedness [Which the Lord will do!]"

The other matter which seems most on his mind is
his Church History, concerning which his prayers and
assurances were frequent throughout the year.   On
the 13th of June came a letter from Mr. Broomfield,
in London: Mr. Robert Hackshaw had agreed to
print the book at his own expense.

[1] In possession of the Massachusetts Historical Society.
[2] This opprobrious mention of a name, a very rare thing in
Cotton Mather's diary, indicates his overwrought condition.
Cf. pages 105, 150.

" I told him," wrote Mr. Broomfield, " *Syr, God has answered* Mr. Mather's *prayers.* — He declared he did it not with any expectation of Gain to himself, but for the Glory of God, and that he might be a means to midwife so good a work into the World. And did you know him so well as I do you would believe him."

But in September came news of some complications about the printing: on the 27th, Cotton Mather held a special fast for the History, being also moved to supplications by the fact that his father-in-law, after the orthodox manner of New England, was already " upon a second marriage." Among his other memoranda for the year, the most notable seems to be that he had started thirteen or fourteen " private meetings." He believed in organizing the work of the Lord : throughout his life he was getting together prayer-meetings, and societies for the suppression of disorders ; working with the commissioners to convert and civilize the Indians ; and so on.

I find but four notes in 1701 which are worth remembering in detail. In September came news that a friend had been killed in the wars. Cotton Mather immediately went to pray with the widow; and found with her another widow, her sister.

" Now in my prayer," he goes on, " I found myself strangely diverted from the Condition of the person to whom only I intended my Visit. I was as it were compelled so to word my prayer as take in all along the condition of her Sister ; even as if my prayer had been cheefly, if not only, for her. I wondered a little at my frame in this matter. But the Spirit of the Lord knew what I did not know. Within Two Days there arrived Intelligence that the young man, the husband of the supposed widow to whom I gave my visit, was yett living."

On the 3d of October, he held a thanksgiving for his health, for the defeats of the "subtil and raging malice" of his enemies, for the safety and prospects of his Church History, and for his opportunities to do good by preaching and printing.

" But there was another signal article," he goes on, " cf my praises to the Lord on this day. And this was the Confluence of Blessings, which I enjoy in my dearest Consort, who bore me company in some of the duties of the day. Her piety, the agreeable charms of her person, her obliging Deportment unto me, her discretion in ordering my and her Affairs and avoiding everything that might be dishonourable to either of us, and the lovely offspring that I have received by her, and her being spared unto me for more than fifteen years : These are things that I should thankfully acknowledge before the Lord."

At the end of the year come two notes without date. The first concerns the Church History, which he had prayed for time and again.

" All that I have to add," he writes, " is That when I am committing my Church History (which great work runs great hazard of miscarrying) into the hands of the Lord Jesus Christ, I receive wonderful Assurances (I think, I know) from Heaven That the Lord will accept it, and preserve it, and publish it, and that it shall not be lost. An Heavenly Afflatus causes me sometimes to fall into Tears of Joy, assured that the Lord has heard my supplications about the matter. And now, its having been thus long delayed, and obstructed and Clogg'd, proves but an opportunity for that prayer and Faith, which if I had gone without, the publication of that book would not have proved near so sweet a mercy to me. But if it should miscarry after all, O my God, what confusion would ensue upon me ! "

The second of the undated entries is a copy of part of a printed letter, expounding from personal experience a passage of Baxter, to the effect that whoever has a special virtue will probably be defamed for the contrary vice.

" It has in some former years commonly happened unto me," he writes, " That when I visited, in the way of my *pastoral Duty*, persons possessed with Evil Spirits, the persons, tho' they knew every one else in the room, yett, thro' the unaccountable operation of the *Evil Spirits* upon their Eyes, I must appear so Dirty, so ugly, so *Disguised* unto them, that they could have no knowledge of me. I have a thousand times thought, That the Lord ordered This for some Intimation unto me, That when *Times of Temptation* come, wherein *Evil Spirits* have so much operation on the *Minds* of my people, as they have on the eyes of Energumens, a Minister of the Lord Jesus Christ that will be faithful unto his Interests, must Look to be all over *Disguised* by Misrepresentation unto the *Minds* of them that are under the power of *Temptation*."

On the cover of the volume are these lines : —

" A Good Note in a Little Book entituled A Spiritual Legacy. Pray for those you Love, And assure yourselves you shall never have comfort of his Friendship for whom you pray not."

It is a very curious fact, that the diary for this most troublous of years shows, on the whole, more spiritual calm than any of the preceding. Mather seems to have realized this himself. On the 6th of December, he was afraid lest he " fall into Security."

In 1701 he published nine works : four volumes of sermons ; a poem addressed to an old gentlewoman afflicted with blindness ; a preface to his friends' answer to Calef ; a book on the Greek Churches ; a book on the Wonders of Christianity; and a book concerning which he writes as follows: —

" Many (it may be, more than seven) years ago, a Bookseller going from hence to *London*, carried certain Manuscripts of mine with him, declaring his Intentions to publish them.   He carelessly left them in the Hands of . . . a Bookseller there; who sometime after dyed; and I could never hear what became of my Manuscripts. . . . A friend of mine going the last Summer for *London*, did . . . Enquire after my Manuscripts; and strangely recovering of them, he carried them to another Bookseller, who published them. . . . The Book, which has had such a *Resurrection* from the *Dead*, has this Title, DEATH MADE EASY AND HAPPY." [1]

The year 1702 brought to Boston Joseph Dudley, the new Governor. As we have seen, it is believed that a letter of Cotton Mather's urging his popularity in Massachusetts — a popularity which there is reason to fear that Mather either invented or imagined — had much to do with his appointment.[2]   Son of the old Puritan Governor, Thomas Dudley, Joseph Dudley had from the first appearance of Randolph in Massachusetts been a pronounced Royalist.   He had been President of the provisional government which held power until Andros arrived.   Under Andros he had held high office; and with him he had been overthrown and sent to England for trial by the Revolution of 1689. Since that time he had been virtually an exile, but had enjoyed several honors. As Chief Justice of New York he had hanged Leisler, the leader there of such a revolution as had driven Dudley from Massachusetts. As

---

[1] Sibley, Harvard Graduates, III. 76.
[2] See page 130.

Lieutenant Governor of the Isle of Wight, and later as a member of Parliament, he had been high in royal favour. And now, as the official representative of Queen Anne, — for William of Orange died in March, 1702, — he returned triumphantly to Massachusetts. This final triumph he perhaps owed to the influence of the Mathers, whose crushing defeats were probably not appreciated in England. They believed that he would be grateful, that with his help something might still be done to preserve the system of the fathers. On June 11th, the day he arrived, there was a grand official banquet at the Town-house, and "Mr. Mather crav'd a blessing and Mr. Cotton Mather Returned Thanks." [1]

But Cotton Mather's diary for 1702 [2] tells little of all this; and much of matters that came nearer to him. "Prophesia quae dicit aliquid tale futurum impletur per aliquid tale," [3] is its motto. His first entry is this : —

"Thursday. On a Thursday just Thirty-Nine years ago, I first appeared in the World. I cannot express either my Amazements at the Goodness and Mercy of God, in sparing me thus far beyond my expectation to enter upon the Fortieth year of My Age: (methinks, *Forty* sounds Old and Big!) or my Distresses in Reflecting upon my Sinful and foolish misspend of my Irrevocable Time. (Alas how little, how nothing have I done in all this Time!) I considered these things a little this Day, in my Supplications before the Lord. But more on the Day following, which was with me a Day of prayer, (albeit I did three Dayes ago keep a Day of Thanksgiving in my Study.) "

[1] Sewall's Diary, II. 59.

[2] In the possession of the Massachusetts Historical Society.

[3] "A prophecy that some such thing shall be is fulfilled by some such thing."

He notes then how he had started a society for the Suppression of Disorders, and another for the Propagation of the Christian Religion. On the 14th of March he held his first recorded vigil: all the rest of his life he held these night-watches of prayer and fasting, as well as those he kept by day. And the same month he began the practice of reading Scotch commentators to his family at evening prayers. The first he took up was Hutchinson on Job.

"And many times after I had begun," he writes, "I had this Darted into my mind; That I might expect some Trials (perhaps of Long Sickness) to come shortly upon my Family; and that the Lessons fetch'd from the Study of Job were to prepare me for those Trials."

The rest of his notes until the 25th of May record only such ecstasies, vigils, activities, as by this time we know well. On that day his consort miscarried, at four or five months. He thought it his duty to humble himself before the Lord; but the dispensation remained mysterious, for

"when I more particularly examined, whether I had ever troubled the Churches of the Lord with any *False Conception*, I could not find myself conscious to any such matter."

For seven months there are few notes in the diary which concern anything but his domestic affairs. What few there are indicate that all the while his busy work went on unchecked. And besides the "Magnalia," which was published this year, he gave no less than eleven books to the press in the course of 1702. But what concerns us now is what went on at his home.

His wife grew worse. On the 3d of June, holding a special fast for her, he had a "sad experiment. . . . I can't Beleeve what I will or when I will." A dulness was on his spirit; impure thoughts assailed him; he feared she was about to die. His distress increased for three days. Then, on the 6th,

"in the Forenoon, while I was at prayer with my Dying Wife, in her Chamber, . . . I began to feel the blessed breezes of a *particular Faith*, blowing from Heaven upon my mind. . . . In the Afternoon, when I was alone in my Study, crying unto the Lord, . . . my *particular Faith* was again Renewed, and with a Flood of Tears, I thought I received an assurance from Heaven, That she should Recover. Whereupon I begg'd of the Lord, That He would by His Good Spirit incline me to be exemplarily wise, and chast, and Holy, in my whole Conversation, when I should again *obtain such favour of the Lord*, as to have my *Good Thing* with me, in former Circumstances."

Next day, for all this, she grew worse; her physician was called out of church to attend her; and Mather "was called up, in the middle of the following Night, because they thought her Dying." At one or two in the morning he retired to his study, where the Lord renewed "assurances of His purpose to Recover her." She lingered on. In a special fast for her on the 4th of July, he prayed too for the town, where small-pox had broken out; for the land, where war had been proclaimed;[1] and for "other sad circumstances we have in our government."[2] On the 12th, he held his seventh fast for her: —

1 "Malbrook s'en va-t-en guerre," etc.
2 See Chapter X.

"On which Day I also made Seven several Addresses for her, wherein I resigned her unto the Lord, and submitted unto all the sorrowful Consequences of a Rejected prayer, and a Defeated Faith, and a desolate broken Family, if He should order them for me. But while I thus *gave up* my dear consort, still I could not *give her over*."

And his particular faith was renewed. On the 21st, as she was still terribly ill,

"I chose . . . to Spread my Distress before the Lord, in the way of a Vigil. I Retired into my Bed-Chamber, and spent good part of the Night, prostrate on the Floor (with so Little of Garment on, as to render my lying there painful to my Tender Bones) crying to God for the Life of my poor Consort. . . . I think, before I went unto my Rest, I obtained some further satisfaction that my God has heard me."

On the 1st of August, she was a little better: —

"And yett, after This, . . . her Feebleness grows again to that extremity, as to render her condition, as dubious perhaps as ever. I am kept up all Night that I may see her Dy, and therewith see the Terrible Death of my prayer and Faith. But in this Extremity, when I renew my Visits unto Heaven, . . . a strange Irradiation comes from Heaven upon my Spirit that her Life shall not as yett come unto an End. — My Heavenly Father will still have me attended with some special Exercise, that shall keep my prayer and Faith employed. And that which His Fatherly Wisdome has ordered for me, in these later weeks, has been the singular Calamity of my poor Consort: and an Illness which none of the ablest physicians know, what to Judge of, or what to do for."

On the 29th, reflecting that his consort had been "strangely upheld, and tho' *chasten'd sore, yett not given over to Death,* for twice seven weeks together," he determined to hold a thanksgiving: it might be, he thought, that "a *Day of praise*, would be followed with salvations, beyond what any *Dayes of prayer* had yett obtained." But though she mended a little hereupon, it was only a little.

So in September he writes:

"I suspect, I have been too unattentive unto the meaning of the Holy Spirit, and His Angel, in the *particular Faith*, which I have had about my Consort's being Restored unto me. . . . When she has been Several Times on or near the Last Agonies of Death, . . . I cry to the Lord, that He will yett spare her. He tells me, That He will do it. Accordingly, to our Astonishment, . . . she stayes yett longer with us. . . . But it may be, after the Lord has given me admirable Demonstrations, of His being Lothe to Deny me anything that I importunately ask of him, and therefore does one Month after another Delay the Thing which I fear; yett I must at Last Encounter the Death which I have so deprecated, when both my wife and myself shall be better prepared for it."

On the 22d of October, matters still unchanged, he held a vigil, at the close of which he writes: —

"I took my *psalm-book* into my hand that I might sing something for the Quickening of my uneasy Mind. And unto my Surprize, the very first Verse, that at the opening of the Book, my Eye was carried unto was that: Psal. 105. 37.

> *And there was not among the Tribes*
> *A Feeble-person told.*

Lord, I thought! — This won't be fulfilled until the *Resurrection of the Dead*. The *Tribes* of the *Raised* will not have one *Feeble person* among them. And must I resign the condition of my Consort at last unto what shall be done in the future state? Lord, *Thy Will be Done*."

The next night his wife had a vision. A grave person appeared to her, — " she supposes, in her sleep," — leading a woman in such " meagre and wretched circumstances " that Mrs. Mather was presently stirred to praise God that " her condition was not yett so miserably circumstanced." The grave person proceeded to suggest remedies that had not occurred to the doctors; the doctors approved the suggestions ; and Mrs. Mather grew better,

"Insomuch that she came twice on Saturday out of her Sick Chamber, unto me in my Study; and there she asked me to give Thanks unto God with her, and for her, on the Account of the Recovery in so surprising a Degree begun unto her. — After this, my dear Consort continued much Refreshed, and yett Feeble. We had Great Hopes of her becoming a Strong person again; and yett great Fears, Lest some further Latent mischief within her, prove after all too hard for her."

On the 30th of October comes this note : —

" Yesterday, I first saw my CHURCH HISTORY, since the publication of it. A Gentleman arrived here from *Newcastle*, in *England*, that had bought it there. Wherefore, I sett apart this Day, for solemn THANKSGIVING unto God, for His Watchful and gracious providence over that Work and for the Harvest of so many prayers, and cares, and Tears, and Resignations, as I had employ'd upon it. My Religious Friend, Mr. *Broomfield*, who had been singularly helpful to me in the publication of that great Book (of Twenty shillings price, at *London*) came to me, at the Close of the Day, to join with me, in some of my praises to God. — On this Day my little daughter Nibby began to fall sick of the small-pox. The dreadful Disease, which is raging in the Neighbourhood, is now gott into my Family. God prepare me, God prepare me, for what is coming upon me. The child is favourably visited, in comparison of what many are."

The pestilence increased through November. So did the fervency of Cotton Mather's prayers. Late in the month, he writes : —

"Humiliations are coming thick upon me! My Study, is tho' a Large, yett a Warm Chamber, (the hangings whereof, are Boxes with between two and three thousand Books in them,) and we are so circumstanced, that my House, tho' none of the smallest, cannot afford a safe Hospital now for my Sick Folks, anywhere so well as there. So I Resigned my Study, for an Hospital to my little Folks, that are falling sick of a Loathsome Disease."

The first patient there was his "godly maid"; Nancy came down on the 24th; little Increase on the 29th.

"The Little Creatures," he writes, "keep calling for me so often to pray with them that I can scarce do it less than ten or a dozen times in a day ; besides what I do with my Neighbours."

Two days later,

"At last, the Black Day arrives. . . . I had never yett seen such a Black Day, in all the Time of my Pilgrimage. The *Desire of my Eyes* is this Day to be taken from me. . . . All the Forenoon, . . . she lies in the pangs of Death; sensible until the last minute or two before her final expiration. I Cannot Remember the Discourses that passed between us. Only, her Devout Soul was full of Satisfaction, about her going to a State of Blessedness, with the Lord Jesus Christ, and as far as my Distress would permit me, I studied how to confirm her satisfaction and consolation. This I Remember, That a little while before she died, I asked her to tell me Faithfully, what

Fault she had seen in my Conversation, that she would
advise me to rectify. She replied, (which I wondred at,)
That she knew of none, but that God had made what she
had observed in my Conversation, exceedingly serviceable
unto her, to bring her much nearer to Himself. When
I saw to what a point of Resignation I was now called of
the Lord, I Resolved, with His Help therein to glorify
Him. So, Two Hours before my Lovely Consort Expired,
I kneeled by her Bed-Side, and I took into my two Hands,
a dear Hand, the dearest in the World. With her thus in
my Hands, I solemnly and sincerely gave her up unto the
Lord: and in token of my Real RESIGNATION, I gently
putt her out of my Hands, and Laid away a most Lovely
Hand, Resolving That I would never touch it any more.
This was the Hardest, and perhaps, the bravest Action,
that ever I did. She afterwards told me, *That she sign'd
and seal'd my Act of Resignation.* And tho' before that,
she call'd for me, continually, she after this never asked
for me any more. She continued until near two a clock in
the Afternoon, And the last Sensible Word that she Spoke,
was to her weeping Father, *Heaven, Heaven, will make
amends for all.* When she was expired, I immediately
prayed with her Father, and the other weeping people in
the chamber, for the grace to carry it well under the present Calamity, and I did Consummate my Resignation, in
terms as full of glory to the wisdome and Goodness and
Alsufficiency of the Lord, as I could utter. She Lived
with me just as many years, as she had Lived in the World,
before she came to me, with an Addition of the seven
months, wherein her Dying Languishments were preparing
me to part with her."

X

COTTON MATHER'S PRIVATE LIFE.—HIS SECOND MARRIAGE.—CHARTER OF HARVARD COLLEGE.—QUARREL WITH JOSEPH DUDLEY

1702–1707

BEFORE proceeding with Cotton Mather's private life, we may best glance at the history of Massachusetts and of Harvard College for the next five years; and first, perhaps, glance back at Cotton Mather's account of his first interview with Governor Dudley.

On the last page of his diary for 1702 is this memorandum:—

"June 16. I received a Visit from Governour *Dudley*. Among other things . . . I said to him, . . . 'Syr, you arrive to the Government of a people, that have their various and their Divided Apprehensions, . . . particularly about your own Government over them. I am humbly of opinion, That it will be your Wisdom to carry an Indifferent Hand towards all parties. . . . I would approve it . . . if any one should say to Your Excellency: *By no means lett any people have cause to say, That you take all your measures from the Two Mr. Mathers.* By the same Rule, I may say without offence: *By no means lett any people say, That you go by no measures in your conduct but Mr. Byfield's and Mr. Leverett's.* This I speak not from any personal prejudice against the Gentlemen, but from a due consideration of the Disposition of the people; and as a service to your Excellency.' The Wretch went unto

those men, and told them, that I had advised him to be no
ways advised by them : and inflamed them into an im-
placable Rage against me."

For some years Mather maintained friendly relations
with the "wretch" in question ; but they were strain-
ing more and more.   The verdict of posterity is that
from beginning to end Joseph Dudley was a self-seeker.
Such verdicts, of course, are to be taken with caution ;
and in estimating this one it is but fair to remember
that Dudley was the first of the native Tories, and that
New England tradition has never done the native Loyal-
ists justice.   At the same time, I have found little to
show that in this particular case posterity has erred.
At home and abroad Dudley's whole training had been
that of a gentleman, — an aristocrat.   In his eleven
years of exile he had been in constant contact with in-
triguing, self-seeking courtiers.   How foreign his temper was to that of the compatriots he came to govern
appears most vividly in a misadventure which befell
him in December, 1705.[1]

"Dec. 7," writes Sewall, "Went to Brooklin. . . . After
Diner met the Govr. upon the Plain ; . . . told me of what
hapened on the road, being in a great passion : threaten'd
to send those that affronted him to England."

What had happened on the road was this.   Driving
in his travelling chariot, Governor Dudley found his way
stopped by two carts loaded with wood.   He ordered
the carters to move aside.   They declined, one of them
saying, " I am as good flesh and blood as you ; . . .

---

[1] See Sewall's Diary, II. 144, *seq.*, and note.   Meantime Sewall's
son had married Dudley's daughter.

you may goe out of the way." The Governor drew
his sword on the man, who snatched it and broke it,
declaring that he acted in defence of his life. "You
lie, you dog ; you lie, you devill ! " cried Dudley. —
"Such words don't become a Christian," said the
carter. — " A Christian, you dog ! " cried Dudley. "A
Christian, you devill ! I was a Christian before you
were born." And snatching the carter's whip he
lashed him. Then he had both carters arrested,
and apparently tried to make their conduct appear
treasonable. The case hung on until the following
November, when the Superior Court discharged the
prisoners. This was the Governor that the Mathers
had fondly hoped to manage.

The temper Dudley thus showed in private appears,
more decorously, in his public conduct. Palfrey[1] tells
in detail the story of his relations with the legislature,
and of the wars which harassed the frontiers. It was
during these wars that Deerfield was sacked, Cotton
Mather's cousin Mrs. Williams killed, and her husband
and family carried off by French and Indians. And
before 1707, the people of Massachusetts had generally
come to believe that Dudley's administration was corrupt ; and that he was personally interested in illicit
trade with the enemy.

Harvard College meanwhile proceeded under the provisional government of Vice-President Willard. From
the time of President Mather's dismissal Cotton Mather
never attended a meeting of the Corporation. On the
10th of August, 1703, he was reckoned to have abdi-
cated ; and Mr. Brattle was elected in his place.[2] As a

---

[1] Book IV. Chapters VIII –X.   [2] Quincy, I. 151.

minister of Boston, he remained an Overseer; but apparently attended only one other meeting of the board. Willard and Dudley had married sisters, — a fact which might well have had influence on such a temper as the Governor's. Whatever the reason, no steps were taken for a new charter during Willard's administration beyond two mentions of the subject in the Governor's messages: one in 1703, the other in 1705.[1]

So we come back to Cotton Mather's diary. It was on Tuesday, December 1, 1702, that his wife died. On Saturday she had been buried; and we find him holding a day of prayer and fasting,

"That I may obtain the pardon of all the sins for which the Lord is now chastening me ; and Grace and Help from Heaven to glorify the Lord with a wise Behaviour, under the Temptations of the Condition which is now come upon me."

Next day he preached on the death of the prophet Ezekiel's wife; and he notes that in many ways the people showed their love to him, — among other tokens of affection subscribing to build Mrs. Mather a costly tomb. A little later, the pestilence began to abate; the children grew better, and escaped scarlet-fever, which was also abroad. Cotton Mather himself remained well. His godly maid recovered, too; but so "distracted" that she had to go.

His next note is very long and curious. The seven months' strain has brought reaction. With a good deal of deliberation, he proceeds to consider the " Dispensations of Heaven, that have been Rolling over" him.

[1] Quincy, Vol. I. Chapter VIII.

" Has not the Death of my Consort," he asks, " that most astonishing Sting in it: *A miscarriage of a particular Faith ?* Truly, Nothing has ever yet befallen me, that has come so near it. But " — he finds reassuring thoughts. In the first place, it was compassionate in God to remove her : she could never have grown strong enough to perform her conjugal and maternal duties. " More than all this. She was a Gentlewoman of a Melancholy Temperament; and there were come dreadful changes in her Father's Family. He had extremely broken her Spirit by bringing home a mother-in-law. . . . Her youngest Brother, and a considerable Interest of mine with him, (some hundreds of pounds perhaps) was newly fallen into the Hands of the French Enemy. Her Second Brother, who was her Darling, . . . was dead in *London.* . . . Her Eldest Brother proves an Idle, profane, Drunken, and sottish Fellow, and a Disgrace to all his Relatives. . . . The sight of these Things, would without a miracle, have brought such a Disorder of Mind upon her, as would have rendered my Condition Insupportable. And now, who can tell, what way may be made for Blessings unto me, and mine, by her Translation to the Heavenly World? " In the second place, she herself had prayed that she might never live to hear of the death of her favorite brother ; and this prayer was granted. In the third place, within a fortnight after her death he had preached on John 4. 47,[1] from which he had expounded the doctrine that " Tho' Faith be no Folly, yett Faith may be mixed with Folly ; and particularly with the Folly of Limiting the Wisdome of God, unto our own way of *answering it*." And a gentlewoman, who heard the sermon, had been so moved as to address him thereupon in verses, ending —

" Your whole Discourse is Swol'n with its own praise,
But this fair Article, does wear the Baies."

[1] " When he heard that Jesus was come out of Judea into Galilee, he went unto him, and besought him that he would come down, and heal his son : for he was at the point of death."

" It may be," he writes at last, " The Lord will ere long
Enable me, to penetrate further into the Nature, meaning,
and mystery of a *particular Faith*. However, I have mett
with enough to awaken in me a more exquisite Caution,
than ever I had in my Life, concerning it."

In January, Nancy was very ill: but when her life was
despaired of, his prayers recovered her. The only other
note I have recorded for this month runs thus : —

"Before the late Weeks of my Life, I had rarely known
Tears, except those that were for the Joy of the Salvation
of God. But now, scarce a day passes me without a Flood
of Tears, and my Eyes even Decay with weeping. One
Day, considering how frequently and foolishly widowers
miscarry, and by their miscarriages dishonour God, I earnestly with Tears besought the Lord, *That he would please
to favour me, so far as to kill me rather* than to leave me
unto anything that might bring any Remarkable Dishonour
unto His Holy Name. (Within a few Minutes, I found
myself grow very Ill. . . . I suspected that the Lord was
going to take me at my word. But anon, I perceived that
it was nothing but *Vapours*.")

The next month began a new trial. He received a
visit from a very attractive young gentlewoman, who declared that she had long admired his public character,
and now felt herself at liberty to confess herself equally
pleased with his person. The state of perplexity into
which this address threw him lasted for two months.

His diary for 1703[1] begins with a birthday fast on
this occasion. His note of it is typical of all on the
subject.

" Nature itself," he writes, "causes in me a mighty
Tenderness for a person so very amiable. Breeding re-

[1] In possession of the American Antiquarian Society.

quires me to treat her with Honour and Respect, and very much of Deference to all that she shall at any time ask of me. But Religion, above all, obliges me instead of a rash Rejecting her Conversation, to Contrive rather how I may Imitate the Goodness of the Lord Jesus Christ in his dealing with such as are upon a Conversion unto him. — On the other side I cannot but fear a fearful Snare, and that I may soon fall into some error in my Conversation, if the point proposed unto me be found after all unattainable thro' the violent Storm of Opposition which I cannot but foresee . . . will be made unto it."

So on the 18th of February he begged her to desist; and, finding her inflexible, devoted himself to the task of converting her. And on the 20th he held a vigil, partly for himself, whom he feared " rejected and abhorred of God," — relatives and friends being displeased with gossip about the gentlewoman, — but partly for his church.

" It was a consolation unto me," he writes, " to think That when my people were all asleep in their Beds their poor pastor should be watching and praying and weeping for them."

On the 27th, he held another fast, in which he gave up to the Lord "the Ingenious Child that sollicits my Respects unto her." On the 6th of March he was in great trouble; the gentlewoman's reputation turned out to be somewhat damaged; to marry her would seriously interfere with his ministry; and her attentions were beginning to cause much tattle.

On the 12th, his state of mind was confused: the Assembly had voted

" the most unworthy man in the world to be Præsident of the Colledge in Cambridge. God knows what further trials

are coming upon me." But at the same time, " the Spirit
of the Lord sometimes does Visit me with Raptures of
Assurances, That He has loved me, and that I shall glorify
Him. I am sometimes even ready to faint away with the
Rapturous prælibations of the Heavenly World."

On the 15th, he definitely renounced the gentlewoman. " I struck the Knife into the Heart of my
Sacrifice by a Letter to her Mother." But next day
comes this : —

" Was ever man more Tempted than the miserable
Mather ? Should I tell in how many Forms the Devil has
assaulted me, . . . it would strike my Friends with Hor-
rour. Sometimes Temptations to Impurities: and sometimes to Blasphemy and Atheism and the Abandonment of
all Religion as a mere Delusion : and sometimes to Self-
Destruction itself. These, even These, O miserable Mather, do follow thee with an astonishing Fury. But I fall
down into the Dust on my Study-floor, with Tears before
the Lord : and then, they quickly vanish : Tis fair weather
again. Lord, what wilt thou do with me ? "

On the 3d of April he held another fast, to guard
against the temptations of widowhood. He would like
to remain a widower, he thought ; but his father and his
friends advised otherwise. On the 13th, 14th, and 15th,
he kept three successive days of fasting and prayer, in
which extraordinary things were done for him.

" The Angels of Heaven are at work for me," he writes,
" And I have my *own Angel*, who is a better Friend unto
me, than any I have upon Earth."

But the " desirable frame " in which this left him
lasted only two days. Still, on the 18th of May he
found himself assured that

"for the sake of the Lord Jesus Christ, whose I am, a
desireable consort should be bestowed upon me ; and a

glorious Angel of the Lord, should be concerned for me (as for Isaac of old) in this important matter."

His friends, it appears, were trying to make a match for him; but succeeded only in getting him distressingly talked about. A "marvellous providence of God" diverted him from "doing a thing whereto . . . Friends had mightily urged" him. On the 19th, he went to Salem for five days. The gentlewoman and her mother took advantage of his absence to call on Increase Mather, who had been suffering with gout; and to urge their case. But Cotton Mather, though distressed, remained resolute. And a little later he writes,

"While the Lord is otherwise laying me exceedingly low, He yett gratifies me with Strange Favours on that point which is the very Apple of my Eye; and that is, my being employed in Service for His Blessed Name."

In other words, his condition had proved unusually favourable to pulpit eloquence.

In June, when gossip began to accuse him of jilting the gentlewoman, she joined her mother in loyally protesting that his conduct had been thoroughly honourable.

"Yea," he writes, "they have proceeded so far beyond all bounds in my vindication, as to say, *They verily look on* Mr. M——r *to be as great a Saint of God as any upon earth.*"

The poor gentlewoman had a worse trial coming, though. Sundry fasts of Cotton Mather's early in July directed his attention to Mrs. Elizabeth Hubbard, a godly and comely widow who lived near by. On the 14th, he paid her his first visit. In a few days more they were engaged. The gentlewoman raged, but relented. People in general approved. And Cotton

Mather's troubles reduced themselves to groundless fears that he should die before his wedding day. On the 18th of August, after spending the day in Heaven, he became in the evening the husband of "the most agreeable Consort (all things considered) that all America could have afforded me."

Of this lady her son Samuel wrote : —

"She was one, of finished *Piety* and *Probity*, and of an unspotted *Reputation ;* one of *good sense*, and bless'd with a compleat *Discretion* in ordering an Household ; one of singular *good-Humour* and incomparable Sweetness of Temper ; one, with a very handsome and engaging *Countenance ;* and one *honourably descended* and related ; . . . the Daughter of Dr. JOHN CLARK. She had been a Widow *four years* when Dr.[1] MATHER married her."[2]

The rest of Cotton Mather's notes for this year show him very busy with pastoral and literary work, and quite relieved of the morbid tension that preceded his marriage.

My summary of his annual literary work in the last chapter should be sufficient. A glance at Sibley's catalogue of his works[3] will show that the years I have summarized are typical. Of this matter I shall say no more, save that his publications in 1703 amounted to twelve ; and in 1704 to the same number. And so he kept on all his life.

His diary for 1704 is not preserved. The only facts I have noted for this year are these. A daughter, Elizabeth, was born to him. It was the year when

---

[1] The title is premature. Cotton Mather was not Doctor of Divinity until 1710.

[2] Life, page 13.

[3] Harvard Graduates, III. 42-158.

Deerfield was sacked. In June, certain pirates were hanged in Boston; and Cotton Mather preached to them and went with them to execution, where, "when the scaffold was let to sink," Sewall writes, "there was such a Screech of the Women that my wife heard it sitting in our Entry, . . . yet the wind was sou-west. Our house is a full mile from the place." In July, Sewall notes that Cotton Mather was at Commencement; on October 12th, that Cotton Mather prayed for the College. Two days before, Samuel Mather[1] tells us, a dying man had sent for Cotton Mather, to beg his forgiveness for wanton slanders. Mather forgave him: and "the Man . . . kept continually crying for him to be with him the next Day in the Forenoon, and he died in the Afternoon." I incline, also, to attribute to the period of his troubles with the gentlewoman of 1703 the anecdote preserved in a vituperative pamphlet of 1707, and probably a good example of the stories told of him by his enemies. It runs thus : —

"A Gentlewoman of *Gayety*, near *Boston*, was frequently visited by the Reverend Mr. *C. M.* which giving offence to some of his Audience, he promised to avoid her Conversation. But *Good* intentions being frustrated by *Vicious* Inclinations, he becomes again her humble Servant: the *Reciprocal* promise being first made, that NEITHER OF THEM SHOULD CONFESS THEIR SEEING EACH OTHER : However it becoming again publick, his Father accused him of it, who after two or three HEMS to recover himself, gave this *Aequivocal* Answer, INDEED, FATHER, IF I SHOULD SAY I DID SEE HER, I SHOULD TELL A GREAT LYE." [2]

[1] Life, page 64.
[2] Sewall's Diary, II. 81*. See page 222.

Which story, having read his diaries, I do not believe.

The diary for 1705[1] records a busy year, more wholesome than usual. I have noted a few entries. On the 16th of March, maligned for falsehood, he held a very earnest day of fasting and prayer.

"And I considered," he writes, "That tho' my whole Time all the Day long, and all the Week long, is employ'd in a continual Contrivance of . . . Zeal to do good, yett few men meet with more clogs in it, from the malignity of Evil people. . . . And if I had jogg'd on in an Indifferent manner as others do, and less thwarted and vexed the Divel in his interests, I might have been as little envied and maligned as they: But I resolved, That I would not at all Abate of my Endeavors to be universally Serviceable."

In May, Nancy had another severe illness.

"I cannot be at rest," he writes, "until I have obtained of the Lord that this Child shall in Spiritual Blessings have an abundant and glorious Compensation for all her Temporal Sufferings."

In May he was specially maligned by a "very wicked fellow," who, with Cotton Mather's approval, had been disciplined by the Church of Woburn. Early in June, then, he examined himself for

"what marks I can find in myself, that might carry me cheerfully thro' the Dark Valley of the Shadow of Death, if I should be (which I have abundance of Reason to look for) immediately called into it." He found eleven, of which the last was compassion for personal enemies. "I am afraid," he writes, "of allowing my Soul a Wish of Evil to the Worst of them All. . . . Q. Whether the man that can

[1] In possession of the Massachusetts Historical Society.

find these *marks* upon himself may not conclude himself *mark'd out* for the City of God?"

At this time he was very busy, starting Societies for the Suppression of Disorders.

"I am well content," he writes, "that I have not the Time, to Record a hundredth part of the *methods to bring forth Fruit* wherein I am endeavoring to *glorify God,* so that they should be utterly buried in oblivion for this world."

In July, hearing in a hymn the words,

"With persons merciful that be
Thou merciful thyself wilt show,"

he was affected to tears by the thought that the merciful dispositions he could discover in himself were but faint rays of the sun of God's mercy. In November, he examined himself curiously.

"A man Bitten with a *Mad-Dog,*" he writes, "has not only his *Body,* but his very *Soul* also poisoned. The poison . . . pervades the Nervous Fluid. . . . The *Spirit* of such a man, will cause him to say to his Friend, . . . *I would not hurt you.* Notwithstanding this, yett when his Fitt arrives the *Spirit* must knock under and ly fettered. . . . The Soul of every man is *Dog-Bitten,* or, which is as bad, *serpent-bitten,* or *Divel-bitten. Original Sin* has depraved it. . . . A *Regenerate Spirit* . . . chuses above all Things, to Glorify God, . . . and it has gotten an *Empire* over the *Soul,* in doing of it."

By this test, he found himself probably regenerate.

In January, there was a thanksgiving for successes in the war with France.

"For the best part of Two Hours together," he writes, "my soul kept soaring and Flaming towards Heaven in the wondrous praises of God. Such length in this kind of Devotions being somewhat unusual, and unto some folks (I fear'd) uneasy, I took occasion in my Sermon to make this Apology for it."

The apology I will not quote; it is very long.

The volume closes with five elaborate notes: one about the dispositions of his mind relating to a great reputation in the world, concerning which he believes himself to care little; one about the education of his children, which is substantially what his son Samuel reports of his practices;[1] one about several points of conduct, in which he resolves to practise Christian humility; and one about his flock, which he purposes to edify by pastoral visits, and by edifying speeches on all occasions, — giving them many books, too, with the charge that they are to remember that he speaks to them whenever the books are before them. The fifth note is similar to that which closes nearly every volume of the diary, — a memorandum of the texts he has preached from this year: it covers four closely written pages.

The diary for 1706[2] opens with a very long memorandum of how his time is occupied: this is digested under thirty-one heads. It appears that he rises at seven or eight;[3] sings a hymn of praise; writes a short paragraph, — "hereby sometimes I have insensibly prepared whole sermons"; adds illustrations to the "Biblia Americana"; prays in private and then with his family; works; dines, edifying the family mean-

---

[1] See page 165.

[2] In possession of the Massachusetts Historical Society.

[3] Thus habitually sleeping eight or nine hours, which is probably what kept him alive.

while; retires to his study for a short prayer; goes
out visiting; about the shutting in of the evening hears
the children say the catechism, and makes an evening
prayer chiefly of thanksgiving; sups at ten, edifying the
adult part of his family; prays and reflects on the day
in his study; and reads himself to sleep with some agreeable book at eleven or so. Sermons, the children, the
sick, calls from all manner of visitors, the fourteen or
fifteen religious societies he belongs to, new books to
be read, frequent days of fasting and prayer, and the
discipline of his church constantly engage his attention.
He notes all this in the hope that by perusing it he may
be kept up to work. Four pages of notes of his cor-
respondents follow: I observe no names of permanent
importance.

His birthday note is worth remembering. He would
like to record thoughts

"that carry in them a peculiar Advancement of my Soul towards the perfection after which I am aspiring. One of
them, which has been of late singularly useful to me in my
pressing after the true temper of Christianity is This. I see
all Creatures everywhere full of their Delights. The Birds
are singing; the Fish are sporting; the Four-footed are
glad of what they meet withal; the very Insects have their
satisfactions. Tis a marvellous Display of Infinite Goodness. The Good God has made His Creatures capable of
Delights: He accommodates them with continual Delights.
These Delights are the Delicious Entertainments of His
Infinite Goodness. His Goodness takes pleasure in . . .
the Delights of His Creatures. — Well: Is there no way
for me to Resemble and Imitate this Incomparable Goodness of God? Yes: I see my Neighbours all accommodated with their various Delights. All have some, and
some have many. Now I may honestly make their Delights

my own. . . . I may make their prosperity, not my *Envy*, but my *pleasure*. . . . Oh, the glorious Joy of this Goodness! Lord, Imprint this thy Image upon me!"

With good resolutions, one against evil-speaking, for example; with prayers and assurances, among others for the prisoners among the French and Indians, the year went on. In March, little Increase having begun school, Cotton Mather wrote a verse daily for the child to get by heart, that he might " improve in goodness at the same time that he improv'd in Reading ": these verses ultimately made a popular book. In April, he was pleased to find that he had "no Fondness at all for Applause and Honour in this World " : for which disposition " in the midst of . . . Humiliations," he gave thanks. Late in May, languishing in health, he hurried work and finished the first draft of the " Biblia Americana." He kept adding to it, however, for years. As late as 1720 he wrote John Winthrop [1] that he had inserted in the " Biblia Americana " an account of the discovery in New England of a water-dove, probably the species employed by Noah. The manuscript of the " Biblia Americana," by far the most voluminous of Cotton Mather's works, is preserved by the Massachusetts Historical Society. He could never find subscribers enough to publish it; and I have not had the time or the courage to examine it. At a superficial glance, it seems to be a marvellously industrious, uncritical collection of every scrap of learning he could find which might by any chance have bearing on Holy Writ. It includes a great deal of such matter as is most familiarly known

[1] Mather Papers, 436.

nowadays in Burton's "Anatomy of Melancholy"; and a great deal, too, of that eager observation of nature[1] which some years later made Cotton Mather a Fellow of the Royal Society.

His next work, printed in June, was an essay to promote the Christianizing of Negroes.[2] He determined to give a copy of this to every family in New England who possessed a Negro, and to send copies to the West Indies.

In July, he was much disturbed about illicit trade with hostile Indians. These Indians made a descent this very month on the Andover road, over which he had passed a few days before. On this journey, he writes,

"being desirous to do some Good on the Road in the Woods, I called some children to me, which I met there, and bestowed some Instructions with a little Book upon them: which I understood afterwards made no little Impression upon the Family. But it proved a family which in a few Dayes the Indians visited, and murdered the mother, and several of the children."

So the year went on, busier than ever. In October I find two notes worth recording. On the 17th, he writes : —

"One of my more special Actions . . . was to make my Children, Four of them,[3] successively to come into my

[1] For examples of this, see Cotton Mather's letters to John Winthrop, in the Mather Papers.

[2] See Sibley, III. 93; and in regard to Cotton Mather's relations to negroes in general, see a paper by Professor Haynes in the Proceedings of the American Antiquarian Society.

[3] Katharine, Abigail, Hannah, and Increase ; their ages ranged from fourteen to seven.

Study, and observe and mention to me the special mercies which they were sensible they had received of God; and then charge them immediately to Retire and give Thanks unto the Lord, and beg to be possessed by the Spirit of the Lord."

On Wednesday, the 30th, he writes: —

"With many favourable Circumstances for which the Lord had been sought unto, my Consort fell into Travail; and after a Wondrous Good and Quick Time, was about three-quarters of an hour past nine at Night, happily delivered of a Son; to appearance a hearty and an handsome Infant. — On the Lord's-day following I Baptized this my Son, and called him SAMUEL. Tis my desire to have him devoted unto the Service of the Lord as long as he lives."

That night, accordingly, he held a vigil for his whole family. This Samuel lived to grow up into a very commonplace divine, whose biography of his father is probably the most colourless book in the English language.

In November, Cotton Mather's assurances were rewarded by the return of his cousin, Mr. Williams of Deerfield, from captivity. In December some gentlemen gave Mather a negro, named Onesimus, worth forty or fifty pounds.

"I would use the best endeavours," he writes, "to make him a servant of Christ, and also be more serviceable than ever to a flock which laies me under such obligations."

The same month comes a note that shows his temper up. He has two wicked brothers-in-law, he writes: —

"The first of these prodigies, namely J. O.,[1] married my Lovely Sister Hannah, a most Ingenious and sweet-Natured,

[1] John Oliver.

and good-carriaged Child : one that would have been a Wife, to have made any Gentleman Happy ; but married unto a Raving Bruit. The Fellow, whom they called, Her Husband, perfectly murdered her, by his base and abusive way of treating her ; and he chose to employ in a special manner, the ebullitions of his venome against me, to weary and worry her, out of her Life, who Loved me dearly. . . . At last on 1d. 10m., . . . the pangs of Death came upon her. Her Death was Long and Hard, and has awakened me more than ever, to pray for an Easy Death. She kept in her dying Distresses much calling on me : her *Brother*, her *Brother !* As I had heretofore used all possible Diligence and Contrivance, to prepare her for her Death, so I now assisted her, as well as I could, in her last Hours. I prayed with her Six Times this Day : and in the Night following she died. The Monster, to whom she owes her Death, now with Anguish, bears a most honourable Testimony for her ; as the best Wife in the World ; and a great example of piety. And from a convinced conscience, he now also speaks of *me*, with no little pretence of Honour and Acknowledgement. Indeed, she had Cause to Bless God for the Wretch, for he was a great occasion of her growing a serious and gracious Christian, weaned from this World and fitted for a better."

The other wicked brother-in-law was a Phillips, whose offences seem less a matter of opinion. On the 10th of January, Cotton Mather writes : —

" My Father-in-Law at Charlestown has of late been in a very froward and Evil Frame. The elder of his Two wicked Sons, has been lately Fined by the General Assembly of the Province for his unlawful Trade with the Enemy. The crime of the Traders, whereof he was one filled the Countrey with a mighty Inflammation. On that occasion, it was necessary for me, to bear my part with the other ministers, in a faithful Testimony. And I did my part as easily and as modestly, tho' as Faithfully as I could. The Humoursome Old Man is so very unhappy, as to be enraged at me, and express himself, as I hear, very Enragedly and Abusively. . . . His Two Wicked Sons do also strangely manage him."

So Cotton Mather was afraid that old Mr. Phillips would disinherit his Mather grandchildren and offered up prayers accordingly.

The very next note, however, is of different tenor : —

" My little Son waits upon his Grandfather every day, for his Instruction, as well as upon other Tutors and Teachers. This day I sent him on an Errand, where the person imposing on his Flexible Temper, detained him so long that his Grandfather was displeased at him, for coming so late ; and his punishment was, that his Grandfather, did Refuse to Instruct him, as he uses to do. The child, unable to bear so heavy a punishment, as that his Grandfather should not look favourably upon him, repairs to me, full of weeping Affliction. Hereupon, I applied myself with a Note, unto my *Father*, as an *Advocate* for the Child. I pleaded all that could be said by way of Apology for the Infirmity of the Child. I asked, that I might bear the displeasure due for it, because of what had passed relating to it. I assured my Father, the child should no more in this way displease him. So the Child was presently received into favour with my Father : My Father looked on him with a pleased Aspect, and bestowed agreeable Illumination upon him. I thought, the Lord ordered this little Accident this Day, to raise in my mind, the Thoughts of the Reconciliation, which the Son of God, who is my Advocate with the Father, would obtain for me, with God."

The diary closes with a painful record of how Cotton Mather was persistently vexed with vile thoughts : but he fought them hard, he resolved that they should not tempt him to forbear testimony against sin in others, and he meditated

"on the inexpressible evil, which there would be, . . . if one of my . . . many and mighty obligations, to the most unspotted Sanctity, should harbour or indulge in myself any wicked Thing in the World."

Of the diary for 1707 only a fragment remains, [1] in which I have remarked nothing of more note than that Cotton Mather was praying fervently for the expedition against Port Royal that came to nothing. For the notable events of this year, then, we must turn to other authorities.

Palfrey tells with great clearness the story of Joseph Dudley's administration.[2] Frequent notes of Sewall's, a member of the Council, a judge of the highest court in the Province, and closely connected by marriage with the Governor, become very vivid when we keep in mind the state of politics. In brief, with his overbearing temper, so thoroughly foreign to the temper of New England, Dudley had been doing his best to strengthen the power of the Crown. Without much success, he had been carrying on the war against Canada; in 1707 a fruitless expedition was sent against Port Royal, restored to the French by the Peace of 1697. Meantime, like other men in office before and since, he had taken good care of his personal friends; and was suspected of connivance with some of them in illicit trade with the enemy. As Cotton Mather wrote in 1706, a number of illicit traders, among whom was

---

[1] In possession of the Massachusetts Historical Society.
[2] Book IV. Chapters VIII. to X.

John Phillips, brother of the first Mrs. Mather, had been condemned by the General Court to pay heavy fines for their offence. It is certain that Dudley wrote to England in their behalf; and that the Privy Council ultimately ordered the fines to be repaid, on the ground that the General Court of Massachusetts had no cognizance of the offence. Before this decision, certain men of New England, mostly resident in London, had addressed to the Queen a formal petition for the removal of Dudley, for corruption, injustice, and oppression.

Harvard College,[1] meanwhile, had been proceeding under the charge of Vice President Willard, who had retained meantime his charge of the Old South Church, and seems to have given little more attention to academic duties than Increase Mather had given. Apparently, however, he was much less vigorously conservative in temper; and so far as records show, made no particular efforts to secure a new charter. As we have seen, Dudley twice suggested that application be made for one to the Crown. But no notice was taken of these suggestions: the friends of the College, Quincy thinks, were convinced that no satisfactory charter could be secured from any more foreign source than their own elected Provincial legislature.

Willard's health was now failing. He managed to preside at Commencement, but gave the degrees so feebly that Sewall, who was not far off, could not hear a word he said. In the middle of August he went to Cambridge for the last time, where he found so few scholars that he returned home before prayer-time.

[1] Quincy, Vol. I. Chapter VIII.

And on the 12th of September, a friend informed Sewall that the President was very sick.

"I hoped it might go off," writes Sewall, "and went to Diñer; when I came there Mr. Pemberton[1] was at Prayer, near concluding, a pretty many in the Chamber. After Prayer, many went out, I staid and sat down: and in a few minutes saw my dear Pastor Expire: . . . just about two hours from his being taken. . . . The Doctors were in another room Consulting what to doe. . . . Tis thought cutting his finger, might bring on the tumultuous passion that carried him away. There was a dolefull cry in the house."

Three days later Mr. Willard was buried; both of the Mathers were among his bearers. And on the 2d of October, a fast day, the Mathers conducted afternoon exercises at the Old South.

The first business of the Corporation of Harvard College was to elect a President. Increase Mather was nearly sixty-nine years old. But Cotton Mather was only forty-four. His learning, his piety, his orthodoxy, and his devotion to the old principles of the College, made him, in his own opinion, the proper successor of Mr. Willard. There is reason to think that the want of deliberate judgment which naturally came from his overworked, overwrought habits of life, led his hopes to run high. So what happened on the 28th of October must have stung him to the quick.

"The Fellows of Harvard College meet," writes Sewall, "and chuse Mr. Leverett President: He had eight votes, Dr. Increase Mather three, Mr. Cotton Mather one."

Within the week Sewall saw for the first time a document that gave rise to much excitement in Boston.

[1] Willard's colleague at the Old South.

This was " A Memorial of the Present Deplorable State
of New England," [1] lately published in London, and
stating with great distinctness every charge against
Dudley. These were supported by sundry affidavits,
and by a long letter, evidently written by Cotton
Mather. It is dated October 2, 1706 : [2] it specifically
mentions the proceedings against Phillips and the other
illicit traders, and contains this passage : —

" Our Present Governour is not without a number of
those, whom he has by Promotions and Flatteries made
his Friends ; but this hinders not a much more considerable number, from wishing, that we had a Governour, who
would put an end unto the horrid Reign of Bribery, in our
Administration, and who would not infinitely incommode
Her Majesty's Service, by keeping the People in continual Jealousies of his Plots, upon their most Valuable
Interests."

On the 1st of November, the day when Sewall saw
this pamphlet, the Governor produced in the Council
a copy of the petition for his removal, and requested
the Council to vote their abhorrence of it. Sewall
pleaded for delay, but the vote was passed. The Deputies refused to concur in it. At a Conference of the
Houses on the 20th,

" Gov. made a long speech, begining from his father,
who laid out a Thousand pounds in the first adventure,
was Governour. He himself the first Magistrat born in
New England . . . Took an opportunity to say, he heard

---

[1] Reprinted at the beginning of the second volume of Sewall's
Diary, and summarized by Palfrey, Book IV. Chap. VIII. It is
in a reply to this pamphlet that the scandalous story appeared
which I lately cited, page 209.

[2] Sewall's Diary, II. 40*-42*.

some whisper'd as if the Council were not all of a mind:
He with courage said that all the Council were of the same
mind as to every word of the Vote. This gall'd me; yet I
knew not how to contradict him before the Houses." At
another conference next day, "the Govr. had the Extract
of many of Mr. C. M. Letters read, of a later date than
that in the printed book, . . . giving him a high character." On the 25th of November, "The Govr. read Mr.
Cotton Mather's letter . . . in Council. . . . When the
Govr. came to the *horrid Reign of Bribery:* His Excellency said, None but a Judge or Juror could be Brib'd, the
Governour could not be bribed, sons of Belial brôt him
no Gifts. Moved that [a committee] go to Mr. Cotton
Mather with the Copy of his Letter, . . . and his Letters
to the Govr., and speak to him about them: this was
agreed to. I shew'd some backwardness, . . . hinting
whether it might not be better for the Govr. to go to him
himself: That seem'd to be Christ's Rule, except the Govr.
would deal with him in a Civil way. . . . p. m. I desired
the Governour's patience to speak a word: I said I had
been concerned about the Vote pass'd Novr. 1. 'At the
Conference his Excellency was pleas'd to say, that every
one of the Council remain'd steady to their vote, and every
word of it: This Skrewing the Strings of your Lute to
that height, has broken one of them; and I find my self
under the Necessity of withdrawing my Vote; . . . and
desire the Secretary may be directed to enter it in the
Minutes of the Council.' And then I delivered my Reasons for it,[1] written and sign'd with my own Hand. . . . The
Govr. directed that it should be kept privat: but I think
Col. Lynde went away before the Charge was given. . . .
Nov. 26, Mr. Secretary reports the Discourse with Mr.
Cotton Mather favourably; It seems they stay'd there

[1] Borland, one of the convicted traders, had given Sewall to
understand that the charges against Dudley were true; but
subsequently denied Sewall's construction of his words. See
Sewall's Diary, II. 215, 216.

more than two Hours ; and Dr. Mather was present. Mr.
Mather neither denys nor owns the Letter : Think his
Letters to the Govr. and that . . . not so inconsistent as
they are represented. . . . The Council invited the Govr.
to Diñer ; . . . I drank to his Excellency, and presented
my Duty to him. . . . In the evening by Candle-Light I
fell asleep in the Council-Chamber : and when I waked
was surprised to see the Govr. gone." [1]

On the 28th, Dudley wished the vote of November
1st published, to prevent the spreading of false reports.

" I said," writes Sewall, " I could not vote to it because
I had withdrawn my vote. The Govr. said, I pray God
judge between me and you ! . . . Lord, do not depart from
me, but pardon my sin ; and fly to me in a way of favourable Protection."

On the 6th of December, there came before the
Council a bill fixing the salary of the new President of
Harvard College. To this was subjoined the following
provision,[2] which we should now call a " rider " : —

" And inasmuch as the first foundation . . . of that
House [3] . . . had its original from an act of the General
Court, made and passed in the year one thousand six
hundred and fifty, which has not been repealed or nulled ;
the President and Fellows of the said College are directed
. . . to regulate themselves according to the rules of the
constitution by that act prescribed."

Dudley and his Council approved this bill. The
charter of 1650, thus revised, governs Harvard College
to the present day. And thus it came about that Harvard College, in spite of all the labours and prayers of
the Mathers, has become, for better or worse, the per-

---

[1] Sewall's Diary, II. 199-204.
[2] Quincy, I. 159.   [3] I.e. Harvard College.

petual nursery, not of priests, but of ever more earnest Protestants.

How the defeated party took this matter appears in a note of Sewall's for December 18th : —

" Mr. Bridge [1] . . . takes Job 15. 34,[2] for his Text ; especially that clause, — Fire shall consume the tabernacle of Bribery : From which he preach'd an excellent sermon. . . . Dr. Mather not at Lecture. Governor . . . there."

In spite of sermons, Leverett was inaugurated on the 18th of January. The Mathers were not present. Sewall gives a minute account of the ceremony.

" In the Library the Governour found a Meeting of the Overseers . . . according to the old charter of 1650. . . . Took the President by the hand and led him down into the Hall. The Books of the College Records, Charter, Seal and Keys were laid upon a Table running parallel with that next the Entry. The Govr. sat with his back against a Noble Fire ; . . . President sat on the other side of the Table. . . . The Govr. read his Speech and (as he told me) mov'd the Books in token of their Delivery. Then the President made a short Latin Speech, importing the difficulties discouraging, and yet that he did Accept. . . . Had a very good Diñer upon 3 or 4 Tables : . . . Got home very well. *Laus Deo.*"

On the 23d of January, Sewall attended a funeral. " When had gone a little way," he writes, " Mr. Cotton Mather came up and went with me." From the burying place they went to make a call, where they had some very pious talk.

[1] Minister of the First Church.
[2] " For the congregation of hypocrites shall be desolate, and fire shall consume the tabernacles of bribery."

"As went thence," continues Sewall, "told me of his Letter to the Govr. of the 20th Inst. and Lent me the Copy. . . . Dr. Mather it seems has also sent a Letter to the Govr. I wait with concern to see what the issue of this plain home-dealing will be ! "

Palfrey[1] and Quincy[2] summarize these letters. Assuming all the spiritual authority of their ministry, the Mathers reiterate every charge that has been made against Dudley; and rebuke him with every anathema of Puritanism. The letters are the agonizing death-cry of old New England.

Two or three more notes of Sewall's tell what this "plain home-dealing" seemed to the victors.

"Jany 31. Mr. Pemberton . . . talk'd to me very warmly about Mr. Cotton Mather's Letter to the Govr., seemed to resent it, and expect the Govr. should animadvert upon him. Said if he were as the Govr. he would humble him though it cost him his head; Speaking with great vehemency just as I parted with him at his Gate. The Lord apear for the Help of his people. — Feb. 2. . . . Somebody said, . . . That no man was admitted to be a Captain without giving the D. of Marlborough, or his Dutchess five hundred Guinys : the Govr. took it up, and said, What is that ! Speaking in a favourable, diminutive way. And said that there had not been any admitted these thousand years but in a way like that; mentioning his own experience in the Isle of Wight. His Excellency seems hereby to justify himself against those who charge him with Bribery. — Febr. 5. Mr. Colman preaches the Lecture . . . from Gal. 5. 25. If we live in the Spirit, let we also Walk in the Spirit. Spake of Envy and Revenge as the Complexion and Condemnation of the Devil. . . . 'Tis reckoned he lash'd Dr. Mather and Mr. Cotton Mather and Mr. Bridge

---

[1] Vol. III. pp. 295, 296.   [2] Vol. I. pp. 201, 202.

for what they have written, preach'd and pray'd about the present Contest with the Govr."

Next day, after a fortnight's waiting, Joseph Dudley sent his answer to the Mathers.[1] With Scriptures as good as theirs, he recommended self-scrutiny to them. And he went on thus : —

"Every one can see through the pretence, and is able to account for the spring of these letters, and how they would have been prevented, without easing any grievances you complain of. . . . I desire you will keep your station, and let fifty or sixty good ministers, your equals in the province, have a share in the government of the College . . . as well as yourselves. . . . I am an honest man, and have lived religiously these forty years to the satisfaction of the ministers in New England, and your wrath against me is cruel, and will not be justified. . . . The College must be disposed against the opinion of all the ministers in New England except yourselves, or the governor torn in pieces. This is the view I have of your inclination."

And this is the view posterity has accepted, with what justice the records I have quoted may help to show. While the Mathers were reading this letter, Samuel Sewall, " in the uꝑer Chamber of the North-East end of the House, fastening the Shutters next the Street," was holding a solemn fast. But though he prayed for so many things that the record covers a closely printed page, I found my eye caught chiefly by one passage : —

"Save the Town, College, Province from Invasions of Enemies open, Secret and from false Brethren: Defend the Purity of Worship. Save Connecticut."[2]

[1] Palfrey, III. 297.
[2] Diary, II. 217. 10 February, 1707–8.

XI

COTTON MATHER'S PRIVATE LIFE TO THE DEATH OF HIS SECOND WIFE

1707–1713

FOR the next six years Joseph Dudley remained Governor of Massachusetts. His quarrel with the Mathers seems never to have been settled. Throughout these years, Cotton Mather was busier than ever in his pastoral work, and his endless plans for doing good in general; and Increase Mather, growing old, and not gaining buoyancy of temper, preached and prayed,— not a little about the good old time. With public offices and with the College, which prospered under the care of Leverett, neither seems to have had much to do. So the course of public affairs has little to do with us. In his relations with the General Court, Dudley seems, in his later days, to have been less aggressive. The war went on with varying success: Port Royal was taken in 1710, but there were disasters later, Indian massacres all along. In fifty years, Hutchinson estimated,[1] the population did not double: in 1709, Dudley estimated it at about fifty thousand, increasing at the rate of a thousand a year; Hutchinson thinks that from five to six thousand of the youth of the country

[1] Palfrey, III. 303.

fell in the wars which ended with the welcome peace of Utrecht in 1713. Meanwhile, according to Palfrey,[1] a new generation was growing up under the Provincial charter, far more loyal to the Crown than the old independent Dissenters of the Colony.

In this chapter our business will be to follow the private life of Cotton Mather until 1713.

Cotton Mather's diary for 1708 is not preserved. But in the collection of the American Antiquarian Society is a copy in his handwriting, with the date 1708, of Swift's burlesque prophecy of the death of Partridge, etc., which Cotton Mather seems to have taken in sober earnest. In Sewall I find but one note worth recording here. In June Mr. Bromfield received an anonymous letter, "putting him upon enquiring after Debaucheries at North's, the Exchange Tavern," and urging him to ask Sewall's advice. Cotton Mather's constant eagerness to suppress disorder, his intimate relations with Bromfield and Sewall, and his frequent practice of "doing good" anonymously, make it not unlikely that this letter came from him. I cannot refrain from citing one more note of Sewall's, though — a little glimpse of manners: "Govr. calls and smokes a pipe with my wife at night 9r. 1."

Sewall's diary for 1709 gives a few glimpses of the Mathers, with whom his relations were now cordially intimate.

"June 22. . . . Going to visit sick Mr. Gerrish . . . I met Dr. Mather, who tells me that yesterday, he was 70 years old. — Octobr. 6. . . . Mr. C. Mather preaches from Prov. 14. 14. Backslider in heart shall be filled with his

[1] Vol. III. p. 302.

own Ways. Mention'd the indulgence of Adonijak; the prophet Micajah; not the prophet, but the King was hurt by his estrangement."

There are glimpses of Dudley, too, giving no new traits; and on January 28th, this note : —

" The Govr. told me of News from Albany, as if the French of Canaday were coming against us. The good Lord stop them ! "

Cotton Mather's diary for 1709 [1] is on the whole not noteworthy. On the 20th of June he makes an entry that is typical of the year : —

" I am so full of employments; and in such a happy way of continually every day doing a variety of services, which yett I do not ask to have remembered, that I have not the Leisure, which else I might have to replenish these memorials."

Little Sam had a fever. Another son, Nathaniel, was born to him on the 16th of May, and died on the 24th of November. I find but two other notes worth recording. In March, Mather was

" assaulted with Solicitations [from Hell] to look upon the whole Christian Religion as — [I dare not mention what !] " but resolved to " Beleeve Him wise and Just and good, and confess myself unable to Judge of His Dispensations, but Refer all unto a Time when He shall please to entertain His people in another world with a Discovery of what He has done and meant in His former Dealings."

At this time Mather was very poor, he remarks, — literally in rags. In September, the other ministers dined with the " Wicked Governor."

[1] In possession of the American Antiquarian Society.

"I," writes Cotton Mather, "have by my provoking plainness and Freedom in telling this Ahab of his wickedness procured myself to be left out of his Invitations. I rejoiced in my Liberty from the Temptations with which they were encumbered while they were eating of his dainties, and durst not reprove him. . . . And considering the power and malice of my enemies, I thought it proper for me to be this day Fasting in Secret before the Lord."

At the end of the diary is a long account of how he is accustomed on rising every morning to enter in a book "Good Devices" for the day: of them we shall hear more by and by. The volume closes, as usual, with notes of the course of his preaching for the year: among which is one telling how when his sermon was three quarters preached his meeting was broken up by a fire, and how when the congregation returned he began afresh and preached a brand-new sermon extempore.

His diary for 1710 is not preserved. Sewall tells a little of what happened to the Mathers. On the 3d of April there was difficulty in finding a minister to preach the election sermon: and though Mr. Pemberton finally agreed to do it, his temper — a very excitable one — was up. So when "word was brought that Dr. Mather was chosen to preach the Artillery Sermon, Mr. Pemberton said Must choose agen." Several notes of Sewall's this year show the infirmity of Pemberton's temper: the divine had an unconfortable way of accosting his parishioner in public places and upbraiding him at the top of his voice.

Towards the end of the year Cotton Mather received from the University of Glasgow the degree of Doctor

of Divinity.   Even in Samuel Mather's lifeless book we
can see how grateful the good man found this honour :
for one thing he immediately began to wear a signet-
ring bearing " a Tree with Psal. 1. 3 [1] written under it ;
and about it *Glascua Rigavit*.[2]   The Cast of his Eye
upon this, constantly provoked him to pray. . . . *O
GOD, make me a very fruitful Tree.*" [3]   But he was not
permitted to enjoy his title unmolested.   One John
Banister wrote thereupon the following verses.

" ON C. MR's. DIPLOMA.

" The mad enthusiast, thirsting after fame,
　By endless volum'ns thought to raise a name.
　With undigested trash he throngs the Press ;
　Thus striving to be greater, he's the less,
　But he, in spite of infamy, writes on,
　And draws new Cullies in to be undone.
　Warm'd with paternal vanity, he trȳs
　For new Subscriptions, while the Embryo [his two vol-
　　umns] [4] lyes
　Neglected — Parkhurst [5] says, *Satis fecisti*,
　My belly's full of your Magnalia Christi.
　Your crude Divinity, and History
　Will not with a censorious age agree.
　Daz'd with the stol'n title of his Sire,[6]
　To be a Doctor he is all on fire ;

　[1] " And he shall be like a tree planted by the rivers of water,
that bringeth forth his fruit in his season ; his leaf also shall not
wither ; and whatsoever he doeth shall prosper."
　[2] Glasgow has watered it.
　[3] See S. Mather's Life, pp. 74–77.　　[4] Biblia Americana.
　[5] The publisher of the　Magnalia.
　[6] Increase Mather, it will be remembered, was made Doctor
of Divinity under the Harvard charter of 1692, subsequently disapproved by the King.   See pages 135–137.

Would after him the Sacrilege commit
But that the Keeper's [Leverett], care doth him affright.
To Britain's Northern Clime in haste he sends,
And begs an Independent boon from Presbyterian friends;
Rather than be without, he'd beg it of the Fiends.
Facetious George brought him this Libertie
To write C. Mather first and then D. D." [1]

On the 25th of November Increase Mather laid this libel before Sewall. On the 28th, Sewall had Banister and others before him in consequence, and, in spite of a letter from Cotton Mather in favor of Banister, imposed a fine on him. This greatly stirred up Mr. Pemberton, who had lately been abused by a certain Captain Martin, against whom no proceedings had been taken.

"Mr. Pemberton," writes Sewall, "with extraordinary Vehemency said, (capering with his feet) If the Mathers ordered it, I would shoot him thorow. I told him he was in a passion. He said he was not in a Passion. I said, it was so much the worse. . . . The truth is I was surpris'd to see my self insulted with such extraordinary Fierceness, by my Pastor, just when I had been vindicating two worthy Embassadors of Christ (his own usual Phrase) from most villanous Libels. . . . These Things made me pray Earnestly . . . that God would vouchsafe to be my Shepherd, and . . . bring me safely to his Heavenly Fold."

And the same evening Sewall visited Madam Pemberton, and gave the nurse three shillings; which did not prevent Mr. Pemberton from giving out next Lord's day a most invidious psalm.[2]

[1] Sewall's Letter-Book, I. 407. Cf. Diary, II. 290–295.
[2] For all this matter, see Sewall's Diary, II. 290–295.

The only other note of Sewall's I have recorded for this year runs as follows : —

"Mid-week, Jany. 31. Went and heard Mr. Bridge, and Dr. Cotton Mather pray and preach, at the said Dr's House. . . . Dr. Mathers [text was] The whole world lyes in Wickedness. Had Cake and Butter and Cheese, with good Drinks, before parting."

In Sewall's diary for 1711, I find little that concerns us. The Mathers were as busy as ever. On the 31st of May, Mr. Wadsworth gave a dinner for the Governor, to which he invited both the Mathers : and both came, — a fact which throws a little fresh light on Cotton Mather's secret fast in September, 1709.[1]

Cotton Mather's diary for 1711[2] is different from all the preceding ones. Those, as I have said, are not the original copies, but abridgements made by himself ; rather annual autobiographies than diaries proper. This volume and the six others that remain are original copies, hastily written from day to day, and little revised. They differ in character from the others, too. Instead of being records of what has happened, they are generally daily entries of good devised for each day, — with the letters "G. D." prefixed. Now and then he inserts a passage that he thinks worth remembering. So we have now, for the years whose records are preserved, a daily note of what he means to do, and occasional notes of what has actually been done. One troublesome fact about the diary for 1711 is that he usually enters there only the days of the week, leav-

[1] See page 231.
[2] In possession of the American Antiquarian Society.

ing the month to be calculated as best it may. The truth seems to be that, about this time, he concluded that he had wasted too much time on the records of his life : there were other things better worth doing.

His birthday note, with which this volume, like all the rest, begins, shows this state of mind. Hereafter he will keep no separate book of good devices : they shall be entered in his regular diary. He had devised a set of questions to ask himself each day : on Sunday, for example, he asked what he should do as a pastor ; on Monday, what he should do for his family ; and so on.

"There is no need of Repeating here," he writes, "The questions assigned for each day of the Week. My answer to each of them will be a Good Devised, for which a G. D. will be the Distinction in these Memorials."

Daily good devices fill the pages of this volume, which is twice as thick as any of the preceding ones. Perhaps his most curious note hereabouts is this : —

"Having some Epistolar Conversation with Mr. De Foe I would in my letters unto him, excite him to apply himself unto the work of collecting and publishing an History of the persecutions which the Dissenters have undergone from the Ch. of E. — And give him some Directions about the work. It may be a work of manifold usefulness."

Somewhat later, curious reflections follow a fit of cholera morbus and a morning cough : the latter moves him to ejaculate, "Oh ! that I may always cast up and throw off, whatever may be inimical to the Health of my Soul !" On the 2d of October there was a great fire in Boston, which aroused proper reflections in Cotton Mather ; and which Increase Mather attributed to the growing profanation of the Sabbath. Later in the same month we find Cotton Mather writing to Sir Richard Blackmore and to Dr. Watts, whose hymns he greatly admired. At intervals through the year he mentions his cousin, Eunice Williams, a captive among the Indians, whose mode of life she ultimately adopted. At Christmas he was greatly disturbed by some young people of both sexes belonging to his flock, who had "a Frolick, a Revelling Feast, and Ball, which discovers their corruption." And a month later he writes : —

"Fast. . . . I took the catalogue of the Books which I have been the Author of. The Number in the Catalogue is Two hundred and five. On each of the Titles I made a pause. And I obliged Every one of them, to suggest unto me some Remarkable Article of Humiliation, which I thereupon with an Abased Soul mentioned before the Lord."

But the most interesting notes this year concern his family. Early in the year he notes a good device not to use his influence against a merchant who has injured him.

"No sooner had I written these words," he goes on, "but there was a pretty occurrence in the Family which carried with it a fine picture and Emblem . . . of the Disposition which I am Endeavoring. My little son Sammy did not carry it so kindly to his little sister Lizzy as I would have had him. I chid him for his crossness, and gave her a piece of *pome-citron*, but would give none to him, to punish him for being so cross to her. I had no sooner turned my back but the good-conditioned creature fell into Tears at this punishment of her little Brother, and gave to him a part of what I had bestowed upon her."

Somewhat later, he writes that his son Increase, now

about twelve years old, is giving him trouble. Later
still, he writes that the time is come for his daughters
to be "fixed" in "the opificial and Beneficial mysteries
wherein they should be well instructed." Katy, he
decides, shall be taught medicine; the inclinations of
Nibby and Nancy shall be consulted before he reaches
a decision about them. Another daughter, Jerusha,
was born this year. But towards the end of the year
Increase is most in his mind.

"My Son Increase," he writes, "now being of Age for
it, I would often call him into my Study, especially on the
Lord's-day Evenings, and make him sitt with me, and hear
from me such Documents of piety, and of Discretion, as I
shall endeavor to suit him, and to shape him withal." A little later : " It may be of excellent consequence to my son
Increase if he may turn into Latin, after the rate of one
Question p. day, my *Supplies from the Tower of David.*
It may also supply me with an Engine, which after my
bestowing further Additions on it, may do inexpressible
good in other Countreys." And his last daily note for the
year runs thus : "G. D. Now my son Increase is arrived
unto the exercise of making Themes, at the School, I would
make this become an Engine of piety for him ; and I
would procure such subjects to be assigned unto him, as
may most assist the study of goodness and virtue in him."

An active, busy year this seems to have been ; less
morbid than most. His final summary of it is perhaps
worth recording : —

"Thus I am come to the end of another year, overwhelmed with confusion, when I look back on the Sin and
Sloth constantly attending me in it. It is true I have been
helped by Heaven this year, To Lett not One Day pass,
without Contriving and Recording, some Inventions to do

Good; And those which have pass'd thro' my pen are but
a few of the projections which I have had: . . . To lett
not One Day pass, without actually expending something of
my Revenues . . . on pious uses: To write some Illustrations for the most part Every Day; doubtless . . . I
have this year added unto the *Biblia Americana* . . . more
than a thousand: To preach many Sermons . . .: To
publish near as many books as there have been Months in
the year: . . . To make many hundreds of Visits; but
never One, without some Explicit Essays or Desires to Do
Good in it: To manage some scores of Correspondencies;
and . . . to propose the Service of my Glorious Lord in
every one of them: . . . To read over many Scores of
Books, and gather into my Quotidiana from them: etc. etc.
etc. But after all, o my dear Saviour, I stand in infinite
need of thy Sacrifice. I have been a most unprofitable
Servant. God be merciful to me a Sinner!"

Mather's diary for 1712 is not preserved. In Sewall's I find nothing especial about him, except that he
went to Commencement. From a note in Quincy,[1] it
appears that a new Catalogue of the College was printed
at this time. Leverett asked Dudley if Mather had
ever apologized for the " undutiful " letter of 1707: if
not, Leverett supposed Cotton Mather's new title had
better not be recognized in the Catalogue. But Dudley told him not to leave out the title on any such
account. And in Harvard Catalogues ever since Cotton
Mather has been Doctor of Divinity. In the Mather
Papers [2] are preserved some of his letters this year to
John and to Wait Winthrop: they show him deeply interested in the European news of the day, which chiefly
concerns the approaching Peace of Utrecht. And Sib-

---

[1] Vol. I. p. 520.   [2] Pages 407–415.

ley names fifteen books published by Cotton Mather during the year.

So we come to his diary for 1713,[1] an eventful year in Cotton Mather's domestic life. At the very beginning of the year, we find him in much disturbance of mind because some of his flock had been inspired by Satan with the idea of starting a new meeting. He did his best to reason with them, but to little purpose. And towards the middle of March he writes : —

"I ought to . . . grow in my Thankfulness to the glorious Lord, in that I have my mind preserved from Hypochondriac Maladies, which, considering my Studies and Sorrowes, tis a wonder, they have not utterly overwhelmed me. The view I have of some other men, unhinged and ruined that way, very much awakens my gratitude."

One of the other men in question was probably the Rev. Ebenezer Pemberton. But a note on the 24th of March shows trials nearer home : —

"Still my aged parent must be the object of my cares ; To make him easy under his Resentments of the proceedings about the New Church; and to procure him Releefs against Bodily Distempers that somewhat incommode him ; and to gett his mind raised unto the points of Resignation to God and Satisfaction in His Will, which become us in the Suburbs of the Heavenly World." — "God calls me," he writes a few days later, "in an extraordinary manner to be armed for the Trials which I may undergo in a church, breaking all to peeces, thro' the Impertinencies of a proud crew, that must have pues for their despicable Families."

So he prayed and fasted, and had his son Increase

---

[1] In possession of the American Antiquarian Society.

come in and pray too.   Not long afterwards he realized that he was growing too impatient of slights, and
resolved to govern his temper.

In April he was still in high excitement.

"There is one point in my Conversation," he writes,
early in the month, "wherein I must press after much
greater Sanctity and purity; and have my Behaviour in it
more governed by that Reflexion, *The Eye of the Great
God is now upon me!* . . . And I must go mourning to
my grave, in the sense of the miscarriages, in this point,
wherewith His Holy Eyes have seen me chargeable."

A little later comes the vigil in which he begged to
know the meaning of the descent from the invisible
world so many years before.[1]

Education is the next thing in his mind.   Increase,
it is clear, must be "applied unto Saecular Business,"
and he must cry to Heaven thereabout.   The tutors at
the College must be reminded that they ought to "in-
still good principles into their pupils, and be concerned
for their Orthodox and Religious, as well as Learned
education."   And a little later, he notes that he has
"litt on a person" to restrain "profaneness in a considerable number of Unruly children on the Lord's day
in our Congregation."   About this time returned the
hypochondriac notion that he was near his end, which
often assailed him; he must select guardians for his
children.   A little later, he determined to write physicians "to obtain for me, as much as may be, of the
knowledge of the Botanicks of the countrey: as also of
rare cures or cases occurring to them."   And a little
later still comes this: —

[1] See page 123.

"My poor son *Increase!* Oh! the Distress of mind with which I must lett fall my daily Admonitions upon him, even with a continual Dropping, especially on these Two points : Conversion to God, in a Sincere compliance with His Covenant: And, The Care of Spending Time so as to give a good Account of it."

Then the new church troubled him again : —

"When any persons . . . fall into errors and evils, and great miscarriages, I must keep a guard of meekness and wisdom on the expression of my zeal. . . . Violent, Boisterous, Intemperate Expressions . . . will not work the Righteousness of God. I am afraid lest I am sometimes too vehement." In answer to this resolution the Lord helped him to treat "the swarming Brethren" in an obliging manner, — "the best thing I can do to prevent the wiles of Satan." A few days later, "in a wicked book I readd a fling at clergymen, as a Revengeful generation of men, who never Forgive such as have offended them. I do not remember, for my own part, that ever I designed the Revenge of an Injury in my life. However, this Venemous Fling, shall quicken my Watchfulness, upon this Article."

Within a few days he had a chance to quicken it : —

"G. D. There are Knotts of Riotous Young Men in the Town. On purpose to insult piety they will come under my Window in the middle of the Night and sing profane and filthy Songs. The last night they did so, and fell upon people with clubs taken off my wood-pile. Tis high-time, to call in the help of the Government . . . for the . . . suppressing of these disorders."

On the 1st of July, he took his son Increase to Commencement.[1] On the 4th, he held a vigil for the

---

[1] Sewall's Diary, II. 390.

" Impurities which my life has been filled withal. . . .
From the Depths I cried unto the Lord, for his grace to be
given unto my children: particularly my son Increase."

The youth, now about fourteen, was beginning to
show himself what he ultimately proved, — a sadly
riotous young man. And this may have been what
prompted another good device, a few weeks later.

" I have shown too much Respect unto Wicked Men in
my Conversation. . . . Though my Intention has been to
show all Gentleness to all men . . . yett I doubt, less Freedom with such Wretches, less Familiarity with such Devils,
would have been better."

So the year goes on, his family more and more on
his mind. On the birthdays of his children, he resolves, he will

" not only discourse very proper and pungent things . . .
relating to their eternal Interests, but also oblige them to
consider; first, *what is their main Errand into the World;*
and then, *what they have done of that Errand.* And such
of them as are old enough to Write, shall give me some
Written Thoughts upon these things."

His negro servant was best governed by reason : he
would assay to reason him into good behaviour.[1] His
" aged parent " — the phrase by which he names his
father from this time on — was out of order.

" I would persuade him to a frequent use of the *sal vola-
tile,* which God has blessed unto me for more than ordi-

[1] In the library of the American Antiquarian Society is an interesting memorandum of the conditions on which, a little later,
this negro, Onesimus, bought his freedom. He was to see that
his place was properly supplied, and to turn up every day
accordingly.

nary Benefit, and I would prevent him with a Bottle of it."
And when the remedy worked, he resolved "mightily to
double my diligence, especially in Afternoon-Studies, for
the Dispatch of those things I would fain finish before
I Dy."

Meanwhile Increase was always on his mind: one
day he made him read the life of a pious youth; again,
while seeking a place for him, he would have him
"preserve learning," and would daily inquire if he has
made secret prayers; a little later, when the youth had
blown up himself and his sister Lizzy with gunpowder,

"I would improve this occasion to inculcate Instructions
of piety in them and the rest; Especially with Relation to
their Danger of Eternal Burnings. Cressy [1] must also
employ the leisure which this had occasioned for him, in the
most profitable manner": there had been lately an opportunity "to gett . . . Increase cultivated with many points
of polite conversation, in his Evening-Hours." Another
note runs thus: "Oh! Why don't I in my Family more
livelily keep up the Temper and Conduct of a parent expecting to be Speedily taken from his Family?" Another
still: "My youngest little daughter [2] is a marvellous
Witty, Ready, Forward Child": he would set the others
to teaching her maxims of piety. Towards the end of
September, the death of an "aged and pious Matron (the
First-born of this Town) . . . affords me an opportunity to
discourse with my mother, upon her preparation."

A little later, he was trying to get Increase a place
with a religious merchant, in good business; and
selecting guardians for his children; and praying to
the Lord that He would return to them what their
father had spent in charity.

---

[1] Increase.   [2] Jerusha, born in 1711.

I find but three other notes before October worth recording. The first runs thus : —

"G. D. Perhaps by sending some Agreeable Things to the Author of the *Spectator*, and the *Guardian*, there may be brought forward some Services to the best Interests of the Nation."

The second expresses an intention to help an old man in the town, eighty-eight years old and needy, "who was a souldier in the Army of my admirable *Cromwel*, and actually present in the Battel of *Dunbar*." The third is a resolution to counteract the corruption spread by "filthy ballads," by having cheap hymns hawked about, — "some from the excellent Watts."

The rest of his story for this year is more notable in his personal history.

"12d. 8m.[1] This Day, in Ships arriving from London, I receive Letters from the Secretary of the Royal Society, who tells me, That my *Curiosa Americana* being Readd before that Society, they were greatly Satisfied therewith, and ordered the Thanks of the Society to be returned unto me ; They also Signified their Desire and purpose to Admitt me as a Member of their Body. And, he assures me, that at their first lawful Meeting for such purposes, I shall be made a A FELLOW OF THE ROYAL SOCIETY. . . . This is a marvellous Favour of Heaven ; . . . One that will much Encourage me . . . in my Essayes to Do Good : and add unto the Superiour Circumstances, wherein my Gracious Lord places me above the Contempt of Envious Men." So he cried to the Lord hereby to quicken his "Diligence in His Holy Service "; and resolved to improve his " Correspondence with the Secretary of the *Royal Society*, to sett

[1] October 12th.

afoot among the members thereof, such studies as may be for general Benefit, and have hitherto been but little prosecuted."

In less than a week he writes : —

"A very deep storm . . . my family may expect in the common calamity of the spreading Measles."

Increase fell ill on the 18th : on the 30th, Katy and Nibby came down. The same day Mrs. Mather was brought to bed of twins, — a boy and a girl.

"The Glorious God," he writes, "in the Surprising Increase of my Family, rebukes my sinful Fears of having them all well-provided for. Thro' the Assistance of his Grace, I find my Soul rejoicing in the View of my having in my Family more Servants born unto my Saviour. . . . I must march against the least Tendencies of Unbelief."

On the 1st of November the twins were baptized : the girl was named for her maternal grandmother, Martha, which

"signifying Doctrix may the better suit (as my Father said) a Doctor's Daughter. I then thought, who was *Martha's* brother ; and that *Eleazar* was the same with Lazarus ; and a priestly name ; and the child must be led to look for the *Help of God*, which is the signification of the Name. I also had an excellent uncle of that Name.[1] So I called them ELEAZAR and MARTHA."

In three days measles had attacked his wife, Nancy, Lizzy, Jerusha, and the maid.

"8. 9.[2] This Day, I entertained my Neighbourhood with a Discourse on Joh. xviii. 11. : *The cup which my Father has given me, shall not I drink it*. And lo, this Day, my Father is giving me a grievous and Bitter Cup, which I hop'd had pass'd from me. . . . When I saw my

---

[1] See page 25.   [2] November 8th.

consort safely delivered, and very easy, and the Measles appearing with favourable symptoms upon her . . . I flattered myself that my Fear was all over. But this Day we are astonished at the surprising symptoms of Death upon her; after an Extreme want of Rest by Sleep, for Diverse whole Dayes and Nights together. — To part with so desirable . . . a companion — A Dam from such a Nest of young ones too ! — . . . Tho' my dear Consort had been so long without sleep, yett she retained her understanding. I used my opportunities as well as I could, . . . with Discourses that night . . . to prepare her for what was now before us. It comforted her to see, that her children in Law, were as fond of her, as her own could be ! God made her willing to Dy. . . . I prayed with her many Times, and left nothing undone, that I could . . . do for her consolation. On Monday, 9d. 9m., between three and four in the Afternoon, my dear, dear, dear Friend expired. — Whereupon, with another prayer in that Melancholy Chamber, I endeavoured the Resignation to which I am now called. . . . It comforts me to see how extremely Beloved and Lamented a Gentlewoman I now find her to be in the Neighbourhood."

" 10. 9. In the midst of my Sorrowes . . . the Lord helped me to prepare no less than Two Sermons, for a public Thanksgiving, which is to be celebrated the day after tomorrow."

" 11. 9. This day, I interred the Earthly part of my dear Consort. She had an Honourable Funeral."

And Sewall tells us that among her bearers were Pemberton and Colman.

" 14. 9. This morning, the first thing that entertains me, after my Rising, is, the Death of my Maid-Servant. . . . Tis a satisfaction to me, that tho' she had been a Wild, Vain, Airy Girl, yett since her coming into my Family, she became disposed unto serious Religion : . . . and my poor

Instructions were the means that God blessed for such happy purposes."

Next day Jerusha and the twins lay dying; Eleazar died at midnight on the 17th, Martha on the morning of the 20th.

"21. 9. This Day I attended the Funeral of my Two — Eleazar and Martha. Betwixt 9 and 10 at night, my lovely Jerusha expired. She was Two years, and about Seven Months, old. Just before she died, she asked me to pray with her; which I did, with a Distressed, but Resigning Soul; And I gave her up unto the Lord. The minute that she died, she said, *That she would go to Jesus Christ.* She had lain speechless, many Hours. But in her last Moments, her speech returned a little to her. Lord, I am oppressed: undertake for me!"

"23. 9. This Day, I followed my dear Jerusha to the grave. But having a mind, full of Resignation, with Resolutions more than ever to glorify my dear Saviour; especially in what I may do for my own, and other children."

There were none in his family now, he remarked, under seven years old. Much might be done at table, then, for both their manners and their minds. A little later,

"The Quiet and Easy and unhurried Condition which my Family (by sad things) is bro't unto, gives me now Opportunity to examine more Distinctly my children every night."

Along with religious books, he wrote and published a letter on the "Right Management of the Sick under the Distemper of the Measles."

Cressy was much on his mind: the boy must study fencing, music, geometry, navigation; "his genius stands much that way."

" My two Younger Children,[1] shall before the psalm and prayer, answer a Quæstion in the catechism ; and have their Leaves ready turned unto the proofs of the Answer in the Bible ; which they shall distinctly read unto us, and show what they prove.   This also will supply a fresh matter for the prayer that is to follow."

Late in January he wrote to a gentleman in Connecticut, urging him first to be good, and then to do good : by which it seems probable that he meant give money to the College that was soon to be called Yale. And his last note for the year runs thus : —

"I must in the Society for pure purposes, bring on an Enquiry, what may be done for the suppression of some very wicked Houses, that are the nests of much Impiety. I must also assist the Booksellers in Addressing the Assembly, that their late Act Against pedlers, may not hinder their Hawkers from carrying Books of piety about the countrey. . . . And thus, the goodness, and mercy, of the glorious Lord, has brought me to the end of another year. The Fifty-first year of my age is terminated."

[1] Elizabeth and Samuel, the latter just seven years old.

XII

COTTON MATHER'S PRIVATE LIFE. — HIS THIRD MARRIAGE

1713–1718

THE history of Massachusetts for the next five years has little to do with our story. In brief what happened was this. In 1714, Queen Anne died; and on the 22d of September, George I was proclaimed at Boston. The commission of Joseph Dudley expired six months after the death of the sovereign. Sewall's Diary[1] shows how reluctantly the first of the Tories relinquished power; but relinquish he had to at last, and retired to private life at Roxbury for the rest of his days. Next year, a certain Colonel Burgess was appointed Governor: he was unwelcome to the Province, whose agents paid him a round sum to decline the office. Lieutenant Governor Tailer was at the head of affairs until 1716. On October 4th, Samuel Shute, the new Governor, arrived in Boston. The next two years passed in various misunderstandings with the legislature, about which we need not trouble ourselves.

Our business in this chapter is to follow Cotton Mather's life to the close of 1718.

Cotton Mather's Diary for 1714 is not preserved; but in the Mather Papers are several of his letters to the Winthrops during that year. They show him inter-

[1] Vol. III. pp. 35–39.

ested in scientific and public matters. And one of
them, of the 2d of March, contains a passage worth
quoting. For it shows that after all he might have
been no bad contributor to the " Spectator " : he was
not insensible to the literary style of the new century.[1]

" There has been much Talk," it runs,[2] "about a Duel
fought between the Duke *Hamilton*, and the Lord *Mohun*.
. . . The former finding himself mortally wounded, made
it an opportunity to thrust his Sword up to the Hilt in the
unguarded body of the other. So both perished. . . .— I
am now on a New side of the leaf, and so may take the
Liberty to divert you with a short story ; which therefore
will not necessarily belong to anything in the t'other page.
You knew old Major *Thompson*. He had a story, that
a young Nobleman, travelling with his Tutor, visited a
church in *Italy*, and viewing the Epitaphs, ask'd his Tutor
to read one of them, which was not very legible. He read
ποπυλοκολοθροπον [a word, whereof I am not learned enough
to know the Etymology]. The Nobleman enquired what
the English of it ? And the Tutor answered, *The World
is well rid of a Knave*. And so my old Major, was used,
when he heard of the Death of certain persons, only to Lift
up his hands, and say *Populokolothropon*. And others
also, would quere Major *Thompson's* Greek, as they called
it, on such occasions."

Sewall's Diary gives us a few more facts for this year.
On the 4th of April, Mrs. Increase Mather died after
fifty-two years of wedded life. One of her son's sixteen publications for this year was her funeral sermon.

[1] His "Political Fables " of 1692–3, reprinted in the "Andros
Tracts," are another example of his lighter literary touch.

[2] Mather Papers, 416. Lovers of " Henry Esmond " will find
this talk interesting.

Before very long, the venerable widower married the widow of her nephew, John Cotton, of Hampton : she survived him. On the 20th of October, the "swarming brethren" gathered in their New North Church, founded by "seventeen substantial mechanics"; and Increase Mather gave the charge, and Cotton Mather the right hand of fellowship, Pemberton joining them in laying on their hands. On the 24th of November, "a very cold day," one Mr. George, a merchant of Boston, was laid in Sewall's tomb, "till Madam George have an oportunity to build one." Whether he was the "facetious George" who brought over Cotton Mather's diploma in 1710,[1] I know not : but of the widow we shall hear more. And on the 23d of December,

"Dr. C. Mather preaches excellently from Ps. 37. Trust in the Lord, etc. only spake of the Sun being in the center of our System. I think it inconvenient to assert such problems."

Sewall's Diary for 1715 gives a few glimpses of the Mathers. Early in the year, they were much interested in the discussions about Dudley's tenure of office, which was fast drawing to a close. On the 13th of April, they enjoyed a singular satisfaction : the Governor, on the verge of enforced retirement, dined with the ministers ; and, as had happened at his first official feast in Boston,[2] Increase Mather craved a blessing, and Cotton Mather gave thanks. On the 2d of August there was a fast at Mr. Colman's about calling another minister ; when in the afternoon

---

[1] See page 233.   [2] See page 191.

"Mr. Pemberton pray'd, Dr. Cotton Mather preach'd from Isa. 5. 6. latter clause, I will command the clouds, etc.[1] Excellently: censur'd him that had reproach'd the Ministry; . . . call'd it a Satanick insult, twice over, and it found a kind Reception. . . . I could wish the extremity of the censure had been forborn — Lest we be devoured one of another."

A fortnight later, Mr. Pemberton vexed his parishioner by appearing in a "Flaxen Wigg." On the 26th of September, Mr. Bridge died, — apparently the most cordial ally of the Mathers in the Boston ministry.

"With him," writes Sewall, "much primitive Christianity is gone. . . . His Prayers and Sermons were many times Excellent; not always alike. It may be this Lethargick Malady might though unseen, be the cause of some Unevenness. . . . We may justly fear he is taken away from Evil to Come. Isa. 57."

For about this time trouble in England was expected. But a few days later came welcome news that all tumults were quelled; with which on the 7th of October Sewall visited "utrumque Doctorem."[2]

Cotton Mather's Diary for 1715 is not preserved. But in the collection of the American Antiquarian Society are three long memoranda in his handwriting which bear this date. The first is a copy of a letter to a lady, not named; the following extract will give a notion of its general character: —

"If he [who now addresses you] be One who Looks

1 "And I will lay it waste; it shall not be pruned, nor digged; but there shall come up briers and thorns: I will also command the clouds that they rain no rain upon it."

2 "Both doctors"; that is, the Mathers.

upon Love to his Neighbour, as a very essential Article of his Religion, and who so Loves every man, that the offer of an opportunity for the doing of Good unto any One, is the sweetest pleasure that can be given him, . . . it will be very Reasonably Inferred from hence, that the Gentlewoman who comes one day into the nearest Relation unto him, will be Lov'd by him, as much as can be wish'd by her." And he waxes warm about "Your bright Accomplishments, your shining piety, and your polite education, your superiour Capacity, and a most refined Sense, and incomparable Sweetness of Temper, together with a Constellation of all the perfections that he can desire to see related unto him."

This letter is very long indeed; the second memorandum is short enough to be quoted in full: —

"21d. 1m.[1] 1715. In the Evening. — After some Words of decent Respect unto Mrs. G. — She said, she had thought fitt, to have one Interview alone with me, that I might fully know her mind, about the Matter I had proposed unto her. She remonstrated the Reproach that she had suffered in the Talk of people about that affair; and therefore she thought it time, to lett me know her Desire, that she might hear no more of it, and that I would Speak and Think no more of it. She said, There were other persons that would be more agreeable to me; and in whom the prayers of many good people for me, would be more likely to be answered. She gave me to understand, That if it were not for a Regard she had unto my Character as a Minister, she should forbid my ever making any more Visits unto her. She said, My Visits would have been a consolation and satisfaction unto her if I had mentioned nothing of this affair: But she peremptorily forbad my Writing any more Letters unto her. She many times insisted on it, That I would say to all persons, As for the

[1] March 21st.

Matter talk'd of, there is nothing in it. I offered that I would say to All persons, Tis a Matter which Madam is not at present disposed to hear of. She then said: — But people will say, Why does she Entertain him ? — if she have no purpose hereafter to allow of his Intentions ? — This she express'd herself desirous, that there should be no Occasion for. I represented unto her, some fatal consequences, likely to follow on this conduct. But she would not admitt any Apprehensions of them. The Conversation lasted for several Hours. On my part, it was as Calm, and as pertinent, and as obliging as my dull Witts could render it. With as full Answers as could be made unto the Things that were objected to me; and just Reasons for every step of my conduct. At last I said; *Madam, To give you a full Testimony of my Honour and Esteem for you, My Satisfaction shall be entirely sacrificed unto Yours.* She answered: *Say and Hold.*"

The third memorandum is a copy of a very long letter to the Rev. Thomas Craighead, who had proposed that the pair have another interview. Mather thinks it undesirable for the moment, but begs Craighead

"to assure that excellent person, that my Resolutions to keep out of Sight . . . oppress my own mind with Violence, which could be well borne, by none but One of my Age, and one so much used unto Sacrifices. . . . She may depend upon it, (tho', I know not, whether a Total Deliverance from me, would not make her yett more easy,) that I can by no means lay aside these Vast Respects. But must renew my endeavours one day to make her yett more sensible of them. However, to be free with you, I have strong Apprehensions that my Dying Hour will Intervene (which, Oh! join with me in my praises to our dear Saviour for it,) I often even long for, and hope it will be the best Hour that ever I saw."

Who Mrs. G. was must remain a conjecture. But the following passage from Samuel Mather's book[1] is suggestive : —

" In his *fifty-third* year, July 5. 1715. he was married to his *third* Wife. She is the Daughter of the renowned and very learned Mr. SAMUEL LEE: She was the Widow of Mr. GEORGE, a worthy Merchant, when Dr. MATHER pay'd his Respects unto her in order to be Marry'd. She is a Lady of many and great Accomplishments, and is the *Doctor's* disconsolate Widow.[2] By this last Gentlewoman he had *no* issue."

Cotton Mather's Diary for 1716[3] begins with a birthday fast, in which his most remarkable petitions were for

"the Good State of my Family; the Welfare of my Son abroad; the Rescue of my Daughter-in-Law from her unhappy Circumstances; the comfortable Disposal of my Daughters in the Married Life."

And amid such daily notes of good devised as fill his other diaries are occasional memoranda concerning his family affairs. Early in March he held a very ecstatic thanksgiving, in which, among other things, he writes,

" I celebrated the Favours of Heaven to my Family, especially in the Excellent Mother that He has bestowed upon it."

A marginal note, evidently made later, throws painful light upon this: "Ah! Quam deceptus."[4] A glimpse of the beginning of his undeception comes in the middle of April: —

---

[1] Life, p. 13.
[2] Samuel Mather wrote in 1729.
[3] In the Library of the Congregational House, Boston.
[4] "How I was deceived!"

"My Religious and Excellent Consort meets with some Exercises, which oblige me, (and, oh! how happy am I, in the conversation of so fine a Soul, and one so capable of soaring to the higher Flights of piety!) To treat her very much on the point of having a Soul, wherein God alone shall be enthroned, and all the Creatures that usurped his Throne Ejected."

Sammy at this time was ill of a fever; and Increase, the subject of constant prayers and letters, was off on a voyage.

Early in May, however, an edifying incident occurred.

"A Wondrous Thing is come to pass," he writes on the 6th. "My Consort's only Daughter has had an Husband, who has proved one of the Worst of men; a sorry, sordid, froward, and exceedingly wicked Fellow. His Life would have kill'd the Child: and have utterly confounded, not only her Temporal Interest, but my Wife's also. I was a Witness of their Anguish, And almost a year ago, I began to have some Irradiations on my mind, which I communicated unto them, that before a year came about, they should see a Deliverance. However, I could not bring about my purposes, to beseech the Lord Thrice until towards the Beginning of the Winter. But then, I kept *Three dayes of prayer*, in every one of which, a principal errand unto Heaven was, to putt over this Wicked Creature into the Hands of the Holy God, that in His Way, and in His Time, the poor child might be delivered from his Insupportable Tyrannies. But above all, that it might be by his becoming a New Creature, if that might be obtained. The Supplications were made on these, and on other Dayes, with a proper spirit of Charity towards the miserable Man, and with all possible Resignation to the Will of God. And my excellent Consort often went up with me to my Library, to make a Consort in them. Well: I had no sooner kept my

Third Day but God smote the Wretch, with a Languishing Sickness, which no body ever knew what to make of.
He was a Strong, Lively, Hearty Young Man; a Little
above Thirty: But now, he Languished for *Six Months;*
nor were any of the physicians tho' he successively employ'd no less than five of them, able to help him. In this
while, our Faith, our Love, our patience, and our Submission to the Will of God, underwent many Trials more
precious than Gold. But on the last *Wednesday*, the Glorious God putt a period unto the grievous Wayes of this
Wicked Man. — Now what remains, is for me to make a
very holy Improvement of these Dispensations. . . . *"O
my God, I will call upon thee, as long as I live !"*

The gentleman whose death is thus narrated was
named Howell. Cotton Mather was made adminis-
trator of his estate. Resulting complications, such as
often attend the efforts of unpractised people to
manage money matters, made him uncomfortable for
years.

It was during this same month of May that Katharine Mather's consumptive symptoms became alarm-
ing. And Katharine was very dear to her father: she
"understood *Latin*, and read *Hebrew* fluently."[1] But
other matters were less depressing. On the 22d, Cotton
Mather writes : —

"This Day my son Increase returns to me: much pol-
ished, much improved, better than ever Disposed, with
Articles of less Expense to me than I expected: And,
which is wonderful, with an excellent Business prepared
for him immediately to fall into. I am astonished at the
Favours of the prayer-hearing Lord. Oh my Father, my
Father, how good a thing it is to trust in thy Fatherly

[1] S. Mather, Life, p. 14.

17

Care ! — But Oh !   What shall I now do to fix the returned
Child for the Service of God ! "

A week later, discovering that Samuel had many play
days, he had the happy thought of occupying the youth
in turning into Latin some sentences about "the true
and right Intent of play, and a good use of it."

June found Katharine worse ; and Increase in evident need of " Proper Books, to employ him in the
Intervals of Business . . . and furnish his mind with
valuable Treasures." The elder Increase Mather, too,
was ailing.

" My parent just finishing seventy-seven," writes Cotton
Mather, " I must now more than ever treat him, as one
taking Wing immediately for the Heavenly World."

Harvard College, too, was employing far too much
time in " *Ethicks* . . . a vile piece of paganism."   But
although his troubles were enhanced by the fact that
Nibby fell ill of an ague, he had the satisfaction of
accepting for her the proposals of a " hopeful young
Gentleman, a merchant," whose intimacy with the
Mathers had " brought him into a Business, which is
likely to prove Superiour unto what any young Man in
the Country pretends unto."   So " that it may be to
his Advantage, in regard to his Better part," Cotton
Mather immediately began to administer to him " continual Admonitions and Inculcations of piety."   And
mid-July found the good man in a thankful mood : —

" Except it be the Sickness of my Two Elder Daughters,
I enjoy upon all accounts a most wonderful prosperity.
A most wonderful prosperity ! A valuable Consort ! A
comfortable Dwelling ! A kind Neighbourhood. My son
Increase, vastly to my mind — and Blessings without Num-

ber. Together with my own Health and Strength, strongly recruited. I must be solicitous to hear what the Holy One speaks to me in my prosperity."

On the 14th of August, an accident happened to him, which Sewall briefly notes with the remark that he " received no hurt." But Cotton Mather took it seriously.

" This day," he writes, " a Singular Thing befel me. My God, Help me to understand the meaning of it! I was prevailed withal, to do a thing, which I very rarely do; (not once in years.) I rode abroad with some Gentlemen, and Gentlewomen, to take the Country Air, and to divert ourselves, at a famous Fish-pond. In the Canoe, on the pond, my foot slipt, and I fell overboard into the pond. Had the Vessel been a little further from the Shore, I must have been drown'd. But I soon recovered the Shore, and going speedily into a Warm Bed, I received no sensible Harm. I returned well in the Evening ; sollicitous to make all the Reflections of piety, on my Disaster, and on my Deliverance. But not yett able to penetrate into the Whole meaning of the occurrence. Am I quickly to go under the earth, as I have been under the Water ! — My Consort had her mind, all the former part of the day, and the day before, full of Uneasy Impressions, that this little Journey, would have mischief attending it."

The state of things in September is expressed by his note for the 18th : —

" Of my Two Elder Daughters, The one I am giving up to God, and preparing for the Finishing Stroke of the Sacrifice, which the Death of the dear creature puts me upon. . . . The other, I am giving away to an hopeful young Gentleman, who is tomorrow to become her Husband."

Next day Abigail was married to Mr. Daniel Willard.

But Katharine grew steadily worse. Her temper, however, was serene.

" Death is become Easy," he writes, " yea, pleasant unto her: she rather chuses it, and has a contempt for this World, and a most satisfying Vision of the Heavenly World. It is very Strange to me ; The child feels herself a dying: but has a strong and bright persuasion of her own Recovery. I have none. I expect the Speedy approaches of Death upon her. — I sett apart this Day, for prayer with Fasting in Secret, on the behalf of the Dying Child. And it was a Day of Inexpressible Enjoyments unto me. I obtained pardon for all the Sins, that may have had a share in procuring my present Sorrows. I resigned the Child unto the Lord: My Will was extinguished. I could say *My Father, kill my Child, if it be thy pleasure to do so.* But yett I interceded, that if it might be so, the cup of Death might pass from me."

Through October she grew gradually worse. But Cotton Mather was gladdened by the arrival of Governor Shute.

" Our New Governour," he writes on the 25th, " appears to have a Singular Goodness of Temper, with a Disposition to Do Good, Reigning in Him : He also favours me with singular Testimonies of Regard. Oh ! Let me improve these unexpected opportunities to do good, in such a manner that God may have much Glory, and His people much Service from it."

In November there was little new. Displeased with some proceedings in the House of Representatives, he sent for the members to visit him at his house.

" I would endeavour," he writes, " their Illumination in the things of our peace. I would also Endeavour to reduce our own Frowards from the Error of their way."

The administration of the Howell estate, too, looked as if it were drawing to a close; and he determined to propose to his wife

"what special Service for God and His Kingdome she will do, in case the Administration be well finished, and she find any Estate remaining, that may render her Capable of doing anything."

But the most remarkable thing that happened this month was the merciless blotting, with a madly scrawling pen, of two long passages of Good Devised.

"I could never learn," he writes in the margin, "How or Why these Blotts were made."

Two years later he discovered.

Meanwhile Katharine had been steadily ailing. On the 16th of December came the end : —

"A little before 3h. A. M. My Lovely Daughter Katharine expired gloriously. The Things which her dear Saviour has done to her and for her, Afford a Wonderful Story. . . . Much of my Time, of Late, has been spent in Sitting by her with Essayes to Strengthen her in her Agonies, wherein God graciously assisted me. . . . I have been for many months a dying in my feeling the dying circumstances of my lovely *Katy*. And now, this Last Night, she is actually Dead : But how triumphantly did she go away ! "

And he made many pious resolutions on this occasion, especially in regard to Creasy, whose conduct worried him again. There was another thing to worry him, too : —

"The Health of my Lovely Consort, who is the greatest of my Temporal Blessings, is a particular matter of concern unto me."

The remaining two months of the year passed quietly.

His son-in-law, Mr. Willard, gratified him by joining the church. And on the 3d of February he could write thus : —

" My Heart is exceedingly affected with my most comfortable and undeserved Enjoyments in my Domestic Circumstances. I can scarce desire to be better off, than I am, upon all accounts. An amiable consort, agreeable Children, most accommodated Habitation, a plentiful Table, The Respects of Kind Neighbours, a flourishing Auditory. — I am even distressed, That I may render unto the Lord, according to the Benefits which I have received from Him. Full of Thoughts, what shall I do in a way of extraordinary Thankfulness and Fruitfulness : Full of cries to Heaven, that I may be Directed, Quickened, Assisted unto a Right Behaviour."

It was during this year 1716 that Cotton Mather reduced to writing the affidavit, officially certified, of how an apparition appeared to Anne Griffin and Ruth Weeden. This admirable ghost-story, very like De Foe's " Mrs. Veal," is printed in the Mather Papers.[1] A note of Sewall's for the 13th of February will fitly close the year : —

" Susan brings word that Mr. Pemberton had a good night. . . . Yet afternoon am sent for to him as aproaching his end. When came was finishing his Will. Then I went in to Him : He call'd me to sit down by him, held me by the hand and spake pertinently to me, though had some difficulty to hear him. Mr. Sewall [2] pray'd fervently, and quickly after he expired, bolstered up in his Bed, about ¾ past 3 after noon in the best Chamber. . . . My Son writ

[1] Pages 421–424.
[2] Joseph, son of the Judge, and Mr. Pemberton's colleague at the Old South.

a Letter to Dr. Cotton Mather to preach for him, and before 'twas superscrib'd, he came in, which took as a Token for good."

Cotton Mather's diary for 1717[1] begins with his remarks about Pemberton : —

"Yesterday in the Afternoon, there died the elder Minister of the Old South Church ; . . . who was eight or nine years younger than myself. He was a Man of greater Abilities than many others; and, no doubt, a pious man; but a man of a strangely Choleric and Envious Temper, and one who had created unto me more Trials of my patience, and more clogs upon my Opportunities to Do Good, than almost any man in the world. The younger minister of that church, a dear son, and One of an Excellent Spirit, should have preach'd this Day; But in his Distress he flies unto me to take his place in the public Services. I cannot easily reckon up the opportunities to Do Good, which I find concurring, in this one Invitation to public performance, on such an Occasion. And the Glorious Lord helped me to glorify Him, in the speaking of many Things to serve the General Interests of Religion, as well as in the Testimony which I gave to what was Laudable in the character of the Departed Minister. Præliminary to my public performance, . . . I humbled myself before the Lord, bewayling all the Distempers which the Ill Carriage of the Deceased Neighbour may at any time have thrown me into, and admiring the Divine Goodness and patience which has given me to outlive so many of my younger Brethren."

The year goes on with no more notable matters than a good devise to " Read a Chapter of Egardus unto my Lovely Consort every morning before we Rise " ; and a troublesome accusation of idolatry, based on the fact

[1] In possession of the American Antiquarian Society.

that he spoke civilly to a ship-carver who had made a figure of St. Michael for the French provinces.

"Our Excellent Governor," he remarks in May, "who has delivered the Country from a Flood of corruption, which was introduced by the selling of places, is to be encouraged."

And on the 3d of July : —

"This Day being the Commencement, as they call it; a Time of much Resort unto Cambridge, and sorrily enough thrown away, I chose to spend this time at home," and to pray that "the Colledge, which is on many accounts in a very Neglected and unhappy condition . . . may be restored unto better circumstances."

But all along come notes that show domestic trouble. His family is much on his mind. Finally, on the 14th of July, he writes thus : —

"Suppose that a child of my Singular Love and Hope should so fall into Sin, and be after wondrous meanes of Recovery so abandoned of God, . . . that there may be terrible cause to fear lest he prove a cast-away ; . . . what should be my Behaviour ?" He must guard himself against rebellion of spirit, adore the divine sovereignty, lament his own sins thus chastised, mourn for the sins of the child, and never give over crying unto the Lord.

"My Son Increase !" he writes on the 23d, "With what plainness, . . . but yett with what prudence must I dispense . . . my Admonitions unto him. I take him into my Library; There I renew my Importunities : I obtain from him expressions of Repentance, and fitt Answers to the Demands of piety. I pray with him there, and make him see I feel my Agonies for him. . . . Methinks I hear the Glorious One saying to me, *Concerning thy Son I hear thee !* "

Other things troubled him, as the months went on : "the Venome and malice " of the "Disaffected Rulers

of our Colledge," for one thing; his daughter Abigail
bore his first grandchild; his consort was ill; Sammy's
education puzzled him. Finally, in the middle of October, he felt that he must

"sett apart Three Days [*Beseech the Lord thrice!*] to extraordinary supplications that [Increase] may not go on in
a course of Impiety."

The same week Sewall gives us another glimpse of
him. Mrs. Sewall was very ill.

" Oct. 17. I asked my wife whether twere best for me to
go to Lecture: She said, I can't tell: so I staid at home.
put up a Note. It being my Son's Lecture, and I absent,
twas taken much notice of. — Oct. 19. Call'd Dr. C. Mather
to pray, which he did excellently in the Dining Room,
having Suggested good Thoughts to my wife before he
went down. . . . About a quarter of an hour past four,
my dear Wife expired. — Oct. 20. I goe to public Worship
forenoon and Afternoon. My Son has much adoe to read
the Note I put up, being overwhelmed with tears."

A week later Cotton Mather preached Mrs. Sewall's
funeral sermon.

Meanwhile he had been filled with unhappy fore-
bodings. A few more notes tell the story.

"[Nov. 5.] The Evil that I greatly feared is come upon
me. I am within these few hours astonished with an Information, that an Harlot big with a Bastard, Accuses my
poor Son Cressy, and Lays her Belly to him. The most
sensible Judges, upon the strictest Enquiry, beleeve the
youth to be Innocent. But yett, oh! the Humiliation! —
Oh! Dreadful Case! O sorrow beyond any that I have
mett withal! What shall I do now for the foolish Youth!
What for my Afflicted and Abased Family! My God,
look mercifully upon me."

" 19.   My God has not heard me. . . . My poor Son
has made a worse Exhibition of himself unto me this day
than I have ever yett mett withal.   Oh my God, what
shall I do!   What shall I do!   I will not yett utterly cast
off the wretched child.   But I will still follow Thee with
supplications for what nothing but an Almighty Arm can
accomplish."

" Dec. 22.   The aspect that some occurrences have upon
me tells me, that I have not sufficiently repented of some
Former Iniquities. . . . My God, help me, help me, to
conform unto Thy Dispensations, and ly in the Dust
before Thee ! "

His wife was ill, too : and though Sammy was the
best boy imaginable, his education was puzzling.   Then
his " transcendently wicked brother-in-law " died, and
he had to console the widow.   February found him a
little more calm, determining to have a cold bath set
up for fever-patients ; and, entreating of his " Discreet
Consort " that she would plainly discover to him any
traits of his that she would have otherwise, he had the
satisfaction to be told of nothing.   For his own part,
he thought himself too touchy, —

"tho' I must be blind indeed if I do not see . . . that
. . . I meet with very odd, absurd, and froward usage from
some of the people."

But perhaps the most permanently notable of his good
devices for the year — he made at least one every day
— was that which he made on the 2d of January.

" What shall I do," he asked himself that morning, "for
the welfare of the Colledge at New-Haven ?   I am inclina-
ble to write unto a wealthy East-India merchant at London,
who may be disposed on Several Accounts, to do for that
Society and Colony."

The College in question had been founded in 1700 :[1] without any endowment to speak of, it had distinguished itself from Harvard by maintaining, in pristine austerity, the Calvinism of the fathers. So the Mathers, and Sewall, and all who felt the old time passing from Massachusetts, looked with growing fondness to New Haven. The letter which Cotton Mather projected on the 2d of January, he wrote on the 18th.[2] It was to Elihu Yale. And among other arguments he urged was this : —

"Sir, though you have your felicities in your family, which I pray God continue and multiply, yet certainly if what is forming at New Haven might wear the name of YALE COLLEGE, it would be better than *a name of sons and daughters*. And your munificence might easily obtain for you such a commemoration."

Yale thought so too : he gave a handsome gift to the College ; and ever since, thanks to Cotton Mather, the greatest nursery of New England priesthood has borne his name.

"Yale College," wrote Cotton Mather to Governor Saltonstall next June, "cannot fail of Mr. Yale's generous and growing bounty. I confess that it was a great and inexcusable presumption in me, to make myself so far the godfather of the beloved infant as to propose a name for it. . . . [But] when the servants of God meet at your Commencement, I make no doubt, that under your Honour's influences and encouragements they will make it an opportunity . . . to deliberate upon projections to serve the great interests of education, and so of religion, . . . and not suffer an interview of your best men to evaporate such a senseless, useless, noisy impertinency as it uses to do with us at Cambridge."

[1] Quincy, I. 197–200; Palfrey, III. 343–345.
[2] Quincy, I. 226–229, 524–527.

How things were going at Cambridge appears from a long note of Sewall's[1] in the following November. At a meeting of the Overseers, to consider an enlargement of the College buildings, Sewall arose and said that there was an affair of greater moment: he understood that exposition of the Scriptures in the Hall had not been carried on; he asked the President "whether 'twere so or no." Leverett was much displeased at Sewall's manner, but admitted the charge. After a hot discussion, Mr. Wadsworth moved that "the president should *as* frequently *as he could* entertain the students with Expositions of the Holy Scriptures."

"I mov'd," writes Sewall, "that *as he could* might be left out; and it was so voted. Mr. President seem'd to say softly, it was not till now the Business of the President to Expound in the Hall. I said I was glad the Overseers had now the Honour of declaring it to be the President's duty."

Next day Leverett repeated his view in private to Sewall.

"I said," writes the sturdy Puritan, "'Twas a shame that a Law should be needed: meaning *ex malis moribus bonae leges.*"[2]

In 1718, too, another matter showed how far the College had strayed from the polity of the fathers. A graduate named Pierpont was refused the Master's degree on the ground that he had contemned and insulted the government of the College. He sued for it at law, with the encouragement of the Mathers. And Cotton Mather wrote a long letter in his behalf to Governor Shute. It was of no avail. The courts held that

---

[1] Diary, III. 202, 203.
[2] "Good laws spring from evil practices."

the matter was wholly within the jurisdiction of the College authorities.[1] And this is why, in 1718, Cotton Mather again and again bewails " the wretched condition of the College."   On the 2d of July,

> "this being the Day of the senseless Diversion they call the Commencement at Cambridge, one of my special errands unto Heaven was to ask Blessings for the Colledge, and the Rescue of it from some wretched circumstances in which it is now languishing."

And now and again he has words of counsel for the "good, wise, generous Governor," who, Sewall tells, "gave occasional balls, and went to a horse-race."

Cotton Mather's diary for 1718[2] contains good devices for every day in the year.   It shows his marvellous activity and restlessness at its highest point.   But what seems nearest to him is the condition of his family.   His aged parent was on his mind more and more; he prayed and struggled for Increase with agonizing efforts to achieve an assurance that after all the boy should be saved; and now and again comes the single cry, "My God!   My God!"   Once he writes,

> "Things appeared unto me, as if the Holy Ghost, were coming forth, to take a terrible Vengeance on me for the sins which my life has been filled withal; yea, and as if my Death being at hand I am to Dy on Ill Terms with Heaven, and have the dreadful portion of the Hypocrites assigned unto me."

There are one or two curious notes, — one showing his feeling toward the mother country he never saw: he will write " home," he plans, about Jacobite troubles.

[1] Quincy, Vol. I. Chap. XI.
[2] In possession of the Massachusetts Historical Society.

And late in the year he projects something he never executed, — an

"Enchiridion of the Liberal Sciences . . . which might enable persons easily to attain them : and at the same time consecrate the whole Erudition unto the Designs of piety."

But throughout the year one feels a growing trouble, and knows not quite what it is. This note, written on the 18th of November, is typical : —

"My Family is in astonishing circumstances. O ! the patience, the prudence, the prayer that is called for. If it were not for my calling of a glorious Christ into my mind continually, and the visits which He graciously makes unto my poor, sinful, sickly soul, what, what would become of me ! I here leave this testimony to you, my children, or whosoever Hands these papers may fall into : That a glorious Christ conversed withal, will be the life of the Soul that has Him dwelling in it."

On the 18th of January the volume suddenly breaks off, with a resolution to read Thomas à Kempis,

"a Book of piety, which tis observable, all Christians of all communions have approved and valued."

A little volume of seven leaves, entitled, " The Conclusion of the LVI. Year,"[1] — preserved quite separately from the rest, — tells the secret.

"21d. xim. 1718. Wednesday," runs the first entry. " My Glorious Lord has inflicted a New and a Sharp Chastisement upon me. The consort in whom I flattered myself with the View and Hope of an Uncommon Enjoyment, has dismally confirmed it unto me, that our *Idols* must prove our *Sorrow*. Now and then, in some of the former years I observed and suffered grievous outbreakings of her

---

[1] In possession of the Massachusetts Historical Society.

proud passions; but I quickly overcame them with my victorious Love, and in the Methods of Meekness and Goodness. And, *O my SAVIOUR, I ascribe unto thee all the glory of it, and I wondrously praise thee for it :* I do not know, that I have to this Day spoke one Impatient or Unbecoming Word unto her; tho' my provocations have been unspeakable; and it may be few men in the World, would have borne them as I have done. But this last Year has been full of her prodigious paroxysms, which have made it a year of such Distresses unto me, as I have never seen in my Life before. When the paroxysms are gone off, she has treated me still with a Fondness, that it may be, few Wives in the World have arrived unto. But in the Return of them (which of late still grow more and more frequent) she has insulted me with such Outrages, that I am at a loss, which I should ascribe them to : Whether a Distraction which may be somewhat Hæreditary,) or to a possession; (whereof the symptoms have been too direful to be mentioned.) In some other papers [1] I leave a more particular Account of these Things. But what I have here to Relate is : That she had expressed such a Venome, against my Reserved Memorials, of experiences in, and projections for, the Kingdom of God, as has obliged me to Lay the Memorials of this year, I thought, where she would not find them. It has been a year wherein I have made more Advances in piety, than in many former years. Perhaps, my Journey thro' the Wilderness just expiring, I must ride more way in one year now than in forty before. . . . For every Day I have noted, my purposes of Service for the Kingdom of God. For fear of what might happen, I have not one disrespectful word of this proud woman, in all the papers. But this week, she has in her Indecent Romaging found them, and she not only detains them from me, but either she has destroy'd them, or she does protest, that I shall never see them any more. I have offered unto her, to blott out with

---

[1] These papers I have not come across.

her pen whatever she would not have to be there. But no loving Entreaties of Mine can prevail upon her to Restore them. Only, she gives me hope of Restoring some time or other, the papers of the Four or Five preceding years, which this ungentlewomanly woman has also stolen. . . . I have Lived for near a year in a continual Anguish of Expectation, that my poor Wife, by exposing her Madness, would bring a Ruine on my Ministry. But now it is Exposed, my Reputation is marvellously preserved among the people of God, and there is come such a General and Violent Blast upon her own, as I cannot but be greatly troubled at. I will now go on."

And go on he does, with good devices for every day until his next birth-day. But the secret was out. His wife was mad; and mad she remained all the rest of his life.

XIII

INOCULATION

1721

THE history of Massachusetts during the ten remaining years of Cotton Mather's life concerns us little. In 1720, Joseph Dudley died, in his last days weak as a child. Amid increasing troubles with the legislature, Shute remained Governor until the death of George I; but during the last years of his office he was in England, and Lieutenant Governor Dummer in charge of affairs at home. There were troubles with Jesuits and Indians in Maine; there were financial difficulties, and disputes about official salaries; there were squabbles about the seizure of timber for the Royal Navy. George II's first Governor was William Burnet, still in office when Cotton Mather died. Our business now is to follow Cotton Mather to his end. In this chapter I shall tell of his life to the end of 1721.

His diaries for 1719 and 1720 are not preserved: nor do I find any record of these years that shows him other than what we have seen. Eternally busy with his preaching, his writing, his reading, his scientific study, his endless projects to do what he thought was good; perplexed with the growing infirmities of his aged parent, with the periodic madness of his wife, with the constant misconduct of Increase, he passed through his fifty-seventh and fifty-eighth years. And in

1721, like loyal sons of Harvard since his time, he sent
Sam to college there, with cordial letters to a President
of whom he heartily disapproved.

His diary for 1721[1] records one of the busiest and
most useful years of his life. The daily notes of good
devices, for all manner of things and people in all parts
of the world, crowd the pages. But month by month
there are notes of other matters. It may perhaps be
best to glance at them month by month.

In March, busy as ever, he felt his family much on
his mind; and one good device is worth remembering:
new accomplishments for Cressy must be paid for, —
"to render him a more finished gentleman [Oh! when,
when shall I say Christian!]" So too is a note that
recalls the death of Howell:[2] a "wicked party" had
been raising trouble in the country, and Cotton Mather
had prayed earnestly against them; this month one of
their leaders was stricken with apoplexy.

"Methinks," writes the lifelong foe of witchcraft, "I see
a wonderful token for Good in this matter; and I go on
with my Humble Supplications to the Lord."

Early in April, Increase was arrested for night-riot
with "some detestable rakes in the Town."

"What, what shall I do!" writes his poor father. "How
shall I glorify my Just, Wise, Dear Saviour on this deplorable occasion. And what is my Duty in relation to the In-
corrigible prodigal." — "I must chase him out of my sight,"
he writes, a few days later, "forbid him to see me, until
there appear sensible marks of repentance upon him.
Nevertheless, I will entreat his Grandfather to take pains

[1] In possession of the Massachusetts Historical Society.
[2] See page 256.

for his Recovery." — " I will write a tremendous letter to my wicked son Increase," comes still later ; . . . "I will tell him that I will never . . . look on him, till the characters of a penitent are very conspicuous in him. . . . Lord, Tho' I am a Dog, yett cast out the Devil that has possession of the Child." — "Ah, poor Increase !" he writes at last, " Tho' I spake against him, yett I earnestly remember him, and my Bowels are troubled for him."

Nor was this the only trouble now : many of his flock were leaving for another church, which vexed him sorely. He comforted himself with this reflection : —

"I shall enjoy a bright conformity to my Saviour, . . . if, just before my Death, I suffer a general withdrawal of my hearers from me."

But old Increase Mather was not so patient : —

" My aged father laies to heart the withdrawal of a vain, proud, foolish people from him in his age."

There is one charming note in May : —

" The Time of the year arrives for the glories of Nature to appear in my Garden. I will take my Walks there, on purpose to read the glories of my Saviour in them."

But that very week there was calamity abroad. His note for the 26th of May is probably the most memorable he ever made. He wrote good devices every day, we must remember. Hundreds of these and thousands came, for all we know, to nothing ; but the one he made this day was of lasting good to humanity : —

"G. D. The grievous Calamity of the Small-pox has now entered the Town. The practice of conveying and suffering the Small-pox by Inoculation has never been used in America, nor indeed in the Nation. But how many lives might be saved by it, if it were practiced.   I will . . . consult our physicians, and lay the matter before them."

The pestilence was very severe : it aroused the best activities of his nature.   Nowhere else in his records does he show himself so free from morbid introspection, so active in self-forgetful altruism, as now.   And in June, he laid before the physicians his suggestion of inoculation.   He had read of it, I believe, in some papers of the Royal Society; and his early training as a physician gave him authority.[1]   But the proposal was startling to many of the learned, and to all the vulgar. "It raised an horrid Clamour."

In July, this clamour was all about him.   Quarrels with his step-children, the Howells, whose estate he had tried to administer, vexed him, at the same time; to meet their claims, he had even to sell some of his clothing.   But what troubled him most was the panic of the plague-stricken town.

"The cursed clamour of a people strangely and fiercely possessed of the Devil will probably prevent my saving the Lives of my Two Children from the Small-pox in the way of Transplantation."   And he prayed, "that God would requite me good for all the cursing of a people that have Satan filling of them; and yett appear, to rescue, and increase my opportunities to Do Good, which the great adversary is now making an Hellish Assault upon."   He was assailed with "wild abuse . . . for nothing but instructing our base physicians, how to save many precious lives"; but at the end of the month he could write thus : "I must

[1] The American Antiquarian Society preserves a large manuscript of Cotton Mather's entitled the "Angel of Bethesda." Valueless to-day, this is said to be a good manual of contemporary medicine.

exceedingly Rejoice in my Conformity to my Admirable Saviour : who was thus, and worse Requited, when he . . . came to save their Souls."

So came August. His son Samuel wished to be inoculated. But if the boy should die, thought the father,

"the people, who have Satan remarkably filling their hearts, . . . will go on with infinite prejudices against me and my ministry. . . . His Grandfather advises, That I keep the whole proceeding private, and that I bring the Lad into this method of Safety. My God, I know not what to do !"

"It is the Hour . . . of Darkness on this Despicable Town," he wrote later; but drew his pen through "Despicable" and wrote "miserable" instead.

In the middle of the month, he yielded to Sam's request, and the lad was inoculated. He sickened so fast and so severely that his father was seized with a dread that perhaps, before the inoculation, the poor boy had already contracted the disorder. And the panic against inoculation rose so that the town became "almost an Hell on Earth." Nancy came down with the pestilence, too ; and as the month went on, both grew worse. Yet in all his agony, and with such execrations about him as even in his troublous life he had hardly heard before, he resolved that he would write to England, urging that they try inoculation there. So, with prayers, and faith amid every doubt, he did his duty : and at the very end of the month came relief. Opening his Bible for comfort, Cotton Mather's eye fell on the words, "Go thy way, Thy Son liveth." And thát very day Sam was bled, and began to mend. Inoculation had triumphed.

In September, both Sam and Nancy were convalescent; but a new trial came. There was an interval of comfort; Cotton Mather preached for the bereaved minister of the New North Church, — the church of the "swarming brethren," — thereby introducing "a more peaceable condition of Things in our Churches." But Increase began to misbehave again; and on the 19th, Abigail died in childbed. Cotton Mather's last prayer for the month is typical of his mood: —

"That I may humble myself before the Lord," it runs, "for all the Sins which the Death of my dear Nibby calls me to repentance for. That I may obtain mercy for the Family that she has left behind her. That Nancy may have a perfect recovery; Creasy be made a New Creature; Liza have her life preserved in the Dangers of the Contagion; and Sammy be bless'd in his Education. That I may be supported and preserved in my daily Visits to the Sick Chambers that are so lothsome, and full of Malignity. That I may be directed, assisted, prospered in my whole Ministry. And have a particular Smile of Heaven on the Essays I am now sending beyond sea to serve the Kingdom of God."

And this troubled month he gave no less than three publications to the press.

Early in October comes a different note. Three of his children lived with him, and a kinswoman of his wife's.

"Tho' I will have my Table Talk Facetious as well as Instructive, . . . yett I will have the Exercise continually intermixed. I will sett before them some sentence of the Bible, and make some useful Remarks upon it."

The pestilence was at its height, though: in one week 315 petitions for prayer were put up in the North

Church; the next week, 322. And Increase Mather, in his sorrowful old age, was now "wholly Laid by from all public service." Cotton Mather struggled hard. The petitions for prayers fell to 180. But at the end of the month he wrote: —

"In my Remarks on the Folly and Baseness continually expressed by our Absurd and wicked people, I do not always preserve that meekness of Wisdom, which would adorn the Doctrine of God my Saviour. I will ask Wisdom of God for the cure of this Distemper."

What happened in November he shall tell for himself: —

"My Kinsman, the Minister of *Roxbury*, being entertained at my House, that he might there undergo the Small-pox *Inoculated*, and so Return to the Service of his Flock, which have the contagion begun among them: Towards Three a clock in the Night, as it grew towards the Morning of this Day,[1] some unknown Hands, threw a Fired Granado into the Chamber where my kinsman lay, and which uses to be my Lodging-Room. The Weight of the Iron Ball alone, had it fallen upon his Head, would have been enough to have done part of the Business designed. But the Granado was charged, the upper part with dried powder, the lower part with Oil of Turpentine, and powder and what else I know not, in such a manner that upon going off, it must have splitt, and have probably killed the persons in the Room, and certainly fired the Chamber, and speedily Laid the House in Ashes. But, *this Night there stood by me the Angel of GOD, whose I am and whom I serve;* and the Merciful providence of my SAVIOUR so ordered it, that the Granado passing thro' the Window, had by the Iron in the middle of the Casement, such a Turn given to it, that in falling on the Floor, the

[1] 14 November, 1721.

fired wild-fire in the Fuse was violently shaken out upon the Floor, without firing the Granado. When the *granado* was taken up, there was found a paper so tied with string about the fuse that it might out-live the breaking of the shell, — which had these words in it: — *Cotton Mather, you Dog; Dam you: I'l enoculate you with this, with a pox to you.*"

Cotton Mather had read Foxe's Martyrs all his life. This attack was such as had been made on the saints in Queen Mary's days, and older still; he was almost a martyr.

"I would much rather Dy for my Conformity to the Blessed JESUS," he wrote, "in Essays to save the Lives of Men from the Destroyer, than for some Truths, tho' precious ones, to which many Martyrs testified formerly in the Flames of Smithfield."

And he closed the month by publishing far and wide accounts of inoculation,

"by Which means, I hope, some hundreds of thousands of lives may in a little while come to be preserved."

December brought lesser troubles. An enemy, to deride him, named a troublesome slave "Cotton Mather"; but he placed his hope in heaven, and prayed especially for "the welfare of the unknown person, who sought my Death by the fired Granado." And this month comes almost the last glimpse we have of the riotous young Increase: —

"My son Increase, by a violent and passionate Resentment of an Indignity, which a wicked Fellow offered unto me, has exposed himself to much Danger, and me also to no little Trouble. I must employ this occasion as much to his Advantage, especially in regard to piety, as I can."

The month ended with reaction : —

"By a dark and a faint Cloud striking over my Mind, I begin to feel some Hazards, lest my Troubles, whereof I have a greater share than any Minister in the Countrey, grow too hard for me, and unfit me and unhinge me for my Services."

And in January he told an assembly of ministers that his efforts to do good had brought obloquy on him and destroyed his usefulness. Hereafter he would follow good schemes, not propose them.

"An Ingenious person in the company, Mr. Wm. Cooper, made the first and a quick Reply, . . . in these Words, *I hope the Devil don't hear you, Syr.*"

The last note for the year fitly closes the record : —

"The year being so finished, what can I do better than seriously peruse the memorials of it, and make the Reflections of piety that may be proper upon them."

XIV

THE DEATH OF INCREASE MATHER

1722–1723

In the year 1722, a startling thing happened at Yale College. The Rev. Timothy Cutler, who had been a successful President there for several years, announced his conversion to the Church of England. He was relieved of his office, and proceeded to England: whence by and by he came back as an Episcopal clergyman to Boston.

Whether this fact had anything to do with what went on at Harvard I cannot say. In the time that had intervened since Leverett had been made President, the course of things there had been wholly in the direction of the liberalism, which in growing and changing forms has constantly characterized the older College. As we have seen, the sympathy of whoever held faithfully to the old traditions of New England had been more and more directed to Yale. Quincy[1] shows good reason for supposing that Cotton Mather, without due openness, tried hard to divert thither at least a part of the benefactions of Thomas Hollis. This gentleman, a Baptist merchant of London, was in his time the most generous friend Harvard College had ever had. And the effort which the Orthodox clergy of Massachusetts

[1] Vol. I. Chapter XII.

made to confine the Professorship of Divinity that Hollis founded to their own creed — a creed distinctly different from his — is among the least admirable features of their hopeless struggle to maintain priestly authority in a state committed to constantly more advanced Protestantism.

The passage I cited from Sewall,[1] describing his controversy with Leverett in the Board of Overseers, relates one incident of a controversy that was going on at Harvard. Quincy[2] tells the story in detail. The Corporation consisted chiefly of men in sympathy with Leverett; Colman, for example, was now a Fellow. Two tutors, apparently of more conservative temper, advanced a claim to seats in the Corporation. A fierce dispute broke out, of which the details need not concern us. One of its features, however, was an official inquiry into the actual state of the College, educational, religious, and moral. This was in progress throughout the year 1723 : and Cotton Mather eagerly urged it on. His suggestions on points to be inquired into, Quincy prints in full. It seems possible that the state of the " beloved infant " Yale led him to hope for a return of grace to the mother Harvard.

In the beginning of this paper is a phrase which refers to the event of this year which meant most to Cotton Mather : —

" The performances of a deceased person, and with what industry and fidelity the churches of New England were served in them, 'tis too late to inquire into."

The deceased person was Increase Mather. The old man had died on the 23d of August, 1723.

[1] See page 268.   [2] Vol. I. Chapter XIII.

Cotton Mather gives a long account of his father's latter days;[1] of the constancy and method of his devotions and studies; of his benign charity — a trait of which I find little trace elsewhere; of the grave civility of his carriage in all departments of life. His faults the pious son passes lightly: were it not for Sewall's diary, and the frequent allusions to "my aged parent" in Cotton Mather's own, we should not have the painful picture I can dimly see of the austere Puritan's sad old age. He had given the best energies of a life that had been among the most laborious of his time, to the Colony and the Province and the churches of Massachusetts. He had won for the people the Charter under which they lived less fettered, I believe, than any other colonists in the world. And his reward had been neglect. Political power, Harvard College, his very congregation, had one after the other been withdrawn from him. And plagued with the pains of pedantic old age, he had diffused about his last years, I fear, an atmosphere free from moral or spiritual exhilaration. The greatest of his trials, the most mysterious of all the dispensations he had to bear, was the disappointment of the greatest particular faith of his life. Again and again, wrestling with the Lord, he had been assured that he should once more serve God in England. His son had shared his faith and his assurances. But they came to nothing. The College fell back to the old Charter that fatally failed to secure it to the faith of the fathers. And what God meant, neither of the Mathers could ever guess. There is pathos in Cotton Mather's last note about the matter: after all, was not

[1] Parentator, XXXI., XXXII.

the faith perhaps fulfilled when, in 1715, an assembly
of ministers asked Increase Mather to bear a formal
address of congratulation to George I?

A few of his last speeches Cotton Mather preserves.
Of Boston he said,

"There is yet a number of Godly People in the town;
they may be brought low, But the Town shall be yet preserved": of the times in general, "There will be no settled Good Times, I suppose, till the second coming of the
Lord."

It was he who drew up a loyal address for the Ministers of Boston to King George, delivered from some
Jacobite plot.   And in the last year of his life he wrote
a solemn paper, briefly asserting the old principles of
New England, to maintain which the Colony and the
College had been planted; and earnestly charging
posterity with the duty of preserving them.

In his last days, grievously plagued with the stone,
his spirit, like his father's before him, sank low.

"In a deep Abyss of Humility, there was utterly Absorb'd
with him all *Sense* of his *ever having done any good at all*
in the World."

And he prayed, and begged those about him unceas-
ingly to pray for the free grace of Christ.   And hearing
that Thomas Hollis had written to ask if he were yet in
the land of the living, he bade his son write back: —

"No, Tell him I am going to it; This Poor World is
the Land of the Dying."

Late in July Sewall wrote thus: —

"Fast at the Old North. As I went along towards
Cambridge-Court, I called at the old Doctor's who was
agonizing and Crying out, Pity me! Pity me! I told him

God pity'd him, to which he assented and seemed pacify'd. He prayed God to be with me."[1]

He lived three weeks longer. This is his son's account of his end : —

"At last, he began to fall into the Torments of the *Wheel broken at the Cistern :* Which yet became not Intolerable, and forced no Ejaculation from him till about *Three Weeks before he Died.* Under these, about *Three Days* before his Expiration, coming out of a Dark Minute, he said, *It is now Revealed from Heaven to me, That I shall quickly, quickly, quickly be fetch'd away to Heaven, and that I shall Dy in the Arms of my Son.* After this, he kept very much calling for me ; till *Friday,* the *Twenty-Third* of *August,* 1723, in the Morning perceiving the *Last Agonies* now come upon him, I did what I could after my poor manner, that he might be *Strengthened* by such *Quickening Words* as the *Lively Oracles* of our GOD have provided for such Occasions. As it grew towards Noon, I said unto him, *Syr, the Messenger is now come to tell you,* This Day thou shalt be in Paradise. *Do you Believe it, Syr, and Rejoice in the Views and Hopes of it?* He Replied, *I do! I do! I do!* — And upon these Words he *Dyed in my Arms.*"

Posterity has inclined to deem him a cunning schemer, justly disappointed in such ambition as to-day not a few among us attribute to the priesthood of Rome. That he earnestly longed to see the temporal power of America at the feet of the spiritual, no man can doubt ; nor yet that he saw in himself the man who should by right stand at the head of the spiritual power of his time and country. And there will always be men, and many, who cannot believe that such views can be held for any other reason than vulgar longing for human

[1] Diary, III. 325.

power. But whoever has followed the history of Harvard College, through Unitarianism, to that more shadowy heresy still which calls itself unsectarian religion, — even though he rejoice, as I do, in the unfettered spiritual freedom of the greatest stronghold of American Protestantism, — must know that the grim old man read the future right. If the faith from which he never swerved be true, then assuredly we of the later times are lost. And those who can train themselves to that sympathy without which no man can understand his fellows will not forget, when they sit to judge the greatest of the native Puritans, that not one of his efforts to preserve and strengthen his earthly authority was not also an effort to make their lives, and all the lives still to come, lives which should tread in the paths of salvation.

So, after nearly eighty-four busy, troubled years, he came to his peace. And so the son, who had never faltered in devotion, who for well on to forty years had shared every hope and grief with an affection as brotherly as it was filial, was left alone, to struggle with a world which all his life had been pressing onward from the station where his feet were planted. With a mad wife, with but four of his fifteen children left him, with his eldest son — and to the end his dearest — straying further and further towards perdition, with the New England churches ever straying further and further from the holy traditions they were founded to preserve, Cotton Mather was left alone.

XV

THE LAST DIARY OF COTTON MATHER

1724

THE last of Cotton Mather's diaries preserved is that for 1724.[1] The daily notes of good devices continue until November, when a sharp fit of illness broke them off. And when he grew better, and began to write once more, in a style whose incoherence shows how his troubles had shaken him at last, his first note tells that he will record his good devices no more; in the little time left him on earth, there are other things that call for every moment.

It was a troubled year, this 1724. Yet his first note is not a troubled one. On his birthday he held a fast as ecstatic as any he had known; and among his works for the day was the long Latin epitaph with which he ended the life of his father — the book from which my picture of the old man has chiefly been drawn, and the book which shows how firmly, even in his closing years, Cotton Mather still held the faith which had governed his whole life. And a little later he had a satisfaction: forty years before, Increase Mather had preached against suicide a sermon instigated by the act of one Taylor, father of the Lieutenant Governor to be, who had hanged himself with a snaffle-

[1] In possession of the Massachusetts Historical Society.

bridle. Another notable suicide now occurring, Sewall sent to Cotton Mather, asking whether the sermon were preserved. Cotton Mather found it almost at once: Sewall had it published.[1] And so Increase Mather, though dead, still spoke to the people of New England.[2] But there were many things to vex Cotton Mather, too: Increase was gone to sea; the troubles about the administration of Howell's estate went so far that writs against Mather were issued;[3] and in his house was a niece of his wife, —

"a very wicked Creature, and not only deaf to all proposals of piety, but also a monstrous Liar, and a very mischievous person, and a Sower of Discord, and a Monster of Ingratitude."

Nor did discord need to be sown in the unhappy house: Mrs. Mather's paroxysms were worse than ever. Again and again this year come Latin notes, telling under the thin veil of that learned tongue what the horrors of his last marriage were.

Another matter which troubled him much he mentions thus: —

"I hear of strong Machinations and Expectations among the wicked Church of England Men, to gett our Colledge into their hands; which will be a most compendious way to bring Quick Ruine on our Churches. I would apply myself with all proper Awakenings to the men at Helm on this Occasion." And next day he would "sollicit for Days of prayer . . . in the Colledge-Hall, on the Occasion of the condition . . . it is . . . exposed unto."

[1] Sewall's Diary, III. 331, 332.   [2] See page 26.

[3] The two Howells, who made all his trouble, were drowned, while skating at the foot of Boston Common, Jan. 8, 1727-8. Sewall's Letter-Book, II. 307.

The state of affairs was this.   The Rev. Timothy
Cutler, the converted President of Yale, had come
from England to Boston, as Episcopal Rector of Christ
Church — the church from which fifty years later, by a
curious irony of fate, the lantern was shown that sent
Paul Revere galloping to Lexington and Concord.
One Mr. Myles was Rector of King's Chapel, the official place of worship of the royal Governor.   As
"ministers of Boston," these gentlemen claimed seats
in the Board of Overseers of Harvard College;[1] and
though their claim was never allowed, it was urged
until after Cotton Mather was dead.   And it had to
be fought hard.

It was this, among other things, which led Cotton
Mather to that day of meditation of which Upham has
published the greater part of the record.[2] He asked
himself question after question about his earthly state,
and gave answers; of which this is an example : —

"What has a gracious God given me to do in *good offices*
wherever I could find opportunities for the doing of them?
I for ever entertained them with alacrity. . . . And yet I
see no man for whom all are so loth to do good offices. . . .
Often have I said, What would I give if there were any one
man in the world to do for me what I am willing to do for
every man ! "

But Upham thought irrelevant and not worth quoting the close of these meditations.

"I have a clear and strong persuasion of a *Future State.*
. . . I do most freely . . . consent unto the condition of a
crucified man, . . . without any prospect of any Outgate,

[1] Quincy, Vol. I. Chapter XVII.
[2] Salem Witchcraft, II. 503, *seq*.

but at and by the Dying Hour. Yea, Secondly, I have already received an abundant *Recompense of Christ.* . . . If I never had any other compensation for my Troubles, I have had so much, that I need not ask for any more."

Which words and others like them make the passage seem to me other than to Upham : he finds in it a confession of selfish wickedness which deliberately sacrificed human life in the witchcraft trials, two and thirty years before.

What Cotton Mather had to bear from his wife, these two notes tell : —

August 13. " This night my unaccountable Consort, had a prodigious return of her pangs upon her. . . . After a thousand unrepeatable Invectives, compelling me to Rise at Midnight, and retire to my Study that I might there pour out my Soul before the Lord ; she also gott up in a horrid Rage, protesting that she would never Live or Stay with me ; and calling up her wicked Niece and Maid, she went over to a Neighbour's House for a Lodging. . . . I, with my Son *Samuel,* and my daughter *Hannah,* retired up to my Library, where we together . . . poured out our Supplications. Towards the morning, I went unto my Bed, and enjoy'd some Repose. . . . What was pretended as the Introduction to the present, was, That, forsooth, for a Day or two, my Looks and Words were not so very kind as they had been."

August 23. " In the Evening, . . . my poor Wife, returning to a Right Mind, came to me in my Study, entreating that there might be Eternal Oblivion of every thing that had been out of point ; . . . and that for the . . . further obtaining of this Felicity, I would now join with her in pouring out Supplications to the Lord. . . . I did accordingly. And the Tokens of the greatest Inamoration on her part ensued upon it."

Meanwhile another trial was in progress. On the
3d of May, John Leverett, President of Harvard College, was found dead in his bed. On the 6th, he was
buried, and Cotton Mather was one of his bearers.
Next day, Mather writes : —

"The sudden death of that unhappy man who sustained
the place of president in our colledge, will open a Door for
my doing of Singular Services to the Best of Interests.
Indeed his being within a year of the same Age with myself loudly calls upon me to live in a daily expectation of
my own call from hence. . . . I do not know that the care
of the colledge will be now cast upon me : tho' I am told,
it is what is most generally wished for. If it should, I
shall be in abundance of Distress about it. But if it should
not, I may do many things for the good of the colledge,
more quietly and more hopefully than formerly. . . . Why
may I not write unto the tutors . . ., and Sollicit . . .
That they would exert their powers to make the Students,
become indeed what they are called, and spend . . . their
Time well; and therefore not content themselves with the
daily Recitations (the matter of which also, ought to be further considered) but assign them suitable Books to read,
and see that they Read them. That they encourage So-
dalities among them; to meet every week for the Communications of their Acquisitions to one another. That
they Countenance Industry, with distinguished Rewards
. . . to the Meritorious. That they bring up the use of the
Latin Tongue in Conversation among the Scholars. That
above all things, they do what may be done for the Anima-
tion . . . of PIETY among the young men : . . . cast a kind
Aspect on those who Associate for Devotions ; and . . .
establish them in the *Faith and Order of the Gospel*, in
which the Churches of *New England* have their Beauty
and their Safety."

August 12. "I am now informed that the Six Men who

call themselves the Corporation of the Colledge mett, and contrary to the Epidemical Expectation of the Countrey, chose a modest young man, of whose piety (and little else) every one gives a laudable character. I always foretold these Two Things of the Corporation: First, That if it were possible for them to steer clear of me, they will do so. Secondly, That if it be possible for them to act Foolishly, they will do so. . . . It proves accordingly. Now, tho' the senseless Management of these men threatens little short of a Dissipation to the Colledge, yett I have personally unspeakably to admire the compassion of Heaven to me on this occasion. Tho' I have been a Man of Sorrows and acquainted with Griefs, yett none of the least Exercises I have met withal, was the Dread of what the Generality of sober people . . . desired: the Care of the Colledge. . . . I had a Dismal Apprehension of the Distresses, which a call to Cambridge would bring upon me. . . . But the Sleight and the Spite of my Six Friends, has produced for me an Eternal Deliverance. I doubt, I have expressed myself with a little too much Alacrity on this Occasion. Lord, help me to a wise Behaviour ! "

Next day he wrote : " G. D. Hasten, Hasten, O Slothful Mather, in dispatching thy Treatise of Advice to the Candidates of the Ministry. Thou mayest thereby do more Good, than Twenty presidents of Colledges."

That very night was the one when his wife left his house.

A month later, he had another meditation about the College : Had the care of it come to him, it might have worried him to death ; and who knows but the Lord, designing shortly to call him from earth, purposely delivered the College from a fresh inconvenience ? Again, though as President he might have served God, the

" Grace which I have already received in that kind, especially considering my prodigious unworthiness, may well

be sufficient for me. . . . Finally, The preferring of a
Child before me as my Superior in Erudition, or in
Capacity . . . to manage the Government of an Academy,
or in piety and Gravity, This is what . . . it would be a
Crime in me to be disturbed at."

The "Child" in question was Joseph Sewall, son of
the Judge, and minister of the Old South Church. He
declined the office. In November the Corporation
met again.

"The Corporation of our Miserable Colledge," wrote
Cotton Mather, "do again (upon a Fresh Opportunity)
treat me with their accustomed Judgment and Malignity.
But Oh! may I take pleasure in the Opportunity I have
to glorify my God and Saviour."

The choice of the Corporation fell on Colman, who
also declined. It was not until June, 1725, that a
President was finally found: it was Benjamin Wadsworth, who held office till after Cotton Mather died.

Meanwhile, in August, just when his wife was at her
worst, had come a harder blow still. On the 20th
he writes : —

"While I am this morning, about projecting of Services
for the Kingdom of GOD . . . I have sad Advice of His
going on to pull down mine [House], with dreadful Dispensations. . . . My son *Increase* is Lost, is Dead, is
Gone. The Ship wherein he was bound from *Barbadoes*
to *St. Peter's*, had been out five Months . . .; and some
singular circumstances of the Vessel also . . . confirm the
Apprehension that it is perished in the Sea. Ah! my Son
Increase! My Son, My Son! My Head is Warm, and
my Eyes are a Fountain of Tears. — I am overwhelmed! —
And this at a Time when the Domestic Inhumanities and
Diabolisms which I am treated withal, are so Insupport-

able! — Oh my God, I am oppressed: undertake for me. —
But the Soul of the Child! — If the purposes which he left
in my Hands were Sincere, and His Heart went with his
pen, — All is well! — Would not my God not have me to
hope so? — My Saviour yett affords me this Light in my
Darkness, that He enables me, to offer up all the Sacrifices
He calls me to."

In September came a rumour that, after all, the ship
in which Increase sailed was safe; but a day or two
later comes this note: —

"The Good News of poor Creasy's being Rescued and
Releeved from Death is all come to nothing: Twas another
Vessel. *O my Father, Thy Will be done.*"

Later still comes a supplication "with a special Regard
unto the sad case of my son *Increase;* that I may have
Light arise in Darkness to me under it; . . . and that
the *Discourse*, which it has awakened me to prepare for
the public may be published and prospered."

Late in November, as I have said, Cotton Mather
fell very ill. For five weeks he was unable to make
entries in his diary. As I have said, those he made
when he grew better show him broken in health and
mind as never before. I will cite but one: it is the last;
and one, I think, with which he would have chosen to
bid us farewell.

"February 7. 1724–5. Lord's-Day. When I sitt alone
in my Languishments, unable to Write or to Read, I often
compose Little Hymns agreeable unto my present circumstances, and Sing them unto the Lord. Vast numbers have
I had of these, which are immediately all Forgotten. But
tho' none of them have been hitherto recorded, I will here
insert one of them; inasmuch as I design to use it again,
and often upon occasion. Having found my Mind for

some time without such precious and Impressive Thoughts
of God my SAVIOUR, as are the Life of my Spirit, I thus
mourn'd and Sung unto the Lord: —

> " O glorious Christ of God ! I Live
>   In Views of Thee Alone.
> Life to my gasping Soul, Oh ! Give!
>   Shine Thou, or I 'm undone.

> " I cannot Live, my God, if Thou
>   Enliven'st not my Faith!
> I' m Dead ; I 'm Lost ; Oh ! Save me now
>   From a Lamented Death.

" For the Return of my Health I added:

> " My glorious Healer now Restore
>   My Health, and make me whole.
> But this is what I most implore :
>   Oh, For an Healed Soul."

XVI

The Last Days of Cotton Mather

1724–1728

In this year, 1724, Cotton Mather's youngest surviving daughter, Elizabeth, had married one Edward Cooper. In this year, too, Benjamin Franklin saw him for the last time. In Franklin's Autobiography, the prince of self-made Yankees tells that one of the books that most influenced his youth was Cotton Mather's "Essays to Do Good,"[1] — a work in which Mather insisted on a point that was always dear to him, the importance of combined, co-operative effort. In 1724, Franklin, better dressed than usual, came home for a few weeks from his first expedition to Philadelphia. Among other visits, the young man paid one to Cotton Mather, in the study where a placard bearing the words "Be Brief" warned visitors that they had to do with the busiest of men. When Franklin took leave, Mather showed him out through a dark passage, and, as the youth was walking ahead, suddenly called out, "Stoop!" Not understanding, Franklin took another step and bumped his head against a projecting beam. Whereupon Mather warned him that, throughout life, he would find judicious stooping a great means of avoiding trouble. So they parted. Years after-

[1] See Sibley, III. 102, 103. The book was published in 1710.

wards Franklin wrote Samuel Mather that he had never forgotten the useful counsel.

For the remaining three years of Cotton Mather's life, I find no record that shows him other than we have seen him. Between the beginning of 1725 and the end of 1728, Sibley shows that no less than fifty of his publications appeared, — sermons, books of good counsel, and so on. In general, one may say that his published work was historical, biographical, expository, and hortatory: its chief features are lives of good people, instructions as to how good may be done, explanations of Scripture and of various points of godliness, and such scientific instruction as appeared in his writings about inoculation. Considering how much he wrote and how actively he busied himself with public affairs, it is amazing that he left behind so little controversial writing. The fact is, I take it, that he was from the beginning so convinced of the essential authority of the clergy, that, except under very great provocation, argument of any kind seemed needless in one of his profession.

In August, 1726, his daughter Elizabeth died, leaving children. Of his own fifteen children only Samuel and Hannah survived him.

In December, 1727, he fell ill.[1]

" My *Last Enemy* is come," he said, " I would say my *Last Friend.*"

He lay ill five or six weeks. On Thursday, February 8th, he began to suffer with

"an hard *Cough* and a suffocating *Asthma* with a *Fever;* but he felt no great Pain; he had the sweet *Composure*

[1] S. Mather, Life, VII. 3, 4.

and *easy Departure*, for which he had entreated so *often* and *fervently* the sovereign Disposer of all Things."

On Sunday, writes Samuel Mather,

"I asked him *what Sentence or Word . . . He would have me think on constantly*, for I ever desired to have him before me and hear him speaking to me. He said, ' Remember only that one word *Fructuosus.*' [1] "

On Tuesday, February 13th, 1728, — the day after his sixty-fifth birthday, — he died.

Sewall describes the last scene of all : —

"Monday, Febr. 19. Dr. Cotton Mather is intombed: Bearers, The Rev'd. Mr. Colman, Mr. Thacher; Mr. Sewall, Prince; Mr. Webb, Cooper. The Church went before the Corps. First, the Rev'd Mr. Gee [2] in Mourning alone, then 3 Deacons, then Capt. Hutchinson, Adam Winthrop esqr. Col. Hutchinson — Went up Hull street. I went in a Coach. All the Council had gloves; I had a pair. It seems when the Mourners return'd to the House, Mr. Walter said, My Bror. had better Bearers: Mr. Prince answer'd, They bore the better part."

[1] Fruitful.
[2] Cotton Mather's colleague at the North Church.

XVII

COTTON MATHER, THE PURITAN PRIEST

BEFORE Cotton Mather's tomb was fairly closed, then, men who had known him best were whispering among themselves other than good things concerning the dead. Posterity has held them right. A subtle priest, self-seeking, vain, arrogant, inconsistent, mischievous in his eternal business, many have called him : even if honest, dreadfully deluded and grotesquely lacking in judgment, is what those mostly say who say the best. And if we had only public records to guide us, I should be disposed to assent.

The son of Increase Mather, the grandson of John Cotton and of Richard Mather, sprung of a race of chosen vessels of the Lord, himself a chosen vessel before his boyhood was fairly closed, intoxicated with such adulation as Urian Oakes spoke when, the youngest of Harvard graduates, he took his degree, he began his half-century of earthly work. Full of the traditions of the fathers, he pressed on, divinely authorized to lead the people of God in the path of salvation : whoever would not follow was godless. Then he saw his father's great work in England ; and meanwhile did great work at home. He saw the tyranny of Andros fall : his prayers were answered. He saw Phipps come with the new Charter : New England was saved. Now he might lead on more confidently still. And he plunged into the horrors of witchcraft. And he saw theocracy fall with poor Sir William Phipps. And he saw Harvard College lost to the cause of the fathers. And he saw the very churches of Boston preaching new doctrines, full of delusion. For five and thirty years he saw the clergy of New England started on the course in which they still travel: from a position where the influence of the church was greater than anywhere else in the world, to one where the influence of the church has become almost imperceptible. And he fought against fate with every weapon he could clutch; and he believed his own advancement was what God needed to restore His kingdom; and some of the blows he struck — and for aught I know many of them — may have been foul ones.

But before we can judge him aright, we must strive to see him as he saw himself. This is what I have tried to do. I have told his story perhaps too much in his own words. By no other means could I show so simply what seems to me the truth: that with a depth of human nature which makes him above most men who have lived a brother man to all of us, he never ceased striving, amid endless stumblings and errors, to do his duty.

It was his lot to possess a mind and a temperament more restlessly active than most men ever know. With this nature, it was his lot to live all his life in a petty provincial town, further removed from the great current of contemporary life than any spot to-day in the civilized world. And this he never realized; nor have any of those realized who have sat to judge him. His grandfathers, and the other founders of New England, came

from the midst of the seething England which was soon
to dethrone the Stuarts, full of the passion of a contest
that had been to every one of them the greatest of
earthly realities.   His father's life had brought the
elder man face to face with kings and bishops: Increase Mather had fought hard to preserve and to perpetuate a Puritanism whose pristine freshness was still
within his own memory.   But when Cotton Mather's
time came, Puritanism — like Anglicanism itself — was
already not the great reality it had once been: it had
become a tradition.   The world travels faster nowadays.
The Civil War is already such a tradition to us.

This great tradition of Puritanism he fought so passionately to defend had in it the seeds of a grim, untruthful formalism, which has made it seem to many
men of later times a gloomy delusion, fruitful only of
limitation and of cant.   Those who see in it only or
chiefly this, forget what even to Cotton Mather himself
was its greatest truth.   Few human philosophies have
been more essentially ideal; few systems formulated by
men have so strenuously kept before the minds of those
who accept them the transitory unreality of those things
which human beings can perceive, the eternal and infinite reality of the Divine universe that lies beyond human ken.   Once learn this, and nothing on this earth
is so great as to deserve a care, when we think of the
infinite realities beyond; nor anything on this earth so
mean as not to be a manifestation of divine truth.   At
once contemptible and reverend, this earthly life of
ours is but the fragment of an instant in the timeless
eternities of God.   But to the Puritans, it was an instant in which the infinite mercy of God, with free

grace mitigating His infinite justice, gave every living man the chance and the hope of finding in himself the signs of eternal salvation. It is not every man who can rise to such heights of idealism as this: whoever cannot or will not so rise, whoever cannot feel beneath the austere pettiness of Puritanism the passionate enthusiasm that made things unseen — Hell and Heaven, the Devil, and the Angels, and God — greater realities than anything this side of eternity, can never even guess what Puritanism meant.

On its earthly side, however, Puritanism had a trait which has been more generally recognized, though not, perhaps, more fully understood. In its origin it was Protestant. It began, and it gained earthly strength, in a passionate revolt of human thought from those phases of ecclesiastical tradition which human experience had proved false and wicked. God's word contains God's truth, the first Protestants cried; we will read it for ourselves, none but God shall be our guide. So, Bible in hand, they led the way for who would follow; and when they were gone far enough to muster their forces, they would have cried halt. But what authority had they to stop the progress they had urged? God's world contains God's truth, cried those of their followers whose spirit came nearest to that of the leaders: let us read it there, and read it each for himself; none but God shall be our guide. And those who press ever onward, seeking God's truth each for himself, are the Protestants of to-day. Protestantism can have no priesthood.

This truth Cotton Mather never guessed. To this day honest Protestant Christians are blind to it. Nor did he guess, either, some other truths which modern

Protestant Christianity equally fails to recognize. The
priestly office, let it derive its authority from Rome or
Canterbury, Geneva or Utah, demands in those who
exercise it even most fervently a trait which in its most
obvious form the priests are the first to condemn —
histrionic insincerity. Placed before men as an accred-
ited spiritual leader, the priest — whatever his mood or
his character — must conduct himself, at least in his
public functions, as if he were what no human being
ever was or can be — wholly given up to the service of
God. And the adulation of the worshippers who see
in him an ever-present minister of God strengthens him
year by year in the power in which applause strengthens the actor: the power of seeming at will to be what
in the depths of his heart he is not. To gain this
power, to strengthen it, is part of the priest's duty.
And there is no way of strengthening it so certain as
the way Cotton Mather took, like the saints of Rome
before him. Day after day, week after week, month
after month, year after year, he cast himself in the dust
before the Lord; he strained his eyes for a fleeting
glimpse of the robes and crowns of God's angels, his
ears for the faintest echo of their celestial music. Pure
in motive, noble in purpose, his whole life was one
unending effort to strengthen in himself that phase of
human nature whose inner token is a riot of mystical
emotion, whose outward signs are unwitting manifesta-
tions of unfettered credulity and unmeant fraud.

Yet it is not as a sly and superstitious priest that I
remember him to-day: any more than I think that sly-
ness and superstition to-day make up the character of a
Christian minister. In the first place, the passionate

idealism to which he held with all his heart — like
honest priests since the world began — coloured, and
glorified, and made divine, even the meanest things in
the petty earthly life he knew. A squatting dog brought
him a message straight from the throne of God. In
the second place, the life he lived — with all its grotesque pettiness — was the life which had in it the seeds
of that great continental life in which lies the chief hope
of the modern world. To understand the America of
to-day, we must know the New England of the fathers;
to know the first New England of the fathers, there is
no better way than to study this man — its last, its
most typical incarnation. And as we study him, and
then look back at the figure that emerges from the dusty
books and manuscripts of two centuries ago, the final
trait of him, that hides the rest, is this: strenuously,
devoutly, he did what he deemed his duty.

All about him he saw ever-crescent disappointment
and sorrow and earthly failure; but he never lost heart,
nor ever for a moment ceased effort, with word and deed
alike, to do good to mankind. *Fructuosus* — be fruitful, do God's work here on earth — was his last command to his son. And the incessant training of his
career in the art that in its meaner form he would have
been the first to execrate, — the art of the actor, who
can at will seem to be what in truth he is not, — made
him what it makes good ministers to-day. More than
other men they can sympathize with mankind: in agony,
in sorrow, in sin, men turn to them for aid, for counsel,
for charity in all its divinest forms. And this the saintly
actors give as no other men can, thus doing good unspeakably reverend. The very weakness of their calling,

20

so palpable to those who have not known their benefi-
cence, — so fruitful of obloquy and execration in those
who neither share their faith nor will let themselves
sympathize, — makes them more blessed to mankind
than a thousand of their more candid fellows. Out of
evil God brings good : it is the histrionic insincerity of
priesthood that brings to unhappy men the Divine sympathy of priests. And in his ministry Cotton Mather
never faltered : with ever-growing earnestness, he went
through that grim and sorrowful old New England, in
every deliberate thought and act ministering to the
bodies and the souls of the people of God. *Fructuosus*
— fruitful — is the final word for him.

And what fruit has his priesthood borne that is with
us to-day ? New England is far enough from the stern
creed in which alone he saw hope of salvation. But
not long ago an old friend, talking of the New England
that both of us love, spoke a phrase I like to remember : " We have here," he said, " what the world has
never seen before : we have devout free thought." It
is the Protestantism of the fathers that has won us our
freedom. But freedom alone were a curse. It is the
faithful earnestness of the Puritan priesthood that has
kept our freedom from straying into that pert irrever-
ence which elsewhere than here has made so many who
cast aside the false cast with it the true. And among
the Puritan priests there was never one, I believe, more
faithfully earnest than this Cotton Mather.

One hundred and sixty-three years have passed since
he was laid in his father's tomb on Copp's Hill. And
few of us to-day can believe that he is gone to such
a little company of God's elect as would make the

heaven he preached of. If he be, then, when by chance he looks back at the earth where he laboured, he must see a sight that for the instant should dim the joys of Paradise. But there are not a few to-day who dream of a heaven in whose blessedness all the fetters of humanity are broken; where what is best in men waxes better than men can even dream, amid the ever-growing glories of eternal freedom from sin, and weakness, and sorrow. And if by chance his eyes have opened again in a heaven like this, and if from thence he looks back to an earth where his sins and errors have borne little fruit, but where the devoutness of the free thought of New England speaks still for what was best in his human life, he sees, I like to think, little that should disturb the great serenity of his peace.

AUTHORITIES

THE books I have cited are these : —

Andros Tracts, 3 vols. Boston: Prince Society, 1868–1874.

Calef, Robert: More Wonders of the Invisible World, etc. Salem: Cushing and Appleton, 1823.

Massachusetts Historical Society: Collections:—
Fourth Series, Vol. VIII: The Mather Papers, 1868.
Fifth Series, Vols. V–VII: Sewall's Diary, 1878–1882.
Sixth Series, Vols. I, II: Sewall's Letter-Book, 1886–1888.

Mather, Cotton: Manuscript diaries in possession of the Massachusetts Historical Society, Boston; of the American Antiquarian Society, Worcester, Mass.; and of the Congregational Library, Boston.

—— Magnalia Christi Americana. Hartford: Silas Andrus and Son. Vol. I, 1855; Vol. II , 1853.

—— Parentator. Boston: Nathaniel Belknap, 1724.

—— Paterna (manuscript), in possession of Mrs. Skinner of Chicago.

Mather, Samuel: Life of Cotton Mather. Boston: Samuel Gerrish, 1729.

Palfrey, John Gorham: Compendious History of New England, 4 vols. Boston: J. R. Osgood & Co., 1884.

Peabody, Wm. B. O.: Life of Cotton Mather. Sparks's American Biographies, Vol. VI. Boston: Hilliard, Gray, & Co., 1836.

Quincy, Josiah: History of Harvard University, 2 vols. Cambridge: John Owen, 1840.

Sibley, John Langdon: Harvard Graduates, Vol. III. Cambridge: Charles William Sever, 1885.

Upham, Charles W.: Salem Witchcraft, 2 vols. Boston: Wiggin and Lunt, 1867.

The numerous standard books I have consulted I need not name. I may perhaps, however, mention the remarkable impression of Puritan ways of thought that may be obtained by reading the first two volumes of Stedman and Hutchinson's " Library of American Literature "; and the notable suggestiveness of Mr. Brooks Adams's " Emancipation of Massachusetts."

INDEX

BARRETT WENDELL (1855–1921), an American educator and man of letters, was born in Boston and attended Harvard University, where he later became a Professor of English. Best remembered as a great teacher, he was also the author of many notable works, including his perceptive life of Cotton Mather, *William Shakspere*, *A Literary History of America*, *The Mystery of Education*, and *The Traditions of European Literature, from Homer to Dante*.

DAVID LEVIN is Commonwealth Professor of English at the University of Virginia and currently holds a research fellowship at the Center for Advanced Study in the Behavioral Sciences, Stanford, California. His most recent book is *Cotton Mather: The Young Life of the Lord's Remembrancer, 1663–1703*.